# iPhone and iPad Apps for Absolute Beginners

## Fourth Edition

Rory Lewis

Laurence Moroney

apress·

**iPhone and iPad Apps for Absolute Beginners, Fourth Edition**

ISBN-13 (pbk): 978-1-4302-6361-6

ISBN-13 (electronic): 978-1-4302-6362-3

Trademarked names, logos, and images may appear in this book. Rather than use a trademark symbol with every occurrence of a trademarked name, logo, or image we use the names, logos, and images only in an editorial fashion and to the benefit of the trademark owner, with no intention of infringement of the trademark.

The use in this publication of trade names, trademarks, service marks, and similar terms, even if they are not identified as such, is not to be taken as an expression of opinion as to whether or not they are subject to proprietary rights.

While the advice and information in this book are believed to be true and accurate at the date of publication, neither the authors nor the editors nor the publisher can accept any legal responsibility for any errors or omissions that may be made. The publisher makes no warranty, express or implied, with respect to the material contained herein.

President and Publisher: Paul Manning
Lead Editor: Tom Welsh
Technical Reviewer: Matthew Knott
Editorial Board: Steve Anglin, Mark Beckner, Ewan Buckingham, Gary Cornell, Louise Corrigan, Jim DeWolf, Jonathan Gennick, Jonathan Hassell, Robert Hutchinson, Michelle Lowman, James Markham, Matthew Moodie, Jeff Olson, Jeffrey Pepper, Douglas Pundick, Ben Renow-Clarke, Dominic Shakeshaft, Gwenan Spearing, Matt Wade, Steve Weiss, Tom Welsh
Coordinating Editor: Mark Powers
Copy Editor: April Rondeau
Compositor: SPi Global
Indexer: SPi Global
Artist: SPi Global
Cover Designer: Anna Ishchenko

Distributed to the book trade worldwide by Springer Science+Business Media New York, 233 Spring Street, 6th Floor, New York, NY 10013. Phone 1-800-SPRINGER, fax (201) 348-4505, e-mail orders-ny@springer-sbm.com, or visit www.springeronline.com. Apress Media, LLC is a California LLC and the sole member (owner) is Springer Science + Business Media Finance Inc (SSBM Finance Inc). SSBM Finance Inc is a Delaware corporation.

For information on translations, please e-mail rights@apress.com, or visit www.apress.com.

Apress and friends of ED books may be purchased in bulk for academic, corporate, or promotional use. eBook versions and licenses are also available for most titles. For more information, reference our Special Bulk Sales–eBook Licensing web page at www.apress.com/bulk-sales.

Any source code or other supplementary material referenced by the author in this text is available to readers at www.apress.com/9781430263616. For detailed information about how to locate your book's source code, go to www.apress.com/source-code/.

*I dedicate my work on this book to my wonderful wife, Rebecca, my daughter, Claudia, my son, Christopher, and to the God of Abraham, Isaac, Jacob, and Jesus who makes all things possible.*

—*Laurence Moroney*

# Contents at a Glance

# Contents

# About the Authors

**Rory Lewis** is assistant professor of computer science at the University of Colorado at Colorado Springs. He is often mistaken for a hippie, wearing Dead-head shirts and walking aimlessly around the campus. He is often described as the guy in the office where students are always lined up outside. He is often heralded as the dude that will explain your math and computer code, even when he first checks and sees you've done 800 tweets and 2,700 Facebook comments while you should have been in class! He is described by his adult daughters as a dad who was once a successful microprocessor litigation lawyer in Palo Alto, but couldn't resist his dorkiness and went back to school to become a doctor of geekdom!

**Laurence Moroney** was an independent consultant, specializing in mobile and cloud development, when he started writing this book. By the time it gets into your hands, he'll be enjoying a new role as a developer advocate for Google, specializing in the Google cloud platform. He's been a developer, architect, manager and evangelist for 20 years, having worked in fields as diverse as casinos, jails, financial services, and software companies. He jokes that they aren't as different as you might think. A successful science fiction author and screen writer, Laurence lives in Sammamish, Washington, with his wife, Rebecca, children, Claudia and Christopher, and dog (aka baby), Bucky.

# About the Technical Reviewer

**Matthew Knott** has over 15 years' experience in software development and now leads a team of developers building groundbreaking software for the educational sector. He is a lover of all things C-based and is an experienced C, C#, and Objective-C programmer. Matthew took his passion for developing software that makes life easier and applied it to making iOS apps about four years ago, going on to release a number of apps. A real iOS development enthusiast and lover of all things Xcode, Matthew can regularly be found evangelizing about its virtues on Twitter or on his blog (www.mattknott.com). More than anything else, he loves spending time with his wife and two children in a beautiful part of Wales, United Kingdom.

# Acknowledgments

I'd really like to acknowledge the entire Apress team that made writing this book easy and simple. Mark Powers and Tom Welsh for easing me through the process; April Rondeau and Kumar Dhaneesh for taking my words and making them fly, and of course Steve Anglin for bringing me aboard! Of course, I'd also like to thank my wonderful wife, Rebecca, for being patient with me during long writing sessions!

—Laurence Moroney

# Introduction

*"Ultimately design defines so much of our experience. I think there is a profound and enduring beauty in simplicity. In clarity. In efficiency. True simplicity is derived from so much more than just the absence of clutter. It is about bringing order to complexity. iOS 7 is a clear representation of these goals. iOS 7 brings with it the most significant set of changes to the user interface since the very first iOS. We see iOS 7 as defining an important new direction, and in many ways—a beginning."*

—Jonathan Ive, Designer of iOS

When the original iPhone was released in 2007, it began a wave of innovation in mobility that is far from over. Since then, the user interface has remained largely unchanged—until now, with the release of iOS 7. With this release, Apple has begun the next phase of mobile user interface innovation and has rejuvenated the already vibrant developer market.

If you haven't built for iOS, there has never been a better time to start. This is, as Jonathan Ive mentions above, a beginning.

With this book in your hands, you have everything you need to start on the road to learning the essential skills for iOS 7 development. There are so many concepts that may be confusing to beginners, but when you follow the step-by-step tutorials in this book, you'll begin to knock those concepts down, one by one, until, by the time you end this book, you'll know what it takes to be an iOS 7 developer, and you'll be able to approach online documentation, open source samples, or more complex tutorials confident that you've gotten the foundation down.

This book, like iOS 7 in its way, is a dramatic makeover of the series of "Absolute Beginners" books. It's been rewritten from the ground up to make it more approachable, more intuitive, and more fun than ever before.

I hope you enjoy it, and I look forward to seeing what you can build on iOS 7.

—Laurence Moroney

# Chapter 1

# Getting Started

If you've picked up this book and have read this far, you're likely interested in being an iPhone and iPad developer. Given the popularity of this platform and the stories of how lucrative development for it can be, you've made a great choice. However, you may also have heard stories of how difficult it can be, how you need to learn abstract or difficult languages and concepts, or how you need to use tools that programmers don't like, or indeed you may have heard how difficult it can be to put your work into the app store, where you can make some money.

Unlearn all that. It's really not that bad, and it can be a fun journey. In this book, you'll go through the basics of what you need to know, from getting the developer tools, to learning how to use them to design and code iOS apps, to debugging and fixing your apps before finally deploying them to the app store.

Your focus will be on the brand new iOS 7 platform. iOS is the operating system (O.S.) that powers these devices. It was first released (although called iPhone OS back then) with the first iPhone back in 2007. In 2013, Apple gave iOS its biggest and most revolutionary update with the release of version 7, called iOS7.

This book is designed for iOS7 development, using a programmer's tool called Xcode and a language called Objective-C. The only thing you'll need is a Mac computer, because Xcode runs only on the Mac, and you'll have to ensure that it's an Intel-based Mac running Mac OS X Snow Leopard or later. Any Mac bought in the last three or four years should be fine. As you'll see in the "Getting Xcode" section later in this chapter, you get Xcode from the app store, so you'll need an account there too. It's free to get an account, and Xcode is free to download.

You don't *need* an iPhone or iPad in order to develop for them, as Xcode gives you a simulator for both of these devices. However, if you want to test on a physical device, which sometimes is necessary, you'll need a developer account for iOS development, at a cost of $99 per year.

In this chapter you'll get started by downloading and installing Xcode and taking a look at how it works. You'll also see how to sign up for a developer account and how to access it.

# Getting a Mac

First off, you will definitely need a Mac to work with. It doesn't have to be the latest, most expensive model, but as mentioned in the previous section, it must be an Intel-based Mac running Mac OS X Snow Leopard or later. We wrote this book using two Macs—a 2011 model iMac and a 2011 model MacBook Air.

You can see the different options available to you at http://www.apple.com/mac/, displayed across the top of the screen, as shown in Figure 1-1.

*Figure 1-1.  Buying a Mac*

At the time of writing, the latest version of OS X, called Mavericks, was in preview, as indicated in Figure 1-1. Of course, you don't *need* Mavericks, but if you have it, you're fine to continue.

When buying a Mac, there are several important attributes that you should consider:

- **Processor Speed:** The faster the processor, the quicker your programs will load, the quicker they'll update the screen, and the quicker Xcode will compile your apps

- **Memory:** The more memory the better. OS X will use memory as it runs applications. If it needs to use more memory than is available, it has to temporarily store information on disk. Accessing the disk is slower than accessing memory, so the more memory, the faster your machine will generally operate

- **Disk Space:** As you download or create information, you'll take up disk space. The more space you have, the more time you have before you run out!

- **Disk Type:** Most machines have a hard disk, but some have a flash drive, also known as a solid state drive (SSD). Hard disks are cheaper, so machines with flash drives tend to be more expensive, or, because of the expense, will have less capacity. The big advantage of flash drives, however, is that they are very fast—in some cases, almost as fast as memory. Thus, a machine with a flash drive can be very responsive, but may have less available storage. MacBook Airs use flash drives, which are generally optional on the other machines.

- **Screen Resolution:** Screen resolution is the number of dots on your screen in width and height. So, for example, you might see 1366x768 as the resolution on a machine, indicating that the screen has 1366 dots (pixels) across and 768 down. The bigger the resolution, the more you'll see. When developing, it's good to have a big screen resolution, giving you plenty of room to view Xcode, the simulator, and a browser for the documentation all at the same time.

We like to use an iMac for our main development, because it comes with a large monitor that offers very high resolution. We use a MacBook Air as a backup, because it's light and very fast (due to its flash drive).

# Getting Xcode

OSX Snow Leopard and later include an app store application through which you can get free software or purchase paid software. Apple distributes Xcode using the app store. If you're not familiar with the app store, you can see its icon in Figure 1-2. It's the one in the center with the pencils and ruler arranged like the letter "A."

*Figure 1-2. The Mac app store*

When you launch the app store, you'll see a home screen with the latest "Editor's Choice" applications, as well as others that are new and noteworthy. At the top right side of the screen you'll see a search box. Type "Xcode" into this box and press the "Enter" key. See Figure 1-3.

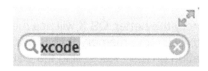

*Figure 1-3. Searching for Xcode*

The app store will return a bunch of apps that match this search term. It should look something like Figure 1-3, but don't worry if it's a little different—apps are being added all the time. Just make sure that you can see Xcode itself, with its "hammer" icon, as shown in Figure 1-4.

*Figure 1-4. Searching for Xcode*

If you have a store account, you can go ahead and get Xcode now. If not, read the next section, where you'll see how to get an account that you can use to acquire and download Xcode.

## Getting a Store Account

With the app store open, select the "Store" menu at the top of the screen, and from this select "Create Account...." See Figure 1-5.

*Figure 1-5. Getting a store account*

You'll be taken to the "Welcome to the App Store" screen. From here, you can click "Continue." You can see it in Figure 1-6.

*Figure 1-6. Step 1 of setting up an app store account*

The next step gives you the terms and conditions of the store, as well as Apple's privacy policy. If you agree to the terms, check the box and then click the "Agree" button. See Figure 1-7.

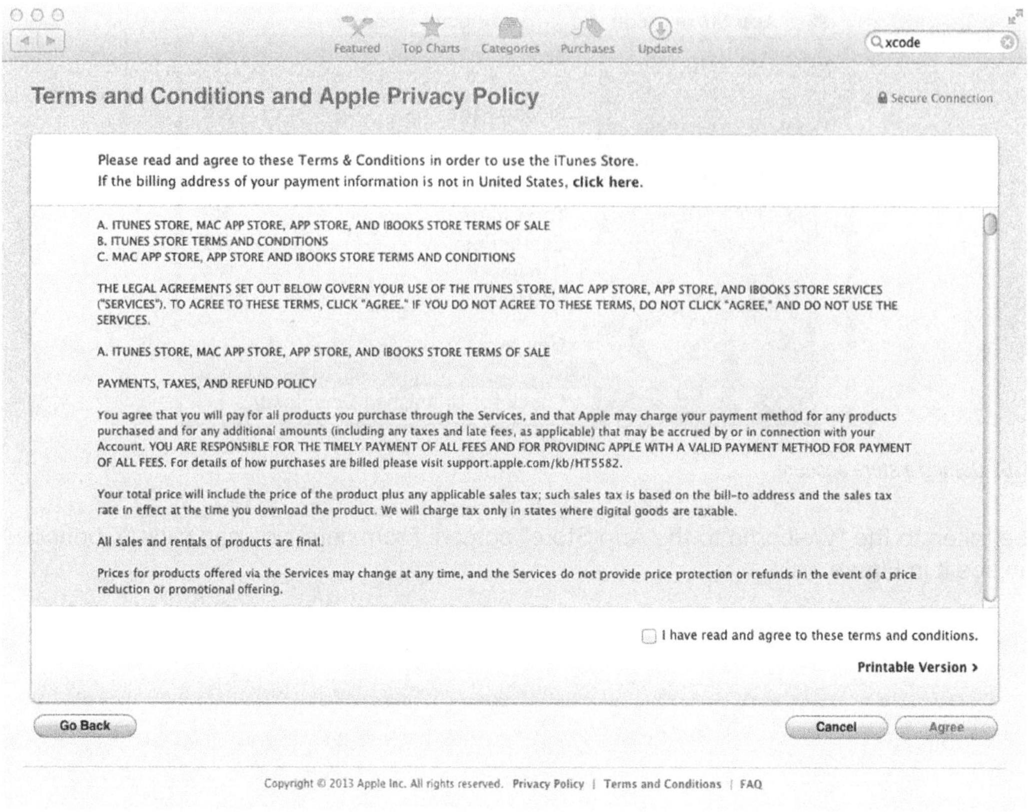

*Figure 1-7.* *Step 2 of the app store signup*

On the following screen, you will set up the details of your Apple ID. You need to provide an email address, security information, a backup email address, and your date of birth. Fill out values for the security info that you'll remember (and not silly answers like ours), and when you're done, click "Continue." You can see all this in Figure 1-8.

*Figure 1-8. Setting up your Apple details*

When you're done with this, you'll reach the final screen, where you will set up your payment method. Fill out the details as shown and click "Create Apple ID." Your Apple ID will be created, and Apple will send an email to the address of the ID. You'll have to click on a link in this email to confirm your address, and then you'll be ready to use your new Apple ID.

# Downloading and Installing Xcode

When you search for Xcode in the app store, you'll see it with a link that allows you to install it (if you've downloaded it before), or notifies you that it's free, as in Figure 1-9.

*Figure 1-9. Accessing Xcode in the app store*

Click on the button, and it will change to a green "Install App" button. Click on this, and you'll be asked to log in with your Apple ID.

*Figure 1-10. Signing into the store*

Use your Apple ID and password. Xcode will begin to download. You'll see its progress from within LaunchPad. See Figure 1-11.

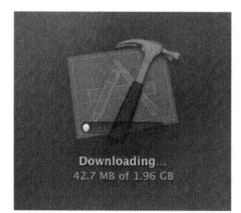

*Figure 1-11. Downloading Xcode*

It's a big download, so it will take a bit of time. While you're waiting, you could check out the page for Xcode in the app store. You can get this by clicking on the word "Xcode" in the search results. Its page looks like Figure 1-12.

*Figure 1-12. Xcode's app store page*

Here you can learn about the features of Xcode, as well as read reviews that other users have posted about it. Previous versions were a little confusing, as the app store only downloaded the installer, and then you had to install explicitly from the download, which wasn't documented very well. This led to a lot of negative reviews.

However, version 5, which you should be installing here, doesn't require this—Xcode will download and install and be ready to use right away!

## Running Xcode

You can launch Xcode from launcher. When you do so, and it runs for the first time, you'll see the "Welcome to Xcode" screen. See Figure 1-13.

*Figure 1-13. Xcode's welcome screen*

This screen allows you to create a new Xcode project, and from there to choose a number of different project types. You'll learn about these starting in Chapter 2, where you'll create your first application. Before doing that, it's good to switch gears for a moment and take a look at Apple's developer portal, which is a great source of information and resources for you as you develop applications.

## The Apple Developer Portal

Apple's developer portal is at `https://developer.apple.com`. It has sections for iOS7, OS X Mavericks, and Xcode 5. See Figure 1-14.

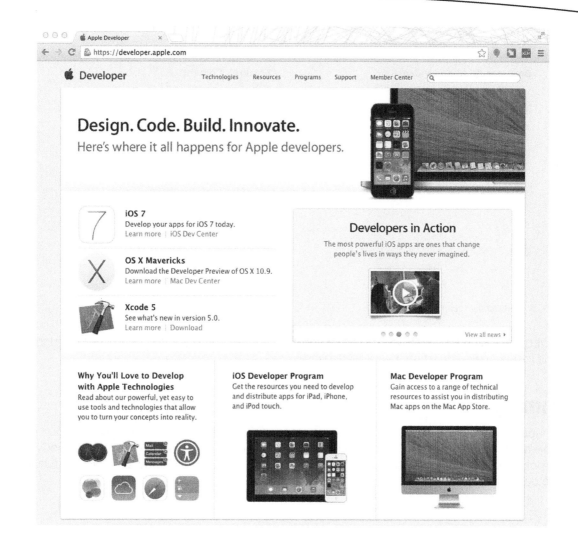

*Figure 1-14. The Apple developer portal*

Click on the iOS dev center link, and you'll be taken to the iOS dev center page, which contains documentation, videos, and more. Most of the information is freely available—you don't need a developer account. If you want to test on physical devices or deploy to the app store, you'll need to register as a developer. This costs $99 per year. You'll step through how to do that in Chapter 3.

The documentation and videos section (see Figure 1-15) is particularly useful, giving you "Getting Started" guides as well as sample code and other references. If you are an absolute beginner, once you've gone through this book and gained some confidence in building iOS apps, go back and visit that section—it's really good, but does require you to have a little knowledge.

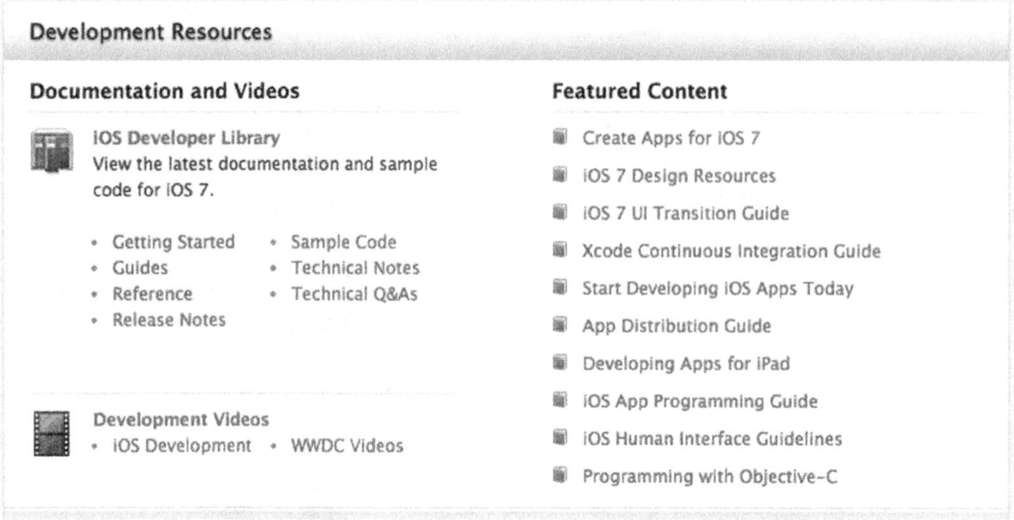

**Development Resources**

**Documentation and Videos**

iOS Developer Library
View the latest documentation and sample
code for iOS 7.

- Getting Started    • Sample Code
- Guides             • Technical Notes
- Reference          • Technical Q&As
- Release Notes

**Development Videos**
- iOS Development    • WWDC Videos

**Featured Content**

- Create Apps for iOS 7
- iOS 7 Design Resources
- iOS 7 UI Transition Guide
- Xcode Continuous Integration Guide
- Start Developing iOS Apps Today
- App Distribution Guide
- Developing Apps for iPad
- iOS App Programming Guide
- iOS Human Interface Guidelines
- Programming with Objective-C

*Figure 1-15.  Development resources*

At the very least, consider looking at the "Getting Started" section once you've worked through the tutorials in this book; you'll find it very rewarding!

# Summary

This chapter was your introduction to development for iOS 7 using Xcode. From it you learned where the tools are available and how to download and install them. Starting in the next chapter, you'll use these tools to build your first app, and in Chapter 3 you'll learn how to deploy it to your hardware using a developer account.

# Chapter 2

# Your First iOS Apps

The first app you'll build is a basic "Hello, World" app where, despite the simplicity of the app, you'll implement some of the functionality that is found in more advanced applications, including taking user input and having your code update the user interface as a result. By the time you finish this chapter, you'll know how to run the app in the following three ways:

**iPhone app on iPhone simulator:** This shows you how to run an iPhone app in the iPhone aspect ratio on an iPhone-sized emulator.

**iPhone app on iPad simulator:** iPhone applications can be run on iPads too, with a special "2x" mode that enlarges the user interface to make it fit the screen. You'll see how to test your iPhone app with the iPad simulator to see how it would look in this scenario.

**iPad app on iPad simulator:** Applications can also be written specifically for the iPad, taking advantage of the larger screen resolutions. You'll see how to do that too!

---

**Note**  Supplementing this book are a number of screencasts of the examples in this book. If you prefer video instead of step-by-step reading, we hope they'll be a great resource for you. You can access these, as well as blogs and help forums around the book, by visiting ios7developer.com.

---

## Creating Your First iPhone App

In this first example, you're going to create an app that gives you a button and a label. When you tap the button, text will appear on the label that says "Hello World!" This is a *very* simple app, but you're going to spend quite a bit of time, and quite a few pages, on it. That is because an app like this, despite its simplicity, implements many of the concepts found in larger, more sophisticated apps, making it a really useful learning tool.

Use Xcode to create your app. Launch Xcode, and the "Welcome to Xcode" screen will appear. See Figure 2-1.

*Figure 2-1.* *The "Welcome to Xcode" screen*

Click the "Create a new Xcode project" option, and you'll see a list of templates for your new application.

Your first application will use the "Single View Application" template. Select it as shown in Figure 2-2, and click "Next."

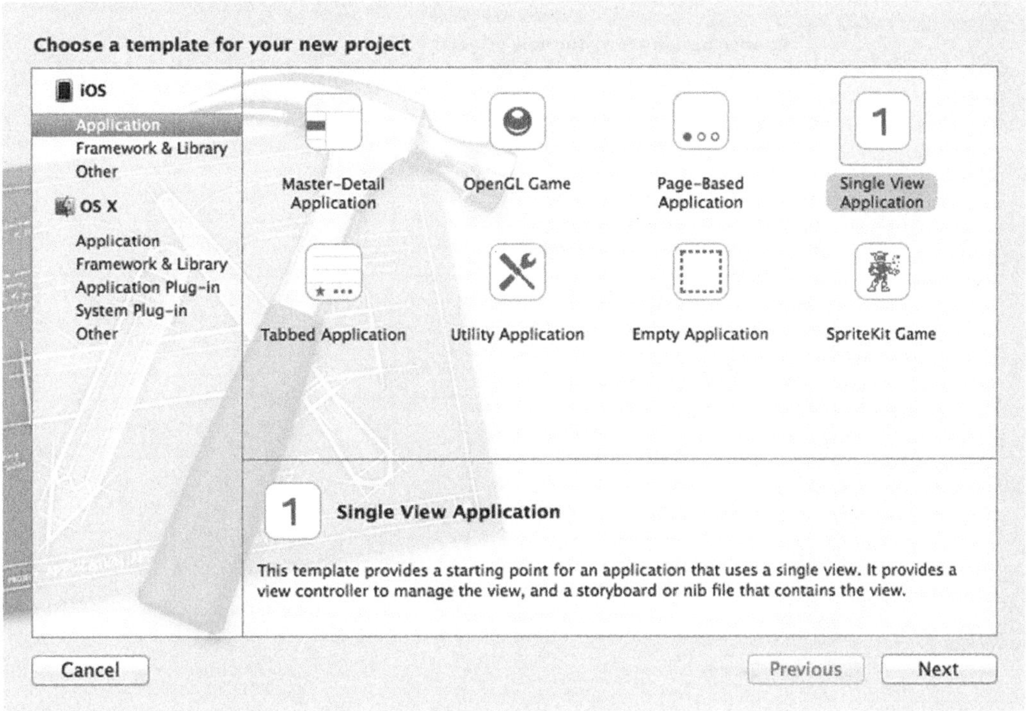

*Figure 2-2. Selecting your application template*

When you click "Next," you'll see a new dialog that requests the options for your new project.

These settings are shown in Figure 2-3, and the recommended settings are:

> **Product Name:** This is the name of your app. For now use "helloWorld_01."
>
> **Organization Name:** This is the name of your organization, or yourself if you are an individual developer.
>
> **Company Identifier:** This is the identifier for your company. It is written in reverse-domain-name format. So, for example, if your company is ios7developer.com, you would use "com.ios7developer" here. The reason for this is that once you deploy your app to the app store, you could have different apps with the same name, written by different people. Our "Hello, World" will be com.ios7developer. helloWorld_01, whereas yours will be different.
>
> **Class Prefix:** This is used to organize your classes into namespaces, which defaults to matching your company identifier. For the sake of simplicity, erase the class prefix. It will make your initial code easier to read.
>
> **Devices:** You'll see the drop-down list giving you the options "iPad", "iPhone," and "Universal." This defaults to "iPhone," so keep it that way. A "Universal" selection is one that runs on both iPhone and iPad.

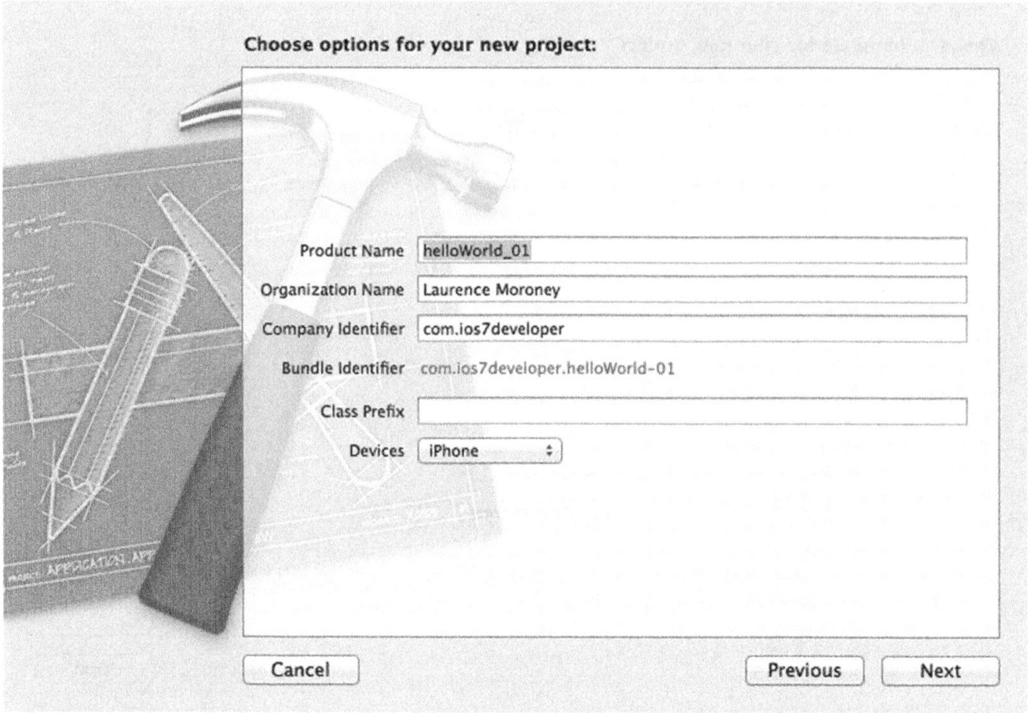

Choose options for your new project:

| | |
|---|---|
| Product Name | helloWorld_01 |
| Organization Name | Laurence Moroney |
| Company Identifier | com.ios7developer |
| Bundle Identifier | com.ios7developer.helloWorld-01 |
| Class Prefix | |
| Devices | iPhone ⇅ |

Cancel          Previous    Next

*Figure 2-3.* *Setting the options for your new project*

Click "Next," and you'll get a dialog that asks you where you want to create your code. It will likely default to your desktop. If not, use the drop-down list at the top of the screen to specify your desktop and click "Create." You can see this in Figure 2-4.

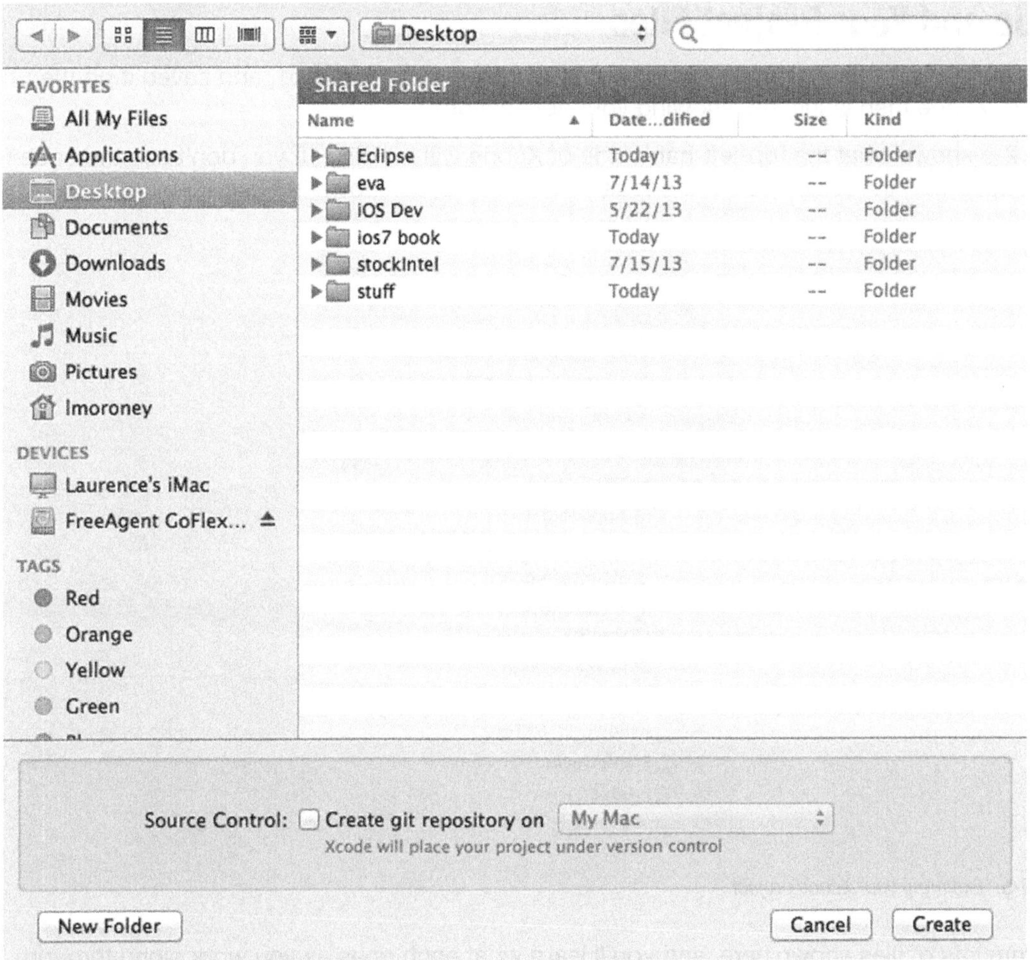

*Figure 2-4. Choosing your source location*

Note that you should keep the "Source Control" checkbox at the bottom unchecked. If you were to check this box, you would be enabling Source Code control through git. This allows you to work with other developers in such a way that you can check changes in and out, avoiding multiple people touching code at the same time. It's beyond the scope of this book, but if you're interested in learning more about git, the 'Pro Git' book by Scott Chacon is available for free here: http://git-scm.com/book.

Once you click "Create," Xcode will create a folder on your desktop containing all the source code and metadata that your application needs. Xcode will also launch the workbench that you'll use for editing your user interface and code. You'll see that in the next section. Congratulations—you've created your first iPhone app project!

# Xcode and Your Project Files

In the previous section you created your first app, called helloWorld_01, and saved it on the desktop. Xcode then launched, showing your application.

Figure 2-5 shows what the top-left-hand side of Xcode will look like. If you don't see the code files listed, make sure the folder icon in the toolbar is selected, as shown in Figure 2-5.

*Figure 2-5. Exploring your Xcode project*

There are lots of files shown here, and you'll learn what each does as you work along through this book. You can see that there are two pairs of files (AppDelegate and ViewController), each with a ".h" and a ".m" file. These are called *classes,* and they have the code for your application in Objective-C. AppDelegate has the code for the shell of your application, and ViewController has the code for the default view of your application. Think about a single-view application as a shell containing a view. The shell handles all the application-level stuff, such as launching, shutting down, and so forth, and each "screen" in your app has a view. The code for this view is called a "controller." As this app only has one screen, it has one controller piece of code, and that's the ViewController.h and ViewController.m files. These terms come from a common pattern used in software development called "Model-View-Controller," or just MVC. Under this pattern, applications can be built by creating a *Model* of your data, a *View* that the user has on your data, and a *Controller* that manages the interaction between the two.

The "Supporting Files" folder contains other files that your app will need, including the ".plist" file that contains metadata about your application and the main.m file that is the starting point of your application as it runs.

Your user interface is the Main.storyboard file. You'll edit that in the next section.

Don't worry if some of this seems overwhelming right now—there are a lot of concepts to take in, and you'll go through them step by step. Before you know it, it will become second nature!

## Using Interface Builder to Create Your "Hello, World" App

Using Xcode, select Main.storyboard, and the storyboard editor will open. On the left-hand side of the screen, you'll see a menu drop down that reads "View Controller Scene."

Drop this down to view all the options underneath it and select the "View Controller" entry, as shown in Figure 2-6.

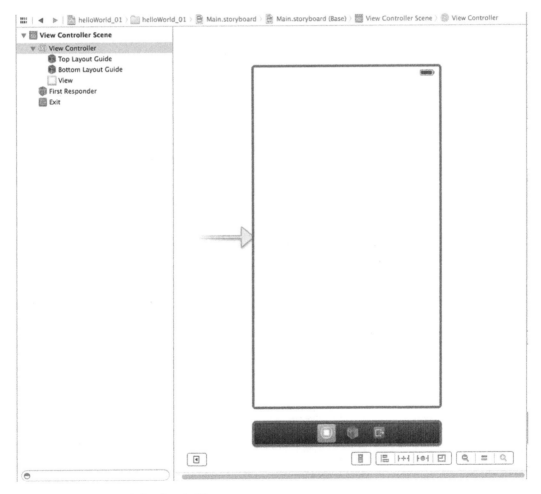

*Figure 2-6. Exploring the scene in interface builder*

To the right of this, you *should* see the utility area, where all the settings for your user interface are kept. If you don't see it, make sure that you click the "View Utility Area" button on the very top-right-hand side. It looks like a square with a shaded area to the right.

You can see the utility area in Figure 2-7.

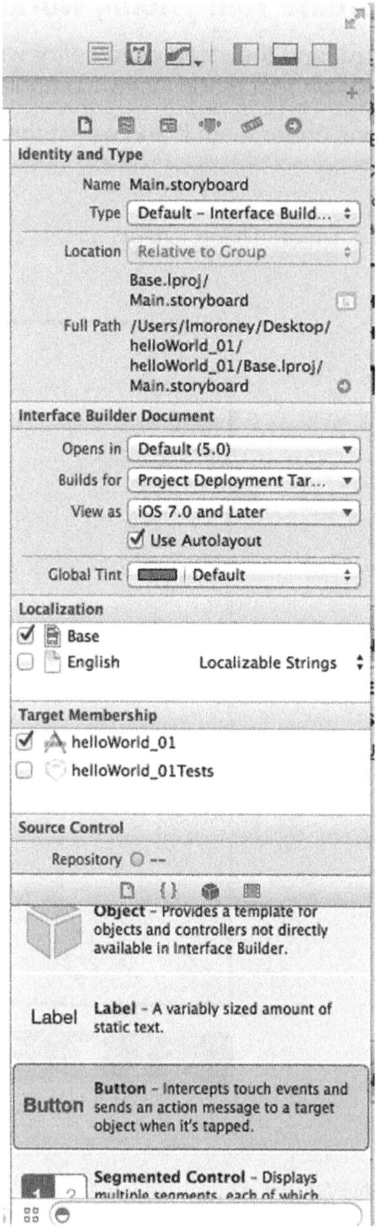

*Figure 2-7.  The utility area*

Across the top of the utility area, you'll see six buttons. These are shown in Figure 2-8.

*Figure 2-8. Utility area buttons*

From left to right, these buttons are:

>    **File Inspector:** Used to set the details including the name, document, language, and localization for the interface

>    **Quick Help Inspector:** Gives context-sensitive help on the currently selected object

>    **Identity Inspector:** Provides details on the class underlying the view

>    **Attributes Inspector:** Displays metadata about the currently selected view, such as background color

>    **Size Inspector:** Shows definitions about how controls should stretch to fit the view

>    **Connections Inspector:** Shows definitions about how the view connects to code

Again, don't worry if you don't understand most of this yet. As you work through this book you'll be using each of these tabs, so it's good to take a quick tour to get a feel for what the controls do.

The important setting that we want you to see here is that which connects the interface that you are designing to the underlying code that you'll write. With "View Controller" selected (see Figure 2-6), make sure the "Custom Class" button is clicked, and you'll see that this user interface will map to a specific class—in this case ViewController. That class is implemented using the ViewController.m and ViewController.h files.

At the bottom of the utility area, no matter which button is selected, you'll see a list of controls. Scroll this list until you see the "Label" control, as shown in Figure 2-9.

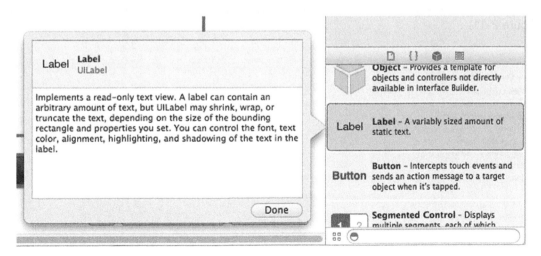

*Figure 2-9. Selecting the "Label" control*

Using your mouse, drag the "Label" control onto the view. As you move it around, you should see blue dotted guide lines that will help you place it. Vertical ones show you the horizontal center of the view and vice versa. Others show you borders around the edge of the screen that you might want to avoid. You can drop the label wherever you like on the view. When you're done, it will look something like Figure 2-10.

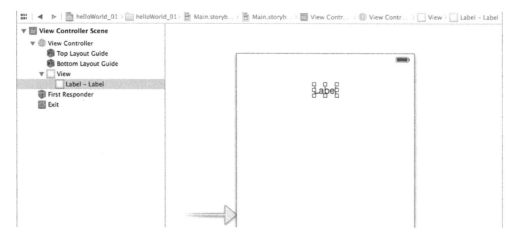

*Figure 2-10.* *Placing your label on the view*

You should then drag the little white dots around the label to resize it. Xcode will crop any text that goes into a label to the size of the label by default, so your "Hello, World!" text will look something like "He . . ." unless you make the label larger.

Experiment until you get the width that you like; you'll notice that the word "Label" appears on the left of the screen. To re-center it, don't move the label—find the "Alignment" setting in the attributes inspector and set it to "Center."

Go back to the controls list and scroll until you see the "Button" control. Select it and drag and drop it onto the view, just like you did with the label. When you're done, your view should look something like Figure 2-11.

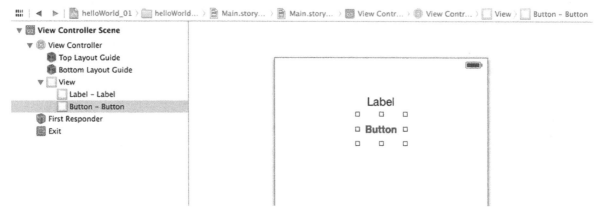

*Figure 2-11.* *Placing the "Button" control on the view*

With the button selected (it will be highlighted on the list on the left and will have dots around it on the designer to the right), select the "Attributes Inspector" button. You'll see the "Title" property that says "Button." You can use this to change the title to "Press Me!" See Figure 2-12. (Alternatively, you could double click on the button in the designer and just type the new caption.)

*Figure 2-12. Updating the button title*

You've now finished with the designer, so save your work before you go to the next step. You can do this by pressing ⌘s or selecting "Save" on the "File" menu.

At the top of the screen, where you opened the utility area, you should now close it and then open the "Assistant" editor. (This is the second icon from the left looking like a tuxedo.) See Figure 2-13.

*Figure 2-13. Opening the assistant*

Note that when an icon is selected it's shaded in light blue. So, in Figure 2-13 you can see that the utility area at the right has been closed, and that the assistant has been opened.

You should see that a code window will open beside the designer.

> **Note**    If the code in the assistant window on the right is for ViewController.m, as shown in Figure 2-14, you'll need to make some changes. This is actually the *wrong* file, but it is often the default file that you get. If this happens, find where it says Automatic > ViewController.m at the top of the assistant window. You can see it in Figure 2-15. Once you've done this, click on ViewController.m, and a drop-down menu will appear that you can use to pick ViewController.h.

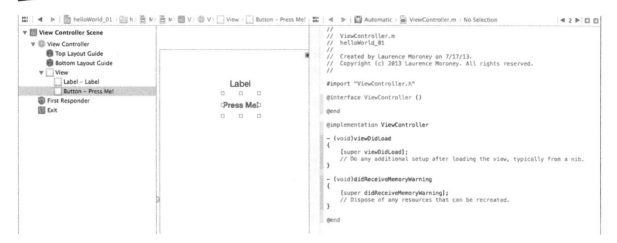

**Figure 2-14.** *Using the assistant window*

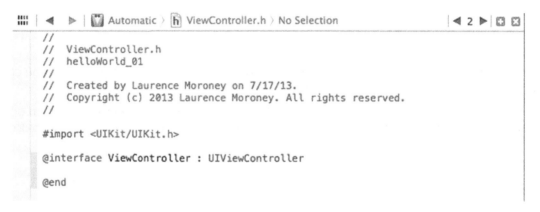

**Figure 2-15.** *Assistant with ViewController.h selected*

As mentioned earlier, classes are defined using two files. The .h (or header) file contains all the information about the class, including the names of the functions and variables used within it. The .m (or implementation) file contains all the logic. To map the controls to functions in the class, you'll need to edit the .h file, so it should be the one selected in the assistant view before you go any further.

When the user presses the button, you want something to happen. You'll write the code for this; Objective-C and iOS call this an *Action*. So, to create an action that happens in response to the user pressing your button, you should hold the CONTROL key and drag the button onto the code window, just below the word @interface. This creates what is called a *connection*.

You'll see a little helper window pop up. It will look like Figure 2-16.

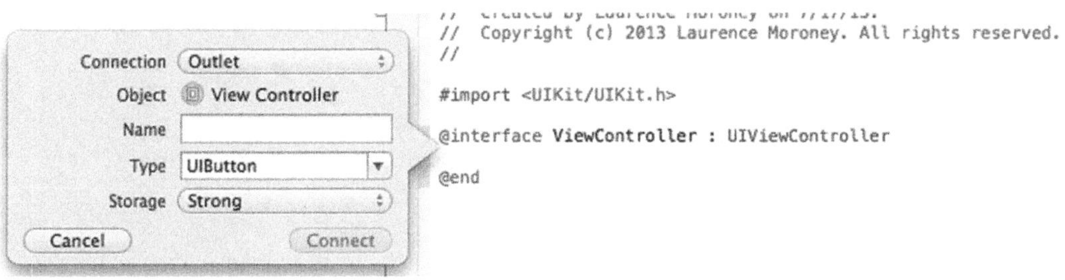

*Figure 2-16.  Connection helper window*

The default type of connection is called an *Outlet*. You'll see what that is for a little later in this chapter. What you want to create right now is an action, so change the "Connection" setting to this. You'll see that the settings change. See Figure 2-17 for how they will look now.

*Figure 2-17.  Connection helper window for actions*

The important parts you want to set up here are the "Name" and "Event" types.

The Name setting is the name of the function that will run when the action happens. Type "btnPressed" into the Name field.

The Event setting is the type of interaction from the user that will trigger this action. Every control has a different set of events that it supports. For a button, "Touch Up Inside" is the default event. It fires, as the name suggests, when the user releases their touch inside the button.

Enter these values ("btnPressed" for Name and "Touch Up Inside" for Event), and click the "Connect" button. You'll see that the code in the assistant window has changed. See Figure 2-18. (If you inspect the .m file, you'll see that code has been added there too. You'll be editing that code in the next section.)

```
//
//  ViewController.h
//  helloWorld_01
//
//  Created by Laurence Moroney on 7/17/13.
//  Copyright (c) 2013 Laurence Moroney. All rights reserved.
//

#import <UIKit/UIKit.h>

@interface ViewController : UIViewController
- (IBAction)btnPressed:(id)sender;

@end
```

*Figure 2-18. Your newly amended code*

When you want to change something on the user interface from within your code, you have to tell iOS how they are connected, and this is where an outlet is used. An outlet is effectively the name of your control as visible to your code. So, in order to change the label's content when the user presses the button, you need to create an outlet to the label.

So, as you did with the button, select the label and then, while holding the CONTROL key, drag it over to the code window and drop it just below the btnPressed line.

The connection helper window will appear, and you will see that you'll need to specify a name for your outlet. Type "MyLabel" into the Name field. See Figure 2-19.

*Figure 2-19. Helper window for configuring the outlet*

Click the "Connect" button and you'll see that some more code has been generated for you in the header file. See Figure 2-20.

```
#import <UIKit/UIKit.h>

@interface ViewController : UIViewController
- (IBAction)btnPressed:(id)sender;
@property (strong, nonatomic) IBOutlet UILabel *MyLabel;

@end
```

*Figure 2-20.* Updated code in the header file

You've now completed the user interface for your application, and you've defined the action and outlet that it uses.

## Writing the Code for Your Application

Before continuing, it's a good idea to review the differences between a .h and a .m file. The .h file is a header file, and in a header file you tell the computer what types of commands you'll execute and what types of data you will use in the implementation file. The .m file is the implementation file in which you program those commands and use that data.

In the previous section, you created the user interface for the application, and you set up the action method that will be called when the button is pressed, as well as the outlet value to allow the label to be changed. When you did this, Xcode generated code for you in the .h and .m files. The .h (where "h" stands for header) file contains the declarations of the data and methods that your program will use. The .m file (where "m" stands for messages, a concept used early on in Objective-C, but which has been greatly expanded on since) is the implementation of your code, where you write your methods. So, for example, when you created the action for handling the button being touched, you'll see that Xcode placed the declaration of the method into the ViewController.h file and an empty method handler in the ViewController.m file.

In the project navigator, select ViewController.m to view the implementation code. You'll notice that there is now an empty function called btnPressed waiting for you to add code to it. See Figure 2-21.

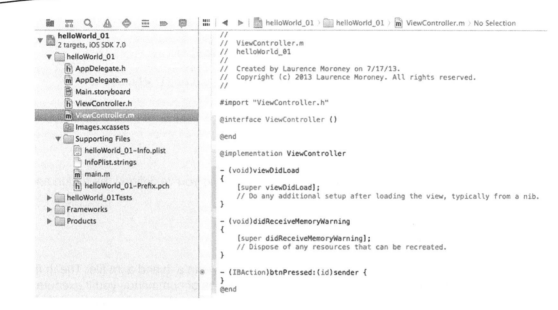

*Figure 2-21. Editing the "View Controller" implementation code*

Now, we said that we want the application to change the text in the label to "Hello, World!" when the user presses the button. We've already identified that pressing the button is the action, and this causes the btnPressed function to be called. We've also seen that an outlet is necessary for us to manipulate the UI from within our code, and we created an outlet to the label called MyLabel. To address the outlet called MyLabel, in code we prefix that with an underscore, so we use _MyLabel.

So, within the btnPressed function, you should enter this code:

```
_MyLabel.text = @"Hello, World!";
```

The entire function should look like this:

```
- (IBAction)btnPressed:(id)sender {
    _MyLabel.text = @"Hello, World!";
}
```

And that's it! You've just written all the code needed for your "Hello, World!" app. In the next section you'll see how to run and test it using the iPhone and iPad emulators.

## Testing the App on the iPhone Emulator

At the top of the Xcode editor, you'll see a toolbar that allows you to pick your run target and to start your application on it. It looks like Figure 2-22.

*Figure 2-22. Running your application*

Clicking the device type—where it says "iPhone Retina (3.5 inch)"—will give you a list of available devices that you can test on. Clicking the "Run" button on the left will compile your code and launch the emulator, if it compiles successfully.

If you've developed in Xcode for iOS before, you might think that the iPad emulator has launched, because it's so large, but don't worry—it's still the iPhone emulator. It's just that in order to fit all the pixels from the retina display onto your screen, you need a much larger surface area. See Figure 2-23.

*Figure 2-23. Using the iOS7 iPhone emulator*

If you need more space on your screen, with the emulator selected, you can select "Scale" from the "Window" menu and reduce the size to 75% or 50%.

Click the "Press Me!" button, and you'll see that the label changes to "Hello, World!" as expected. See Figure 2-24.

*Figure 2-24. The result of clicking the button to get "Hello, World!"*

This is running using the iPhone simulator. Let's now look at running it on the iPad simulator.

Simply drop down the list at the top of your Xcode window and select "iPad Retina." Your screen should look like Figure 2-25.

*Figure 2-25. Configuring Xcode to use the iPad simulator*

When you click "Run", your app will launch as an iPhone app within the iPad. Remember back at the beginning of the chapter, you specified it was an iPhone app? iPad launches iPhone apps in a small, iPhone-sized rectangle in the center of the screen, and the emulator does the same. See Figure 2-26.

*Figure 2-26.  Running in the iPad simulator*

If you want to run full screen, the iPad allows you to do so by pressing the "2x" button. You can see it at the top-right-hand side of the emulator.

Your app isn't written with the iPad screen in mind, so this just "zooms" into your app. See Figure 2-27.

*Figure 2-27. Zooming into your app on the iPad*

And that's it! It's been quite a few pages to build a simple app, but it's a great start to using the tools that are available to you in building iOS apps. But you're not quite done yet. In the next section you'll see how you can build an iPad app with the same functionality. You'll go through it a lot quicker, as you've already covered most of the concepts.

## Creating Your First iPad App

Using Xcode, from the "File" menu, select "New," and then select "Project." You'll see the "Choose a Template" dialog (refer back to Figure 2-2 for details), and, on this, select "Single View Application" and press "Next."

You'll see the "Project Options" dialog. Fill it out as you did earlier, but this time you'll select "iPad" as the device, and of course you'll use a different project name, in this case "helloWorld_02." See Figure 2-28.

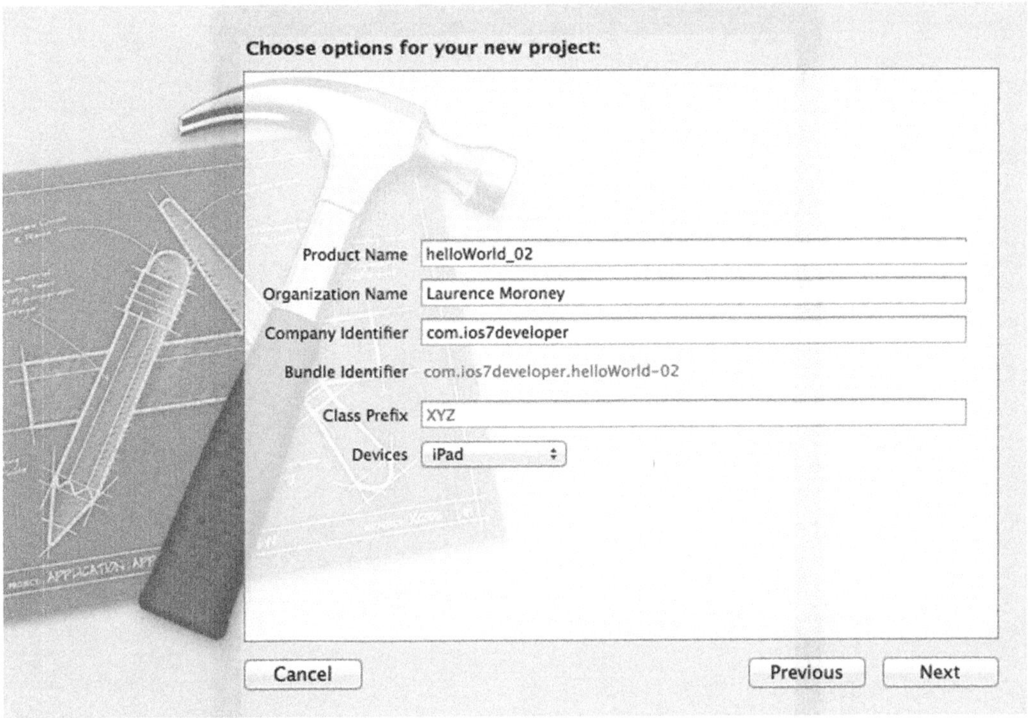

*Figure 2-28. Creating your iPad project*

Click "Next" when you're done, and on the next screen click "Create."

You're now back in Xcode and ready to edit the code to make an iPad application.

Repeat everything you did earlier in this chapter for the iPhone application. The chief difference, of course, is that the view is much bigger when working with the iPad. Drop a label and a button on the view and edit their properties as before. Use the assistant to create an outlet for the label (called MyLabel) and an action for the button (called btnAction), just like you did with the iPhone app.

When you're done, open the ViewController.m file, and edit the btnPressed code as before to this:

```
- (IBAction)btnPressed:(id)sender {
    _MyLabel.text = @"Hello, World!";
}
@end
```

You can now run your app, and you'll see it launches as a full-screen iPad application. See Figure 2-29.

*Figure 2-29.  Running your iPad app*

# Summary

If you've never coded for iOS before, and this is your first venture into this exciting and valuable skillset, we hope you enjoyed it! While the app you built didn't really do a whole lot from a user perspective, you covered many of the basics that a more sophisticated app does. In creating this "Hello, World" app, you've touched on the following:

Project structure

iOS storyboards

Managing user input via actions

Managing programmatic user interface output using outlets

Used headers and classes

Worked with a view

Automatically generated stubs and prototypes

Written your first lines of Objective-C code

Ran an iPhone application on the iPhone simulator

Ran an iPhone application on the iPad simulator

Ran an iPad application on the iPad simulator

**Note**    If you have no idea what stubs, prototypes, or any of these concepts mean right now, don't worry—you will! You did this when you dragged the controls onto the assistant in order to add the declarations of the outlet and action to the .h file and the empty function to the .m file.

That's a lot of ground to have covered, and a great start on getting into more sophisticated development. Congratulations, and see you in Chapter 3!

# Running Your App on a Device

In Chapter 1 you learned how to get the requisite tools to become an iOS developer, and in Chapter 2 you saw how to build your first (albeit very simple) app. Before you go further into app development, this chapter will show you how to sign up for a developer account on apple.com and how to use that account to authorize your device for development work. You'll see how to deploy an application to a device and how to run it on your device from within Xcode.

You don't need to work through this chapter if you just want to learn development. If you don't want to subscribe to Apple's service and just want to continue building apps that run on the simulator, feel free to skip ahead to Chapter 4. You might want to come back here when you've finished some later chapters, particularly those on debugging, so that you can see how to debug an app running on a physical device.

## Signing Up as an Apple Developer

The journey begins at http://developer.apple.com. You saw this site back in Chapter 1. This site is the overall Apple developer site, with resources for iOS, OS X, and Safari development. While it is free to be a Safari developer, OS X and iOS development memberships each cost $99 per year. They are completely separate, so if you only want to develop for one of these, ensure you sign up for the right one!

You can see a section of the site in Figure 3-1.

**iOS 7**
Develop your apps for iOS 7 today.
Learn more | iOS Dev Center

**OS X Mavericks**
Download the Developer Preview of OS X 10.9.
Learn more | Mac Dev Center

**Xcode 5**
See what's new in version 5.0.
Learn more | Download

*Figure 3-1. Apple's developer site*

Be sure to click on the iOS dev center link to be taken to `https://developer.apple.com/devcenter/ios/index.action`. This is the hub of the iOS developer world. At the top, you'll see a section that reads "Access additional resources in the iOS Dev Center." See Figure 3-2.

**Access additional resources in the iOS Dev Center.**    Sign in

Sign in with the Apple ID you used to register as an Apple Developer, or register for free today.

*Figure 3-2. The sign-in banner*

It's a little confusing, as the words "register for free" appear. This is to register for a free Apple ID, as you did in Chapter 1 to use the store. Once you have an Apple ID, and have signed in with it, you will be given the option of registering for an iOS (or OS X, if you like) developer account.

If you don't already have an Apple ID, go ahead and sign up for one with the "register for free" link in the banner, as shown in Figure 3-2. Once you have it, sign in with the blue '"Sign in" button.

Once you sign in with your Apple ID, you'll be asked to review your agreement with Apple. Read through it, and, if you agree, check the box and click the "Agree" button.

You'll be asked to fill out a brief survey about yourself and the type of apps you're developing. See Figure 3-3.

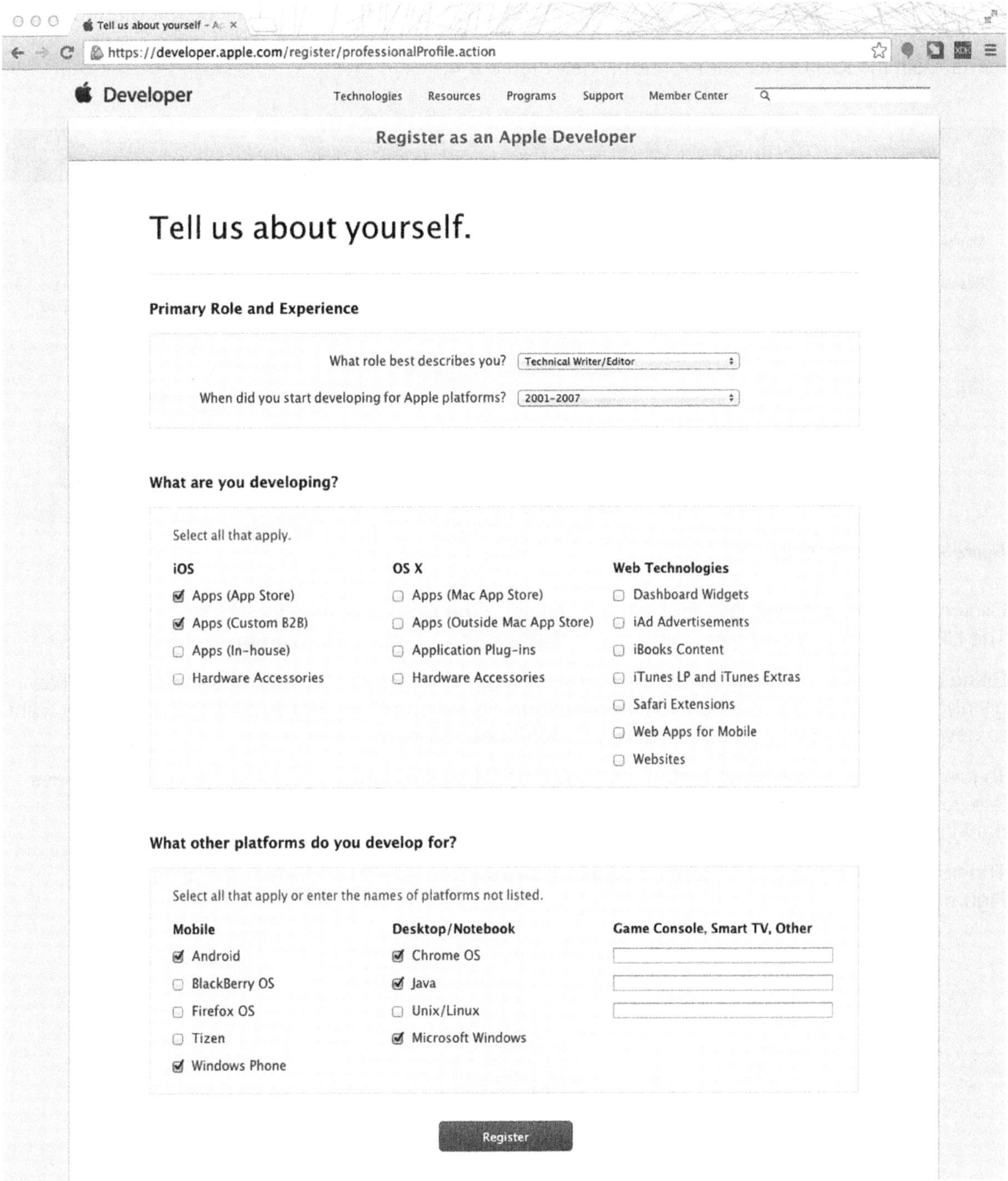


*Figure 3-3. Developer survey*

Fill it out with the appropriate information and click the "Register" button. You'll be returned to the developer center, but it'll look a little different now. On the right-hand side, you'll see a section that reads "Join the iOS Developer Program." See Figure 3-4.

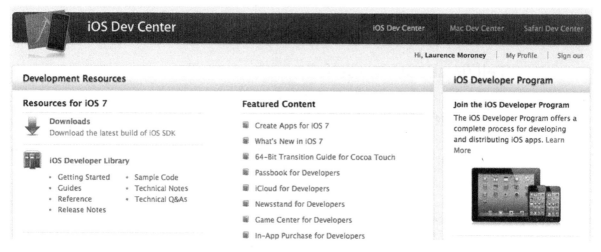

*Figure 3-4. The iOS dev center*

Click on the "Learn More" link, and you'll be taken to the sign-up screen for iOS development. The URL is `https://developer.apple.com/programs/ios/` if you want to go there directly.

Being a member of the program allows you to develop and test your apps on hardware, as well as giving you the ability to distribute iOS applications via the app store. Remember that if you only want to develop without physical distribution, you don't need to join.

To join, click the "Enroll Now" button, and you'll be taken through a process to enroll. This process lets you enroll as an individual or as a company and shows you how to set up details such as banking, through which you'll receive payment as people buy your app through the app store.

The first step is at `https://developer.apple.com/programs/start/standard`, and it looks like Figure 3-5.

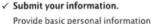

Apple Developer Program Enrollment

# Enrolling in Apple Developer Programs

Get everything you need to develop and distribute apps for iOS and OS X.

**It's easy to get started.**

✓ **Choose an enrollment type.**

Individual: choose this option if you are an individual or sole proprietor/single person business.

Company/Organization: choose this option if you are a company, non-profit organization, joint venture, partnership, or government organization.

✓ **Submit your information.**

Provide basic personal information, including your legal name and address. If you're enrolling as a company/organization, we'll need a few more things, like your legal entity name and D-U-N-S® Number, as part of our verification process.

✓ **Purchase and activate your program.**

Once we verify your information, you can purchase your program on the Apple Online Store. After you have completed your purchase, we'll send you an email within 24 hours on how to activate your membership.

Continue

*Figure 3-5.  Enrolling in the Apple developer program*

When you click "Continue," you'll be given a chance to sign in with your existing Apple ID or to create a new one. By now you should have an Apple ID, so go ahead and use that to sign in.

You'll then be asked if you are enrolling as an individual or an organization. See Figure 3-6.

 Developer                                    Apple Developer Program Enrollment

Enter Account Info      Select Program      Review & Submit      Agree to License      Purchase Program      Activate Program

# Are you enrolling as an individual or organization?

## Individual

Select this option if you are an individual or sole proprietor/single person company.

**Seller Name**
Your personal legal name will be listed as the seller of your apps on the App Store.

Example:
Seller: John Smith

**Individual Development Only**
You are the only one allowed access to program resources.

**You will need:**

- A valid credit card for purchase.
  We may also require additional personal documentation to verify your identity.

## Company/Organization

Select this option if you are a company, non-profit organization, joint venture, partnership, or government organization.

**Seller Name**
Your organization's legal entity name will be listed as the seller of your apps on the App Store.

Example:
Seller: ABC Company, Inc.

**Development Team**
You can add additional developers to your team who can access program resources. Companies who have hired a contractor to create apps for distribution on the App Store should enroll with their company name and add the contractors to their team.

**You will need:**

- The legal authority to bind your company/organization to Apple Developer Program legal agreements.

- An address for the company's principal place of business or corporate headquarters.

- A D-U-N-S® Number assigned to a legal entity.
  D-U-N-S Numbers, available from D&B for free in most jurisdictions, are unique nine-digit numbers widely used as standard business identifiers. To learn more, read our FAQs. Before enrolling, check to see if D&B has assigned you a D-U-N-S Number. If not, please request one.

  Note: We do not accept DBAs, Fictitious Business, Trade names, or branches at this time.

- A valid credit card for purchase.

[ Individual ]                                    [ Company ]

*Figure 3-6. Enrolling in the developer program*

The rest of the enrollment is shown in the steps at the top of the screen. You first have to enter your billing information in order to verify your identity. After that you'll select your desired program, so be sure, for instance, that for iOS development you pick that program. Once you're done, you'll purchase and activate the program.

# Using the Developer Portal

Once you've signed up for the iOS development program, when you sign into the portal, you'll see that the dev center looks like Figure 3-7.

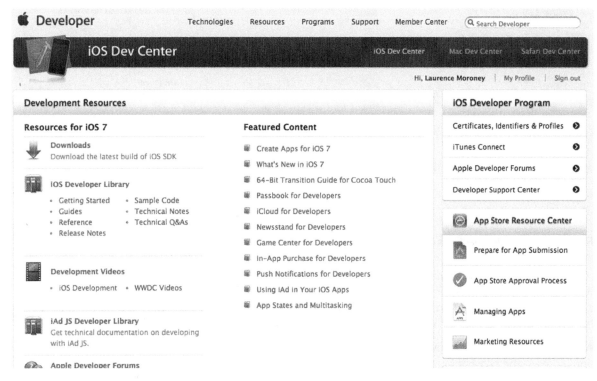

*Figure 3-7. The developer portal*

You'll notice that the right-hand side of the screen has changed; it now gives you options for the likes of Certificates, Identifiers & Profiles, as well as iTunes Connect, Apple Developer Forums, and the Developer Support Center. There's also a resource center, which gives you details on how to handle app submission.

Take a look at the "Certificates, Identifiers & Profiles" link, and you'll be taken to `https://developer.apple.com/account/overview.action`. You can see this in Figure 3-8.

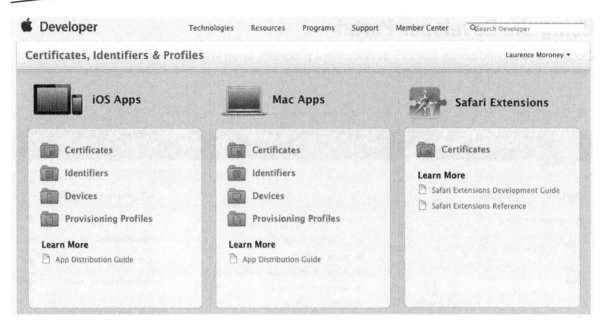

*Figure 3-8.  Certificates, Identifiers & Profiles screen*

"Certificates" are used to identify who you are when you are building for a device. They are matched with devices through the "Provisioning Profile" so that the apps that you build (as signed by the certificates) can run only on the devices for which those certificates have been loaded on (as defined by the provisioning profile), unless, of course those apps are deployed from the app store.

As a developer, you are allowed to deploy your code to 100 devices for testing. So, in the next steps you'll create the provisioning profile for an attached device that contains the certificate that works with your developer profile, as well as an application identifier, which signs that this app will work on this device.

Conceptually it's very confusing. It'll make more sense as you work through the example. Fortunately Xcode 5 does a lot of the heavy lifting for you.

# Deploying to a Device with Xcode

In this section you'll create a new, simple Xcode application and deploy it to an iOS device. The device can be an iPod, iPhone, or iPad. As we work through the examples, we'll be using an iPhone.

Launch Xcode, and you'll see the "Welcome to Xcode" screen. See Figure 3-9.

*Figure 3-9.  Welcome to Xcode screen*

Select the "Create a new Xcode project" link, and you'll be asked to choose a template for your new project, as shown in Figure 3-10.

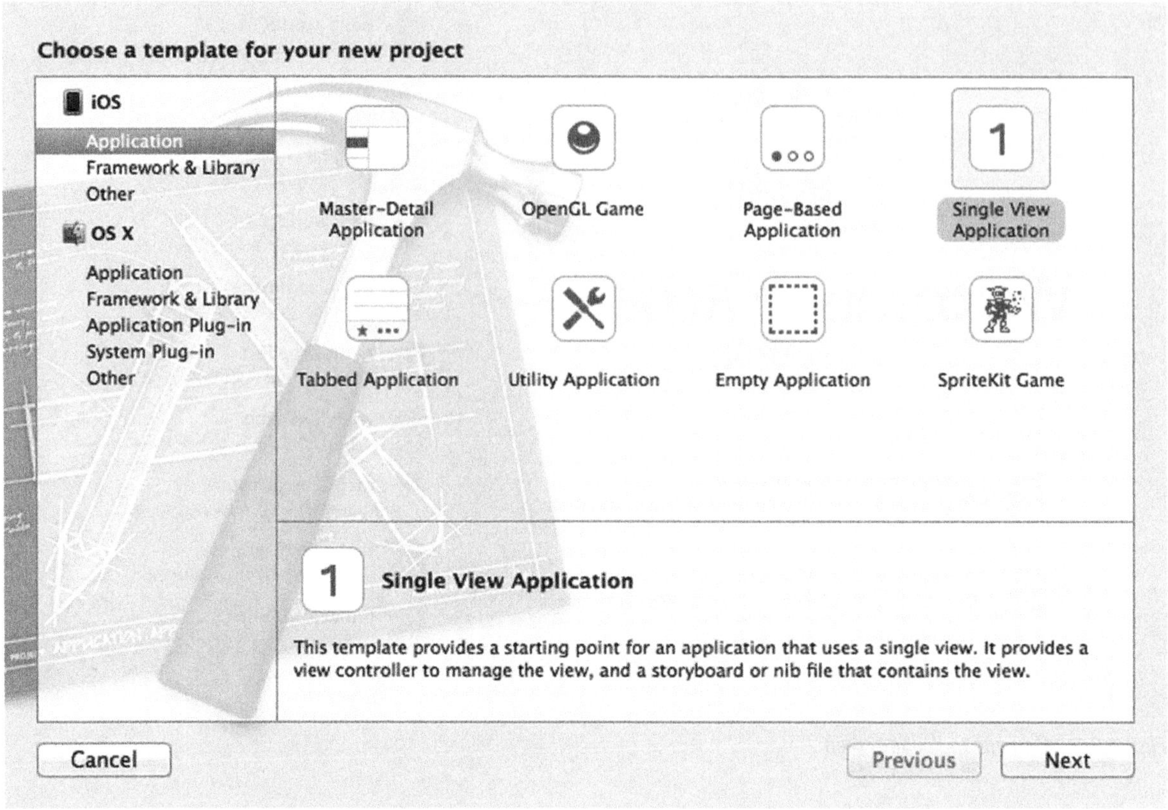

**Choose a template for your new project**

iOS
- **Application**
- Framework & Library
- Other

OS X
- Application
- Framework & Library
- Application Plug-in
- System Plug-in
- Other

Master–Detail Application   OpenGL Game   Page-Based Application   Single View Application

Tabbed Application   Utility Application   Empty Application   SpriteKit Game

**1**   **Single View Application**

This template provides a starting point for an application that uses a single view. It provides a view controller to manage the view, and a storyboard or nib file that contains the view.

Cancel                    Previous    Next

*Figure 3-10.  Choosing a template for your project*

Choose the "Single View Application" template, as shown in Figure 3-10, and click "Next." You'll see a dialog asking you to choose options for your new project.

Fill it out as shown in Figure 3-11, but use your own organization name and company identifier. The company identifier is reverse-domain-name style, so if your domain name is foo.com, you should use com.foo as the company identifier.

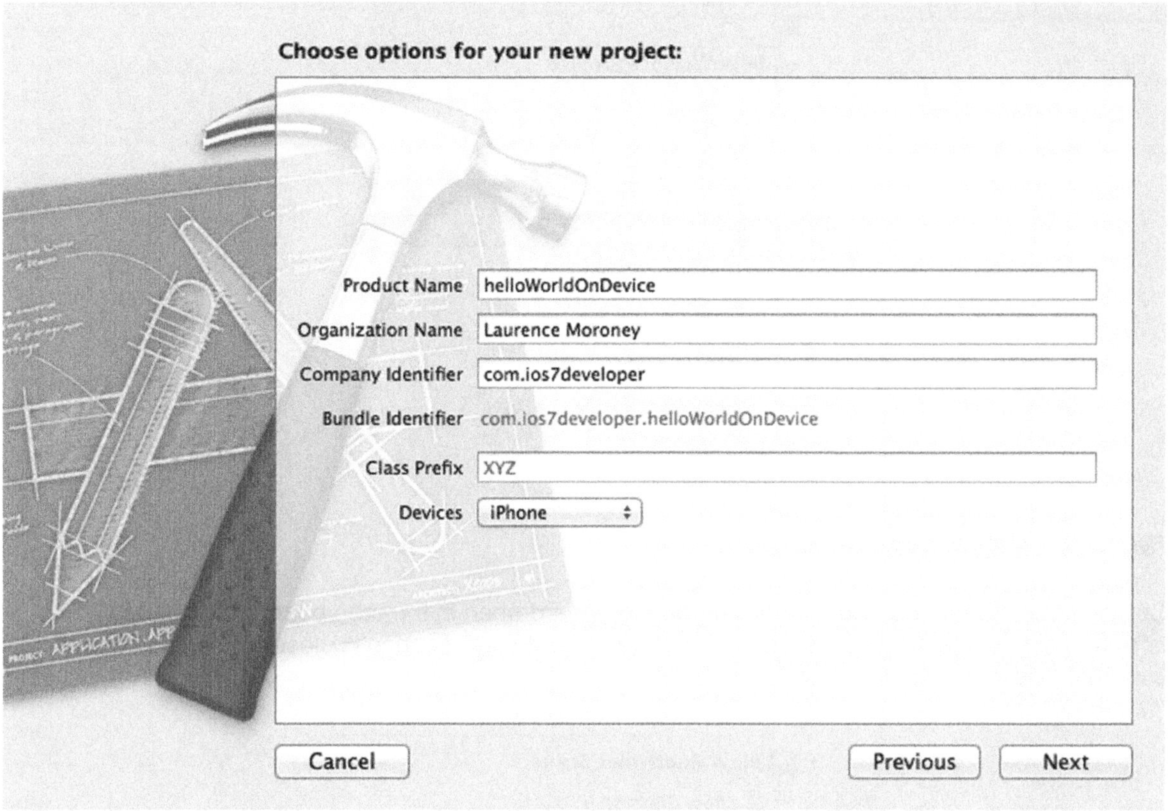

**Choose options for your new project:**

| | |
|---|---|
| Product Name | helloWorldOnDevice |
| Organization Name | Laurence Moroney |
| Company Identifier | com.ios7developer |
| Bundle Identifier | com.ios7developer.helloWorldOnDevice |
| Class Prefix | XYZ |
| Devices | iPhone |

Cancel     Previous     Next

*Figure 3-11. Setting the project options*

Click "Next," and you'll be asked where you want to store your code. Leaving it on the desktop is fine for now. When you click "Create," Xcode will launch.

On the left-hand side of the screen, you'll see your app code in the project navigator. See Figure 3-12 for the list of files.

*Figure 3-12.  List of files in the project navigator*

Select "Main.storyboard," and you'll see the storyboard open in the storyboard editor. On the left-hand side of the storyboard editor, if the "View Controller" section is closed, open it and make sure that "View" is selected. See Figure 3-13.

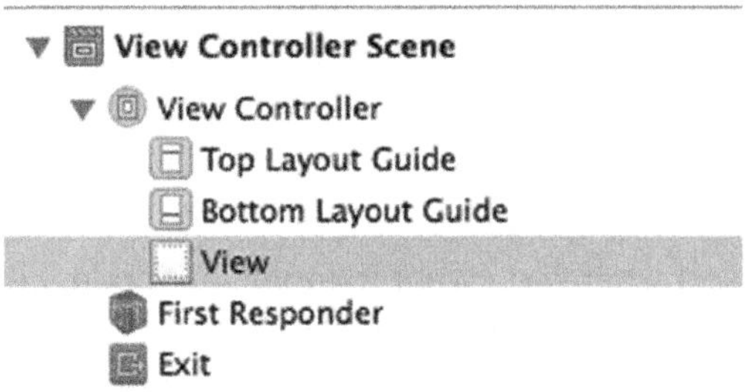

*Figure 3-13.  Selecting the view*

With the view selected, take a look at the attributes inspector on the right-hand side of the screen. It should look like Figure 3-14.

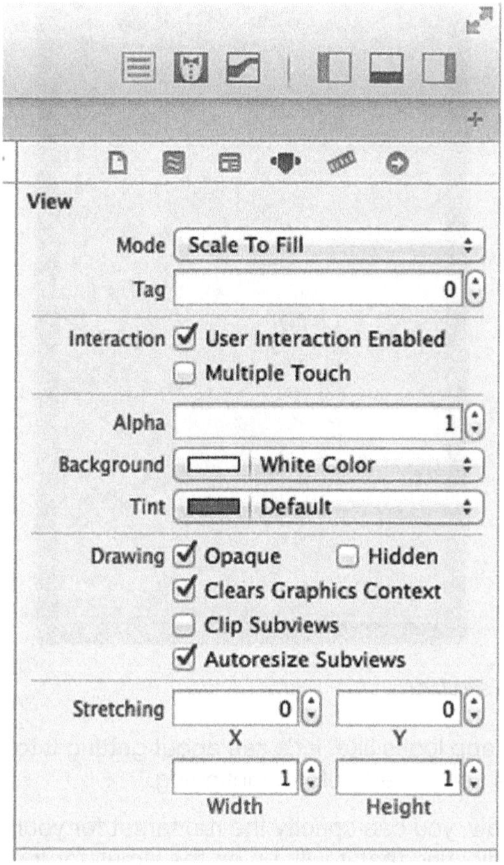

*Figure 3-14. Attributes for the view*

Select the "Background" setting and change the color from "White Color" to something else. In our case, we chose a blue color.

If you run the app now, it will run in the simulator. You should see a simple app with a blue screen. See Figure 3-15.

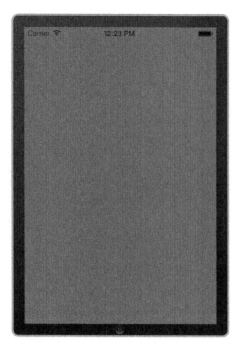

*Figure 3-15. Running your app in the simulator*

Now that you know what the app looks like, let's see about getting it to run on your device. Make sure that your device is connected before continuing.

At the top of the Xcode window, you can specify the run target for your app. By default it reads "iPhone Retina (3.5 inch)," indicating that it will run on the simulator for the iPhone. See Figure 3-16.

*Figure 3-16. Finding the run target*

Click on where it says "iPhone Retina (3.5-inch)" and a menu will pop up. At the top of this menu, you should see an entry that reads "iOS Device." See Figure 3-17.

*Figure 3-17. Selecting the iOS device*

If you try to run the app, you'll now get a message that says there isn't a provisioned iOS device attached. As mentioned earlier, you have a limit of 100 devices that you can deploy apps to, unless you go through the app store, in which case there is no limit. These 100 devices are identified using their provisioning profile.

The message will look like Figure 3-18.

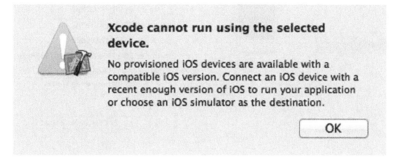

**Figure 3-18.** *No provisioned device is attached*

Next, you'll provision a device. To do this, look at the "Window" menu at the top of the screen while Xcode is selected. You'll see an option to load the Organizer. See Figure 3-19.

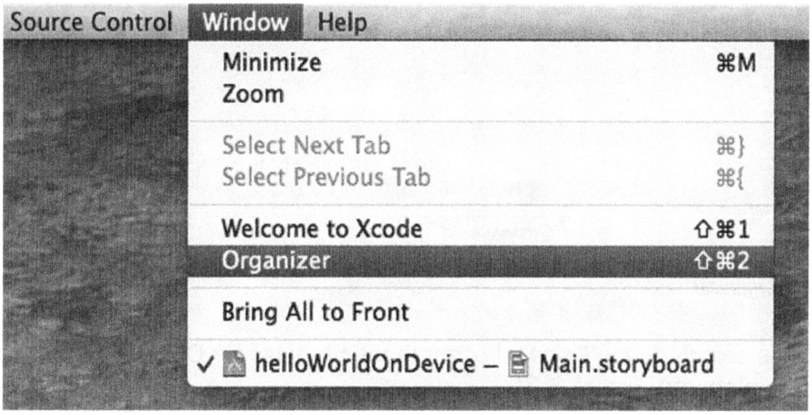

*Figure 3-19. Launching the organizer*

Select "Organizer" on this menu, and it will launch. Across the top of the screen, you'll see icons for "Devices," "Projects," and "Archives." Make sure that "Devices" is selected, and you'll see a list of connected devices. See Figure 3-20, where you can see what the organizer looks like on our machine, with an iPhone 4 device attached.

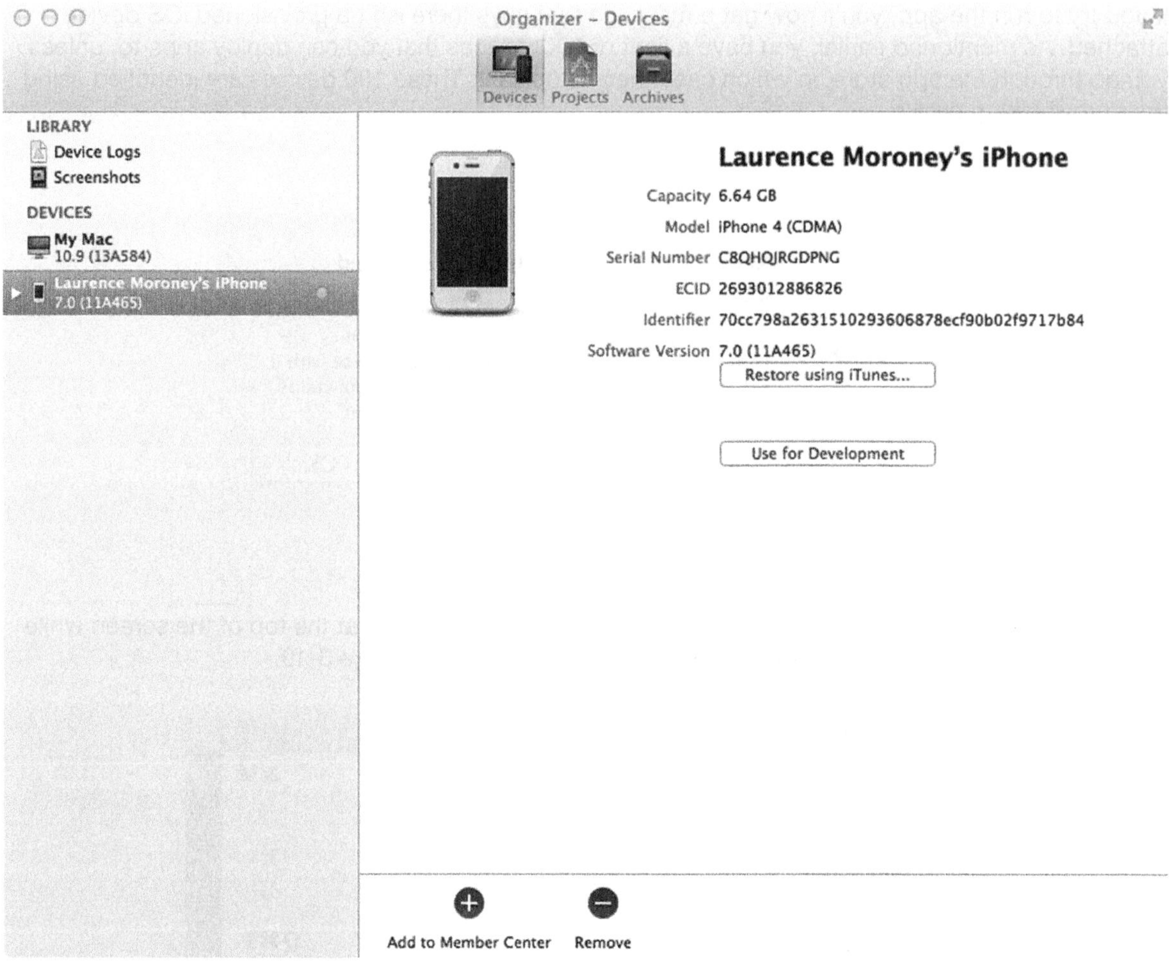

*Figure 3-20. Using the organizer*

When your device is selected, you'll see a button that says "Use for Development." Click this button, and you'll see the dialog from Figure 3-21.

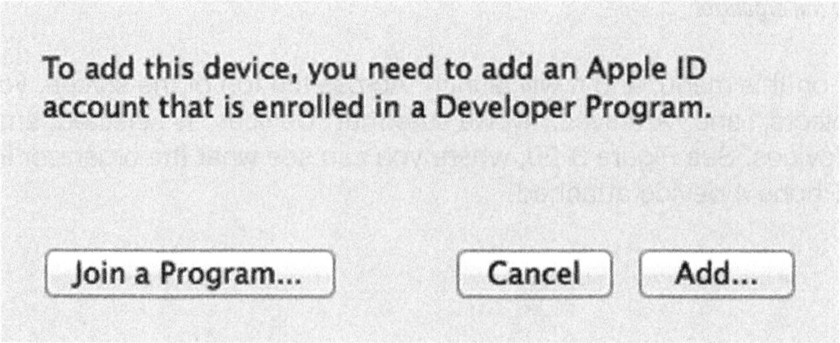

To add this device, you need to add an Apple ID account that is enrolled in a Developer Program.

Join a Program...        Cancel        Add...

*Figure 3-21. Dialog to assign your developer program*

Click the "Add…" button, and you'll be asked to sign in with your Apple ID. When you sign in, you'll see the "Accounts" screen. It should look something like Figure 3-22.

*Figure 3-22. The accounts screen*

This is a useful screen for monitoring stuff about your apps, but right now you don't need it. However, it is most likely obscuring a dialog on the organizer because it popped up after you signed in from that app. Switch back to the organizer, or move the accounts screen out of the way, and you'll see something like Figure 3-23.

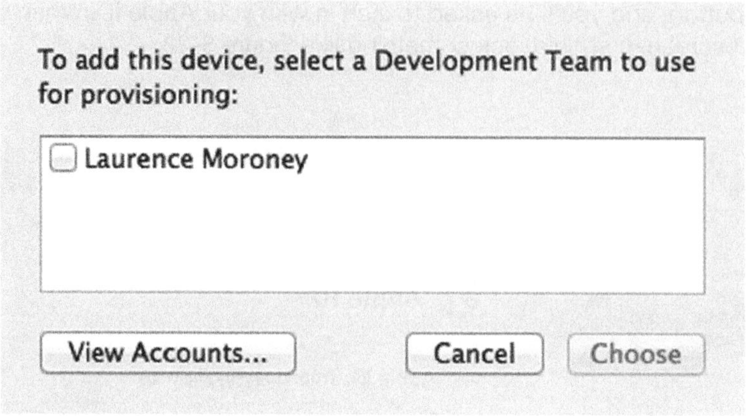

To add this device, select a Development Team to use
for provisioning:

☐ Laurence Moroney

[ View Accounts... ]        [ Cancel ]  [ Choose ]

*Figure 3-23.* *Developer IDs for provisioning*

The name(s) on your dialog will match those in your developer account. Pick one of them and click
"Choose."

Xcode will begin the process of provisioning, but it needs a certificate in order to do so. It will give
you a dialog like that in Figure 3-24.

**Certificate Not Found**

Your iOS Development Certificate for "Laurence
Moroney" was not found on the portal. Xcode can
submit a certificate signing request on your behalf.
Would you like Xcode to do so now?

[ Not Now ]      [ Request ]

*Figure 3-24.* *Getting a certificate*

Clicking the "Request" button will cause Xcode to submit a certificate request on your behalf.
Once it's done, the organizer screen will update, with the option to set the phone up as a developer
machine removed. See Figure 3-25.

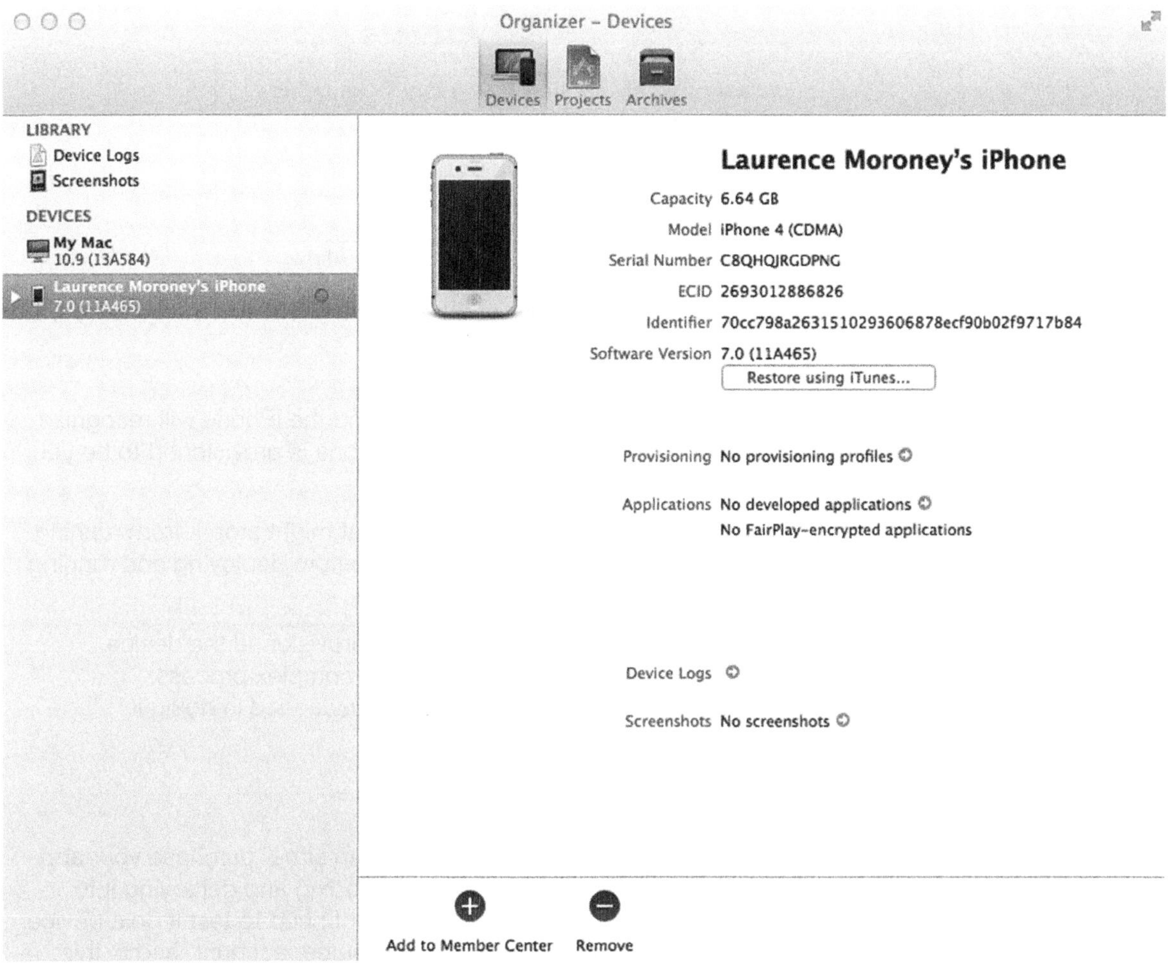

Organizer – Devices
Devices
Projects
Archives
LIBRARY
Device Logs
Screenshots
DEVICES
My Mac
10.9 (13A584)
Laurence Moroney's iPhone
7.0 (11A465)
Laurence Moroney's iPhone
Capacity 6.64 GB
Model iPhone 4 (CDMA)
Serial Number C8QHQJRGDPNG
ECID 2693012886826
Identifier 70cc798a2631510293606878ecf90b02f9717b84
Software Version 7.0 (11A465)
Restore using iTunes...
Provisioning No provisioning profiles
Applications No developed applications
No FairPlay-encrypted applications
Device Logs
Screenshots No screenshots
Add to Member Center
Remove

***Figure 3-25.** The updated organizer screen*

Now, close the organizer and return to Xcode, where you'll see that the option at the top of the screen has changed from the generic "iOS Device" to the specific name of your device. See Figure 3-26.

helloWorldO...
Laurence Moroney's iPhone

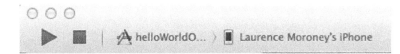

***Figure 3-26.** Your device is now available to Xcode*

Now run your app, and it will compile and begin deploying to your device. It will give a dialog that looks something like Figure 3-27.

*Figure 3-27. The codesign dialog*

Once you click "Allow," your app will be signed with your certificate, and the iPhone will recognize the app using that certificate as one that you have built. And as the phone is provisioned to be your development device, iOS will allow the code to run.

Within a moment the app will execute on your device. One problem that might stop it from running is if your device is locked, so be sure to unlock it with your passcode before deploying and running the app.

Congratulations! Your app is now running on your device. You've just provisioned the device, created a certificate, and compiled your app with that certificate. It's a complex process, but hopefully, with the assistance of the tools, and this book, you've succeeded in doing it.

# Summary

Applications are deployed to iOS devices from the app store. A user can either purchase your app or, if it is free, download it directly, and the app store manages downloading and deploying it to their device. However, before you deploy the app to the store, you might need to test it on a device. In this chapter you learned how to do that. For that you needed a developer account, and in this chapter you saw how to sign up to get one. With this developer account you could get certificates of identity and use these certificates to sign your applications to verify that you have developed them. It also allows you to provision a physical device to be used as a test device on your account. You saw how to do that by creating a simple application and using the organizer to set your device up as a developer device. You then used Xcode to request a certificate from the developer portal on your behalf. Xcode then signed your app and deployed it to the device. In the next few chapters you'll continue learning iOS development, and you can test your code using either the simulator or a device.

# Chapter 4

# Your Second iOS App

Now that you've gotten your feet wet from programming your first two iPhone and iPad apps and running them not only on the simulator, but also on real hardware, the next step is to build some more apps that are a little more sophisticated.

The third "Hello, World!" app introduces you to some more user interaction, as well as if-else statements in code. Objective-C is a sophisticated and complex language, so we are going to take you through this little by little without throwing too many complex concepts at you.

## Creating the Project and Adding a Graphic

In Chapter 2, you wrote helloWorld_01 as an iPhone app and helloWorld_02 as an iPad app. These were single view apps that housed a button, and when the user pressed the button, a label changed to say "Hello, World!" In this section we'll expand on that by building a single view application that asks you if you are a geek and gives different responses as you touch it.

To get started, launch Xcode and create a new project. On the "Choose a template for your new project" screen, choose the "Single View Application" template, as shown in Figure 4-1.

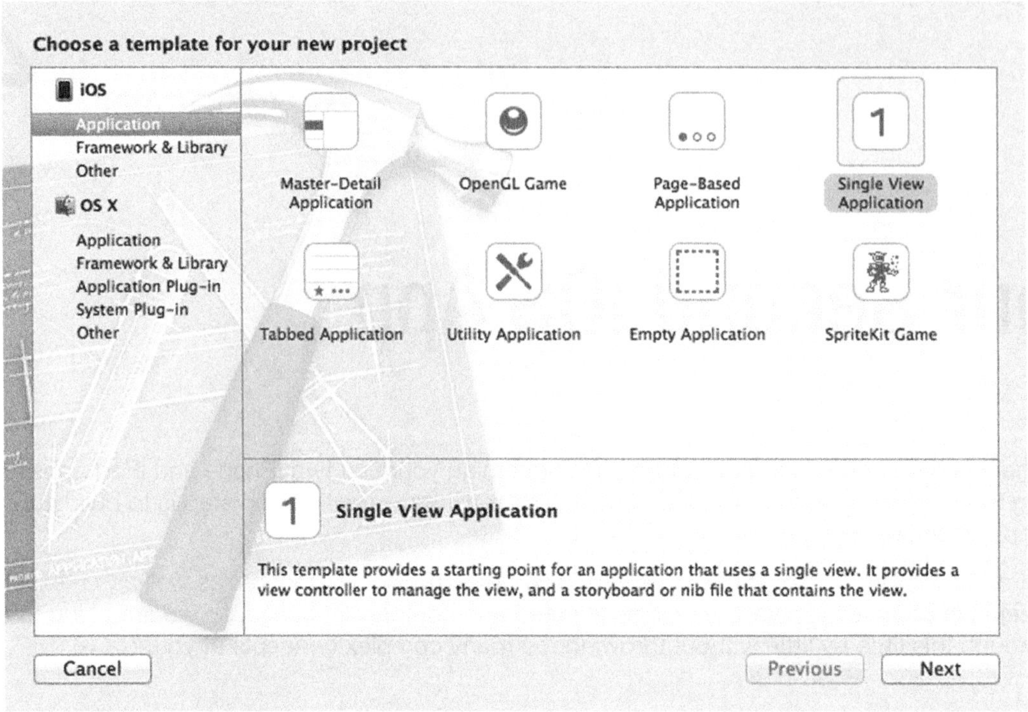

*Figure 4-1.  Starting your new project*

As before, you'll see the options dialog when you click "Next." This will allow you to specify the Product Name, Organization Name, and Company Identifier. Set them up as in Figure 4-2, and make sure that the product name is helloWorld_03 and that the "Devices" setting is set to "iPhone."

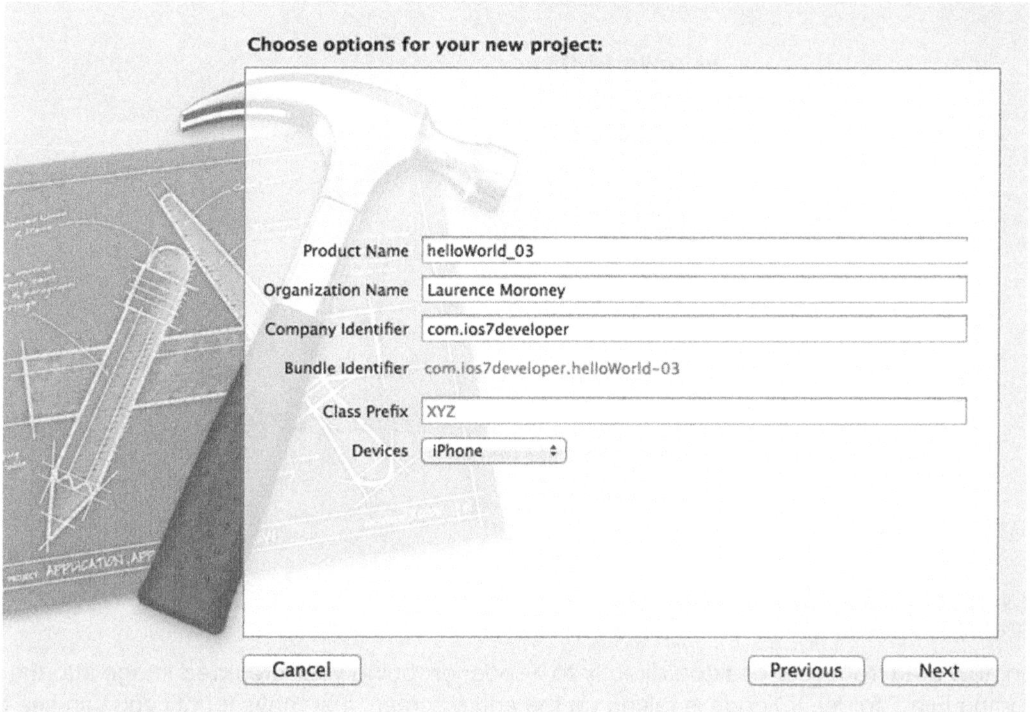

*Figure 4-2. Your project settings*

Click "Next" to be taken to the screen where you'll save your code, which defaults to your desktop. If you want to leave it there, that's fine. Just click "Next," and Xcode will create your project, store it where you specified, and open it for you.

For the next step you'll need a 320x480 image, preferably some type of portrait, in PNG format. If you don't have one, or don't have time to create one, I've created a couple of sample images that you can download and use.

If you prefer your image to be of a female, you can use the one stored at http://ios7developer.com/book/geek1.png. If you'd rather it were a male, you can use the one stored at http://ios7developer.com/book/geek2.png. For the rest of this chapter, I'll be using geek1.png.

Make sure you save the image on your desktop. Using Safari or Chrome, you can do this by visiting your choice of the preceding URLs and right clicking on the image. You'll see an option that says "Save Image As . . ."; you can click this to save the image to your desktop.

In Xcode, on the left-hand side of your screen, you can see all your project files. On this list, you'll see a directory called "Supporting Files." If you can't see it, open the helloWorld_03 folder by clicking the little arrow beside it. See Figure 4-3.

*Figure 4-3. Finding your supporting files folder*

You can now drag from your desktop directly to Xcode, dropping your preferred image into the "Supporting Files" folder. If Xcode is taking up the entire screen, just move it until you can see the file and simply drag and drop the file. Of course, if it is in fullscreen mode, change it so that you can see the desktop too.

You'll see a dialog that says "Choose options for adding these files" (Figure 4-4); make sure that you check the box that says "Copy items into destination group's folder (if needed)," as shown.

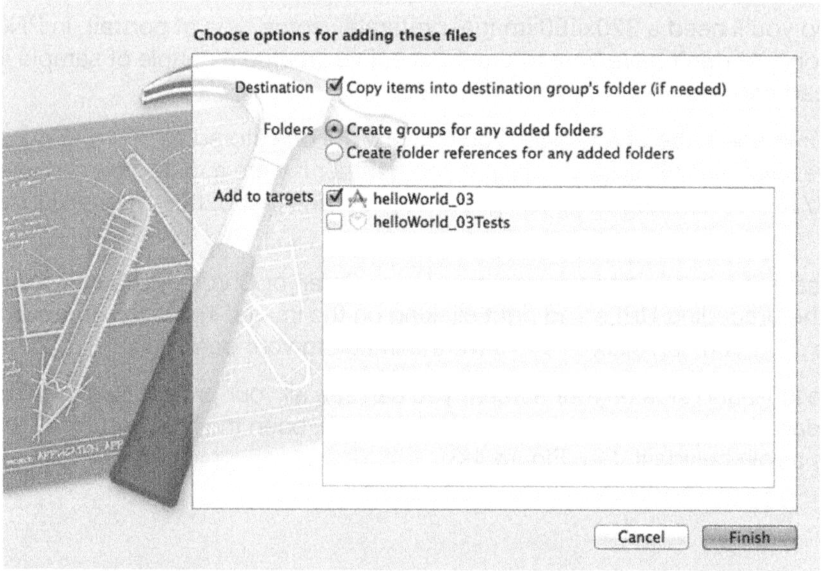

*Figure 4-4. Copy options for your image file*

It's very important to check that box for iOS applications. The reason for this is that when your app runs, it will need to read the image file. If the checkbox isn't set, then running the app in the emulator will *appear* to work correctly, because the emulator is on your machine, and the image is on your desktop. The emulator can then read the file, and everything will look fine. As soon as you try to run the app somewhere else, such as on a device or someone else's machine, it'll fail, because they don't have access to *your* desktop, where the image resides.

By checking the box, you've made a copy of the image in your source code, so that when the app compiles, it will take the image with it, embedded right within the app. Thus, if you distribute the app or the code, you'll also distribute the image, and the app will work correctly.

Once you've copied the image over, you should see it in your "Supporting Files" folder. See Figure 4-5. If you can't see it there, drag and drop again, but also see if you can find where you put it originally so that you can delete it from the wrong location.

*Figure 4-5. Adding the graphic to your "Supporting Files" folder*

# Creating the User Interface

Now that your app is created, it's time to start designing the user interface. You'll see a file called Main.storyboard in your project. Select it, and the storyboard editor will open. You'll likely just see a blank screen with a menu to its left that reads "View Controller Scene." Click the arrow beside it to open it, and you'll see several items. One of these is "View Controller." Click the arrow beside it, and you'll see "View." Select that to begin editing. Your screen should look like Figure 4-6.

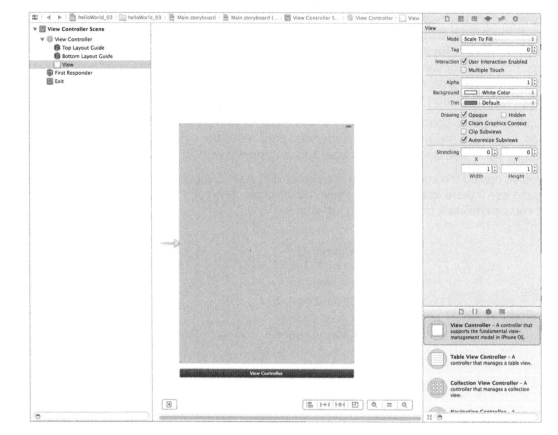

*Figure 4-6. Editing your storyboard*

> **Note**    If you don't see the full view controller, and instead the center area of your screen is all gray, click the
> "Zoom Out" button at the bottom of the screen. It looks like a magnifying glass with a "-" in its center.

## Adding the Image View

Next, take a look at the Utilities pane to the right of the screen and make sure the controls list is
visible. The small blue cube icon should be selected—you can see it in Figure 4-6. Scroll down the
list until you see the "Image View" control. See Figure 4-7.

*Figure 4-7. Selecting the image view*

Drag and drop this to the "View Controller" gray area in the center of the designer. If you have trouble, you can also drag it directly to the "View" entry on the "View Controller Scene" list to the left of the window. See Figure 4-8, where the image view is added to the view, and where it is visible on the storyboard.

**Tip**  You may notice when you try to drag the image view to the design surface that Xcode won't let you, and the control bounces back. If this is the case, click the "View Controller" button beneath the image. You'll see three colored buttons. Select the yellow one on the left, and the problem should go away.

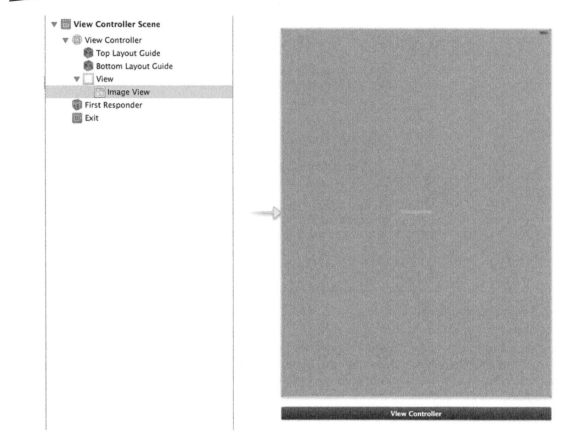

*Figure 4-8.* *Adding an image view to the storyboard*

With the image view selected, you should now look at the attributes inspector at the top-right-hand side of your Xcode window. You'll see a list option called "Image." See Figure 4-9.

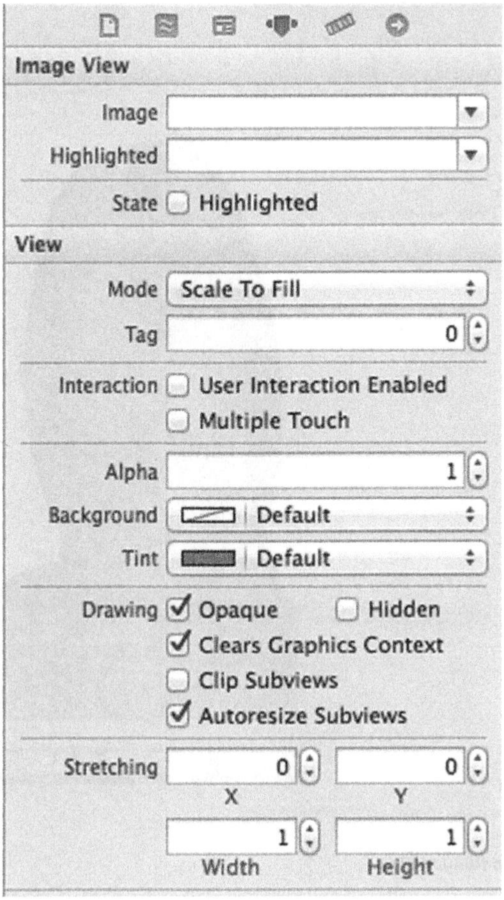

*Figure 4-9.* *The attributes inspector for the image view*

Drop down the list beside "Image" at the top, and you should see an item for the image you added earlier. We used "geek1.png," so you can see that in Figure 4-10. When you select it, the image view will also load your picture and render it.

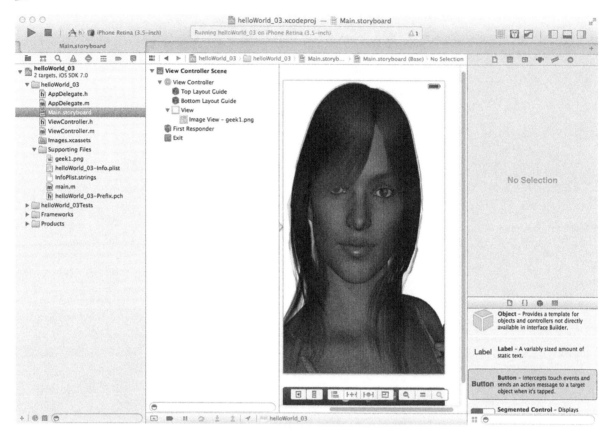

*Figure 4-10. Setting the image on the image view*

## Adding a Label

Next you should drag a label from the library onto the "view design" area, placing it near the center of the view, as shown in Figure 4-11. Make sure it's centered as indicated by the blue line. Later you'll be adding a button, and your code will invoke an action that will change the text on this label.

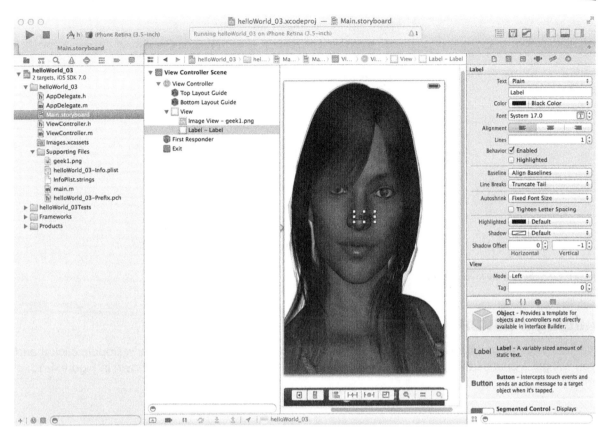

*Figure 4-11. Adding a label to the bottom of the image*

> **Note**   As before, you may notice that when you try to drag the label to the design surface Xcode won't let you, and the label bounces back. If so, click the "View Controller" button beneath the image. You'll see three colored buttons. Select the yellow one on the left, and the problem should go away.

The text is quite difficult to read, so let's fix that. With the label selected, drag the corners to change the width of the label, making it wider, and then go to the attributes inspector and make three changes.

- Change the alignment to centered.
- Change the text color to white.
- Delete the default text (label).

You can see what the attributes inspector should look like for the label in Figure 4-12.

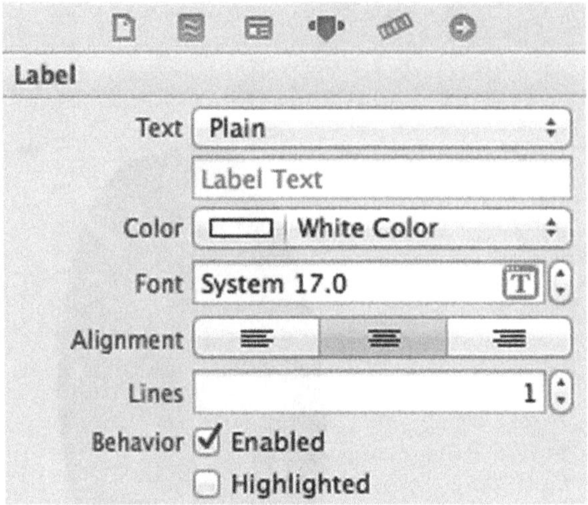

*Figure 4-12. Setting the label attributes*

## Adding a Button

Next up, you should drag a button to the design surface and center it horizontally. Double click it and you will get a chance to change its text. Set the text to "Are you a Geek?" as shown in Figure 4-13.

*Figure 4-13. Setting the button text*

In iOS7, buttons are flat and look like labels, so you'll need to change the text of the button to make it more readable. As it's set against a dark background, the only change you'll need to make is to set the Text Color property on the attribute inspector. We set it to white, as you can see in Figure 4-14.

**Button**

| | |
|---|---|
| Type | System |
| State Config | Default |
| Title | Plain |
| | Are you a Geek? |
| Font | System Bold 15.0 |
| Text Color | White Color |
| Shadow Color | Default |
| Image | Default Image |
| Background | Default Background Image |
| Shadow Offset | 0.0    0.0 |
| | Width    Height |

*Figure 4-14.  Setting the text color property of the button*

Now that you're done with designing the app, the next step is to add the code that you'll use to bring it to life. You'll see that in the next section.

# Writing the Code for Your App

In the previous section you designed the "Are you a Geek?" app by adding an image to your source code and then using an image view on your app to render it. You also added a button and a label. Before writing any code, you'll have to define an action for the button and an outlet for the label.

If you get stuck here, you should refer back to Chapter 2.

First, you should hide the attributes inspector by clicking the rightmost button on the toolbar (square with shaded right side) and then bring up the coding assistant by clicking on the secondmost-from-left button on the toolbar, which looks like a tuxedo. You can see these buttons at the top-right-hand side of your screen. They are also in Figure 4-15.

*Figure 4-15.  Toolbar buttons*

Your screen should now show your files on the left, your design in the middle, and some code on the right-hand side. Ensure that your code shows your ViewController.h code and *not* your ViewController.m code. If it is incorrect, click ViewController.m at the top of the code window and a list will drop down. Select ViewController.h from that list. When you're ready to set the outlet and action, your screen should look like Figure 4-16.

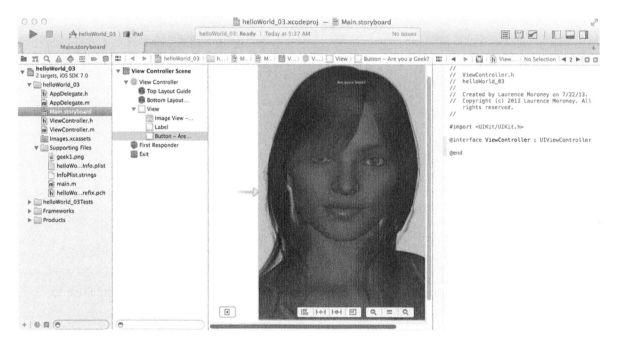

*Figure 4-16. Xcode ready for outlet and action generation*

> **Note**    The following few steps have you selecting the button and label control and CTRL-dragging them to the code window. If it's hard to select them on the design surface because of the image, you can also select them on the "View Controller Scene" drop-down menu to the left of the design surface. Simply click the control there to highlight it, and CTRL-drag.

Select the button control, and while holding the "Control" key, drag and drop it onto the code window just below where it says @interface. A small menu will pop up. Make sure that on this menu you set the Connection type to "Action" and the Name type to "btnClick." You can see this in Figure 4-17.

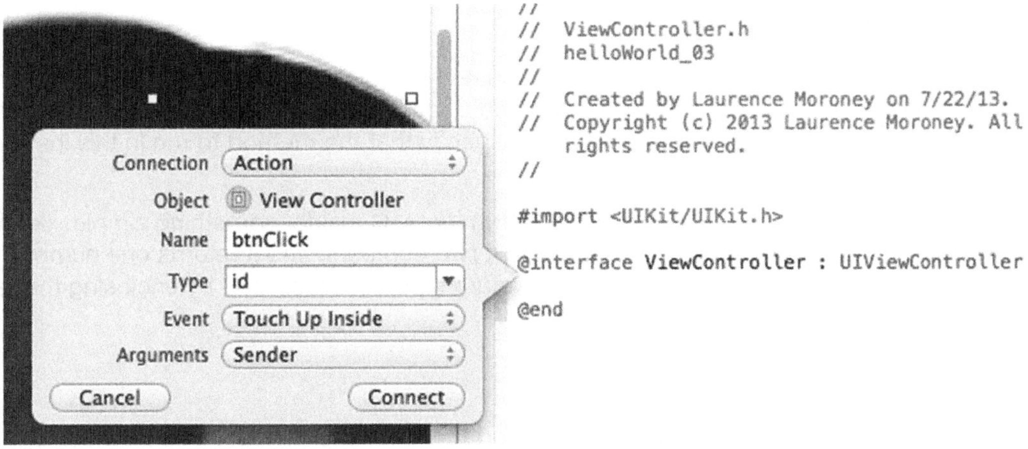

*Figure 4-17. Setting the action for the button*

Click "Connect" and some code will be generated for you in the ViewController.h file. Code will also be generated in the ViewController.m file, and you'll see that in a moment.

Now, select the "Label" control, and while holding down the control key, drag it over the code window, just like you did with the button. If you're having difficulty finding or selecting the label, use the View Controller Scene to the left of the design surface as noted in the preceding note. This time, on the popup menu, leave the Connection type as "Outlet," and enter "geekLabel" in the Name field. This will allow you to refer to the label control in code as _geekLabel, making your code a little more readable than if you just used the generic "label" as the name. See Figure 4-18.

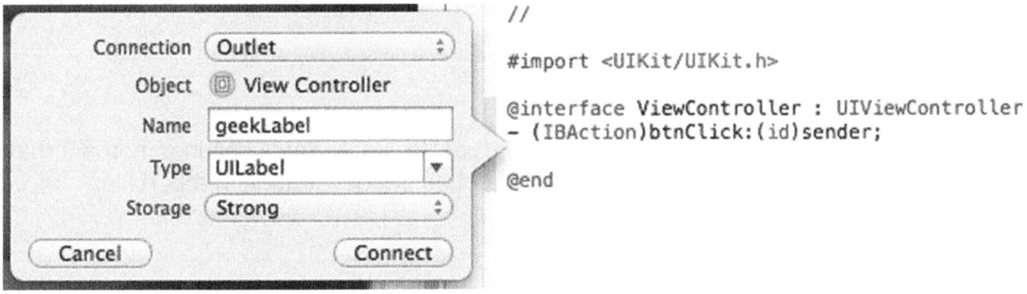

*Figure 4-18. Adding the label outlet*

If you've configured these steps correctly, you should have this code in your ViewController.h file. If not, delete what you have and go back and try again.

```
#import <UIKit/UIKit.h>

@interface ViewController : UIViewController
- (IBAction)btnClick:(id)sender;
@property (strong, nonatomic) IBOutlet UILabel *geekLabel;

@end
```

# Digging the Button Code

When you made the button an action, you created something very important: a *method*. A method is the code that runs in response to an action performed upon an object. In this case, the object is the button, and the action is the user clicking on it. You specify that the method to run in this instance is called btnClick.

A method is also a function, and a function has a return type. Consider something simple, like a function that adds two numbers together—you give it two numbers, and it returns one number, which is the result of the addition. You specify the return type in Objective-C by enclosing the return type in brackets before the method name declaration:

- **(IBAction)**btnClick:(id)sender;

In this case, the return type is IBAction, which is short for "Interface Builder Action," which should make sense, as you specified that this function is an action when you dragged the button to the code surface.

This is a special type of return value, which you don't have to explicitly set yourself. Objective-C now understands that this function is going to be used by controls you put on the designer.

The name of the method comes next. If the method requires values to be passed to it as parameters, the method name will be followed by a colon (":") and a list of those parameters. In this case the method is called btnClick.

- (IBAction)**btnClick**:(id)sender;

Last is the list of parameters or *arguments* that you send to the function. In this case you are sending an argument of type id, with the name "sender." This just allows Objective-C to keep track of which object raised the method, because it knows its id.

- (IBAction)btnClick:**(id)sender**;

The method itself will be implemented in the ViewController.m file. You'll see in a moment that an empty function was created for you there too that matches the declaration in the .h file.

# Editing Your Code

The first step is to add some code to your header file. This will be used to track the state of how the user has pressed the button. The label is going to alternate between two messages, so you can use a Boolean variable, which has only two states, to keep track of them. Boolean variables can be set to false and true, so we'll write some code that says, "If it's true, make it false, and if it's false, make it true." So, in order to set the label to alternate between the two states, we can say, "If it is true, make the text this, otherwise, make the text that."

Variables like this—that you use in your implementation (.m) file—can be defined in your header (.h) file. Thus, to declare a Boolean, you use bool, and give the variable a name. In this case we'll call it ruaGeek.

```
#import <UIKit/UIKit.h>

bool ruaGeek;

@interface ViewController : UIViewController
- (IBAction)btnClick:(id)sender;
@property (strong, nonatomic) IBOutlet UILabel *geekLabel;

@end
```

Now, within your .m file, you can reference ruaGeek, and Objective-C will know that it's a Boolean that can be true or false.

Open ViewController.m, and you'll see the code that was generated for you when you created the action for the button. You called it btnClick, so the code will look like this:

```
- (IBAction)btnClick:(id)sender {
}
@end
```

Earlier, we mentioned that when the button is pressed, we'll check ruaGeek, and *if* it is true, we'll set the text to one value, otherwise we'll set it to a different one. In Objective-C, rules like this are performed using an if-else statement.

The syntax for this statement looks like this in Objective-C:

```
if(condition)
{
    do something;
}
else
{
    do something else;
}
```

The condition is tested to see if it is true, and if it is, the first "do something" is executed, otherwise the "do something else" is executed. This is really convenient, because ruaGeek is a Boolean variable, which can either be true or false. In Objective-C, you use two "=" signs when you are checking if something is equal. This might look a little strange at first, but it's a way to help the computer understand the difference between using "=" to set a value and using "==" to determine if values are equal.

In English, you can say "x=1" and you'd understand that you are making x have the value of one. You can also say if(x=1), and you'd understand that you are checking if x is 1 before going further. Computer languages can't tell the difference here, so for checking if the value is equivalent, you use two "=" signs like this: if(x==1).

So, to check if ruaGeek is true, you can do this:

```
if(ruaGeek==true)
{
    do something;
}
```

```
else
{
    do something else;
}
```

A convenient shorthand is this: if you want to check if a condition is true, you don't need to say ==true. This code is exactly the same:

```
if(ruaGeek)
{
    do something;
}
else
{
    do something else;
}
```

So now, let's set the text of the labels according to the value of ruaGeek:

```
- (IBAction)btnClick:(id)sender {
    if(ruaGeek)
    {
_geekLabel.text = @"No you're not!";
    }
    else
    {
        _geekLabel.text = @"Definitely a geek!";

    }
```

So, what do you think would happen if you ran this code now? Run it and give it a try. The app will launch, you'll press the button, and it will tell you that you're definitely a geek. But then when you press the button again, nothing happens. Why?

Go back to look at the preceding code. When you first run the app, ruaGeek hasn't been set, so it's considered to be false. As a result, the text "Definitely a geek!" gets rendered. But ruaGeek is *still* false. So when you press it again, the same text is rendered. You have to change the value of ruaGeek in code when you click the button.  You do this by setting it to true in the branch of the function where the code goes when ruaGeek is false, and vice versa.

Here's the code:

```
- (IBAction)btnClick:(id)sender {
    if(ruaGeek)
    {
        _geekLabel.text=@"No, you're not!";
        ruaGeek = false;
    }
    else
    {
        _geekLabel.text=@"Definitely a geek!";
        ruaGeek = true;
    }
}
```

Now if you run the app, you'll see that the label changes whenever you press the button. Figure 4-19 shows the label upon pressing the button once.

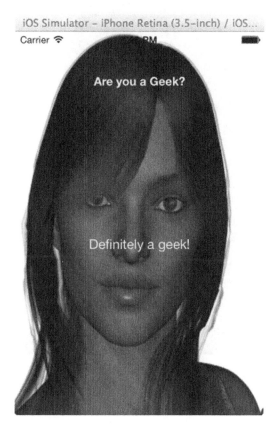

*Figure 4-19.*  *Running the "Are You a Geek?" app*

Pressing the button again, you'll see that the label changes. See Figure 4-20.

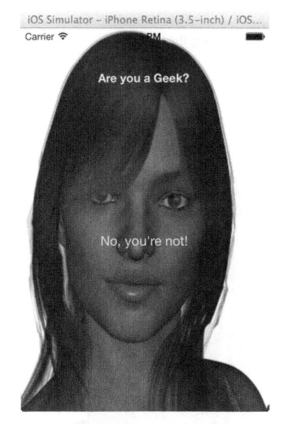

*Figure 4-20.  Clicking the button again changes the label*

> **Note**    In this application, the `ruaGeek` Boolean was never initialized—you checked its value before you ever set it. This is a really bad idea. In the case of Booleans, it's okay, because it will initialize to `false`. But with most other data types, if you don't initialize them, they will be `null`, and when you try to check if a `null` object equals something, the app will crash. A better practice would be to set `ruaGeek` to false explicitly in the `viewDidLoad` function.

And that's it. You've now created an app that, as well as managing user I/O, has conditional logic within the code. It's a quantum leap from your first "Hello, World!" app, but as you move through this book, you'll get introduced to more and more concepts that build upon these foundations! You're well on your way to being an iOS7 developer!

# Pit Stop—Reviewing Some Concepts

Up to now you've had a whole lot of new concepts thrown your way. You may not have understood them all, and that's okay. For now, take a little pit stop from the hands-on coding.

In this section, you'll review some of the concepts you've touched on in this chapter, exploring what's behind them in more detail. You'll be introduced to more technical terms that you'll use in future chapters and in communicating with other programmers.

In helloWorld_01 and helloWorld_02 you took your first steps into development. In helloWorld_03, you started looking beyond the mere basics. From a programming perspective, you looked into the most important parts of software development in Objective-C: methods, outlets, and actions.

There are a few other concepts that you should consider, including storyboards, classes, methods, and header files. You'll explore them next.

## Storyboards

A few times already you've done user-interface work by editing a file that ended with the extension .storyboard. This is a curious name for something that is your user interface—why is it called a *storyboard*? Well, the logic behind that is that it separates, in the developer's mind, the actual user interface and the instructions that are used to construct that interface. In movie making, before the director films anything, the writer, director, and artists get together to sketch out the scenes and what they should look like in a process called storyboarding. When you storyboard a movie, you effectively make the entire movie on paper, showing each scene and how they are all connected. It's similar in iOS user interfaces.

Apple introduced storyboards so that developers could design what they wanted their user interfaces (UI) to look like, and how they connected to each other, and Objective-C would use that to create the actual UI that ran. It's no coincidence that your user interface "screen" that you've been building was called a "scene." See Figure 4-21.

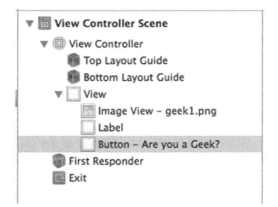

*Figure 4-21. Scenes within a storyboard, just like a movie*

Each app you've built so far is a single view app, so your storyboard had only one scene. It's like a very short movie.

In this book, so far, you've opened your storyboards, and you've dragged and dropped controls onto them. This created the behind-the-scenes instructions that Objective-C uses to construct your user interface, and the storyboard editor gave a graphical interpretation of that to help you design your UI.

You can see what the scene *really* looks like by right clicking on the storyboard file in Xcode, and selecting "Source Code" on the "Open As . . ." menu that pops up. This code is written in a language called XML (Extensible Markup Language). Despite its name, XML isn't really a language in which you can communicate actions, but more one in which data and its structure are expressed together. It's a very useful way to define and exchange information.

Figure 4-22 shows some of this XML opened in the Xcode editor.

*Figure 4-22. Storyboard open in XML view*

XML is commonly used in development for storing data, and, as you can see, your user interface definition is just data. Tweaking the XML by hand is a neat way to quickly edit your user interface if you don't want to use the assistants. But for now you won't do anything with it. It's just good to get an understanding of how the Objective-C compiler reads your design.

# Classes

It's almost impossible to avoid classes when writing software in just about any modern programming language for just about any platform, including iOS. You should think of a *class* as the set of instructions for building an object. An object that is built from a class is an *instance* of that class.

So, for example, if you were to define a cow, you would say that the class of a cow is that it's an animal with four legs and a tail that makes a "moo" sound. It's typically a certain size and produces milk and beef.

An instance of that class is any particular cow.

Of course there are lots of species of cow, so each of these can be designed as a different class. To get around having to define the same things again and again, object oriented (OO) programming provides things such as inheritance, where one class can borrow stuff from its parent class, and interfacing, where common stuff can be put into one class, and other classes extend on that. Indeed, our cow class has already inherited from a base class of type "animal," which would distinguish it from a vegetable or mineral. But that's getting into complex territory, so for now just think in terms of classes as defining objects. Everything in an iOS app is an object, so it's important to start thinking in terms of the classes that define them. For example, in the app in this chapter, the button is a class, and you told the program to create an instance of the button class at runtime. You give it various attributes, such as its text ("Are you a Geek?"), and you listened for actions on that button. Ditto for the label, the image view, and even the view controllers. It's classes all the way down . . .

# Methods

A *method* is a function that you can call to act on an object. So, for example, if you define the class for a car, you'd likely define a method for "accelerate," so that when there's an object for the car, whoever is driving could push it forward by accelerating it. In a real-life car, the interface is the gas pedal, and by pushing on the gas pedal you are "calling the accelerate method."

You saw how to declare a method earlier when you looked at a method and a method signature.

```
-(IBAction)btnClick:(id)sender
```

In this case, btnClick is the name that was chosen for the method. You could have called it anything you liked, as it's not a reserved keyword. It's good practice to give it a descriptive name like btnClick, geekButtonTouched, or btnGeekClicked. That way, when you read your code, you can glean an understanding for what triggered this event.

> **Tip**  It's a bad idea to use a vague name like "button" or "monkey" because code like this would give you no idea what the function actually does, unless of course it's a monkey in your app.

```
-(IBAction)monkey:(id)sender
```

Sometimes as you write code you'll notice that there's a "-" to the left of the method declaration, and sometimes there's a "+."

When there's a "-," that means it's an *instance* method, where the method can be used on any object created from the class.

When there's a "+," that means it's a *class* method, and the method is used on the class itself, typically when constructing an object. When you come across a class method being used later in the book, I'll leave a note showing this.

# Header Files

Some programming languages—and Objective-C is one of them—like classes to be defined using two files—a header file (.h) and an implementation file (.m)—where the header file defines the data and methods that the class is going to use, and the implementation file implements them.

Let's look at our `ViewController.h` a little more closely. Here's the code:

```
#import <UIKit/UIKit.h>

bool ruaGeek;

@interface ViewController : UIViewController
@property (strong, nonatomic) IBOutlet UILabel *geekLabel;
- (IBAction)btnClick:(id)sender;

@end
```

There are lots of concepts here that you'll understand in due course, but two important ones that you'll use a lot are #import and @interface.

#import: Think about all the code that is used to draw the button, handle the messages from the user, lay out the user interface, draw the label, etc. This all seems to happen without you doing anything. That's because you are just using an instance of a button, a label, and other controls, and their code is held elsewhere. Well, Objective-C isn't smart enough to know where that elsewhere is, and that's what the import statement is for. The iOS development environment has many libraries that you can use for different functions, and the library that supports the UI is naturally called UIKit. Thus, when you import the UI kit, you are telling Objective-C to look for code that you haven't written, such as the class definitions for the UILabel and the UIButton as it compiles your app. Putting the # in front of import tells the compiler what to do, and isn't code that will execute in your app.

@interface: Whenever you see an "@" in front of a command, it's effectively a directive to Xcode to do something. In this case, you are defining the user interface of your application as a class called ViewController. The syntax for telling it what *type* of class it should be is a ":" so the following line:

```
@interface ViewController : UIViewController
```

means "Define the interface with the ViewController class. This class inherits from the UIViewController."

That's a funny word: *inherits*. In the real world, you inherit something that belonged to somebody else, and they pass it on to you. In Objective-C it's very similar. Consider a class of type "cow" as before, and then another class of type "Angus cow." It would be best for "Angus cow" to have not only everything a cow has, but also some extra stuff that only an Angus cow has. That's inheritance—your Angus cow class would inherit from the cow, but would have some extras.

> **Note**  You'll also see the "@" character used in Objective-C in front of strings, so be sure to differentiate them.

In this case, your ViewController inherits from UIViewController, and your instance of the ViewController has some extras, such as the button, label, and image.

# Summary

In this chapter you built a slightly more sophisticated "Hello, World!"–type app. You used this to learn many of the important concepts of Objective-C development, including adding functional logic code to your app and using primitive variables. We also looked a little deeper into storyboards, classes, methods, headers, interfaces, and inheritance.

# Chapter 5

# Going Deeper: Patterns and Delegates

In the last few chapters, you've been looking at creating "Hello, World!"–style applications that perform basic tasks, using very simple controls—the button, the label, and the image view. These introduced you to some concepts of development, including actions and outlets. In this chapter, you'll look into more of the concepts that are regularly used in iOS development and that you'll use extensively in this book. They are the concepts of delegates, messages, and patterns.

It probably sounds very high level and confusing at the moment, and you may not grasp it all the first time through, but don't worry—with practice it becomes easier. We'll warn you that this might be the most difficult chapter of the book, particularly if you are new to programming. Don't worry if you can't get through it all. Skipping ahead is okay, but it would be good to come back here from time to time if you are stuck with some of these concepts in later chapters.

We'd also recommend, strongly, that you get very familiar with Chapter 2 and Chapter 4 in particular. In those chapters, you are taken step by step through everything needed to create the single view apps that you'll be using in this chapter, as well as how to use the various tools in Xcode for designing your app. Some of the skills you'll need in this chapter, such as placing and sizing controls, are covered in more detail there.

Don't forget the videos accompanying this book, which are available at http://ios7developer.com/book. The videos will take you through these examples to help you better understand them.

## Building an App for Text Input

The "Text Field" control could have several chapters all to itself, as there is so much to learn about it! In this section you'll build it for a very simple scenario—one in which you can capture text input from the user with the iOS Keyboard, and then dismiss the keyboard when you are done. Despite its simplicity, this task is one that iOS developers commonly get tripped up on, so go through this example carefully and make sure you understand it before continuing.

# Create and Design your App

To get started, create a new single view app called textFieldDemo. Make sure it's an iPhone app. If you're jumping into this chapter and aren't sure of the steps, refer back to Chapter 2 to see how to create one of these apps.

When it's done, open the Main.storyboard file in the editor. Your screen should look something like Figure 5-1.

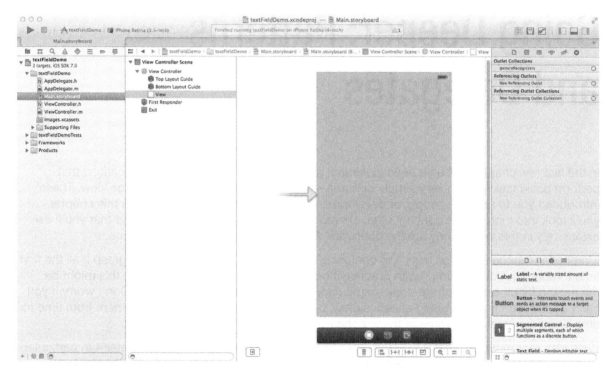

*Figure 5-1.* *The textFieldDemo project*

Drag a button and a label to the design surface of your view and place them near the top. Change the button's text to "Go" by double clicking the button and typing the new text, and then change the label's text to "Output will go here" in the same way. Use Figure 5-2 as a guide for where you should place the controls and how you should size them.

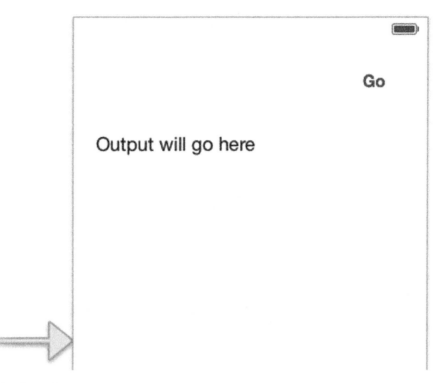

Go

Output will go here

*Figure 5-2.* *Designing the text input app*

Next, find the "Text Field" control in the assistant menu on the lower right-hand side of the screen. Take care, as there is a very similar control called "Text View." Be sure to pick "Text Field," or the following steps in this section may not work. You can see the "Text Field" option in Figure 5-3.

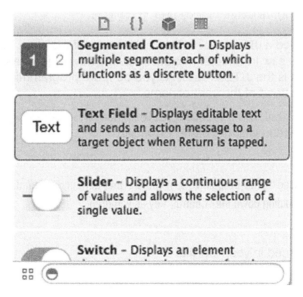

*Figure 5-3.* *Finding the "Text Field" control*

When you find it, drag it and drop it onto the design surface, fitting it above the label and to the left of the "Go" button, as in Figure 5-4.

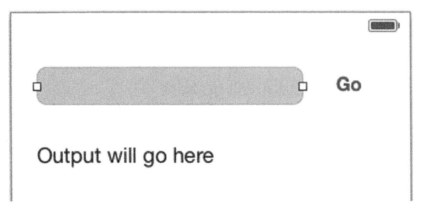

*Figure 5-4.  Designing your UI*

Great! Now you're ready to start wiring up your actions and outlets. Again, if this concept isn't familiar to you, we strongly recommend you go back and take a look at the simple examples in Chapter 2 and Chapter 4 that introduced these.

## Set Up Your Connections and Write Your Code

First, open the assistant and CTRL-drag the "Text Field" control onto the ViewController.h file, and create an outlet connection with the name txtInput.

You'll see code like this placed in your .h file:

```
@property (strong, nonatomic) IBOutlet UITextField *txtInput;
```

Note that the control is called a UITextField. This is the name of the class that gives you the "Text Field" control. As you saw in Chapter 4, classes define how objects are built. The object type is a text field, but the class is the UITextField. As you do more programming, you'll probably find yourself using this name instead of the control name.

Next, you should drag the label to the ViewController.h file, while pressing the "Control" key, and create an outlet connection with the name lblOutput.

> **Note**   This process is called "CTRL-Dragging," so if you see that term in documentation, or in this book, just remember that it means holding down the "Control" key as you drag.

You'll see code like this placed in your ".h" file.

```
@property (strong, nonatomic) IBOutlet UILabel *lblOutput;
```

Again, the "Label" control is declared using `UILabel`, the class within `UIKit` that gives you the label functionality.

The third and final UI step you'll need to do is to create an action for the button. CTRL-drag the button to the header file and create an action connection by selecting "action" from the drop-down menu that appears. If you find this confusing, refer back to Chapter 2 and Chapter 4, in which you are taken through this process in a little more detail. Give the action the name `btnGo`, and you'll see code like this in your .h file:

```
- (IBAction)btnGo:(id)sender;
```

In addition to this, you'll see this code has been added to your ".m" file.

```
- (IBAction)btnGo:(id)sender {

}
```

As you saw in earlier chapters, any code that you write here will execute when the user presses the button.

> **Tip**   It's important to note that when you create an outlet and give it a name, accessing that outlet requires you to prefix the name with an underscore. Thus, to access the `lblOutput` outlet in code, you use `_lblOutlet`.

Xcode helps you with writing your code. As you type, it tries to figure out what you're typing and gives you hints about what you might want to do next. So, for example, if you go to the `btnGo` function in `ViewController.m` and start typing with an underscore (_) character, and then the letter "l" (lowercase "L"), a menu will pop up with everything your code can understand that starts with _l and guess that you want `_lblOutput` because that's an outlet that you created. See Figure 5-5.

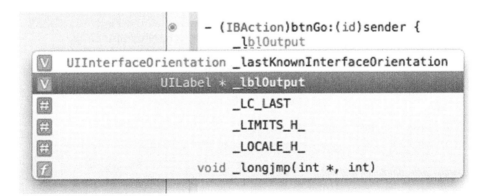

*Figure 5-5. Xcode's autocompletion helpers*

Because the _lblOutput is selected, pressing the "tab" key will take you to the next chunk within your word. In code, words are divided by capital letters; for example, look at _lastKnownInterfaceOrientation, as shown in Figure 5-5. Pressing tab while _lblOutlet was selected will fill out the current word, and give you the same effect as if you typed _lbl. Once you do this, there's only one option left on the list. See Figure 5-6.

**Figure 5-6.** *Autocomplete highlights the _lblOutput when you press "tab" key*

Consider how this would look if you had several labels, and you named them consistently with something like "lbl" in front of the name—the "tab" functionality would very quickly give you a list of the available objects that you might want to code against.

Select the object you want to insert in the code and press "tab" again; the object name will be filled in for you.

But auto completion doesn't end there. This code is going to set the text property of the label, which can be accessed using the "dot" syntax. This syntax allows a property of an object to be addressed by selecting it with a dot, as in object.property. As a result, the text property of _lblOutput is _lblOutput.text.

Press the "." key, and Xcode will give you a list of available properties. You can see this in Figure 5-7.

```
- (IBAction)btnGo:(id)sender {
    _lblOutput.class

M              BOOL canBecomeFirstResponder
M              BOOL canResignFirstResponder
P           CGPoint center
M             Class class
M          NSArray * classFallbacksForKeyedArchiver
M             Class classForCoder
M             Class classForKeyedArchiver
M             Class classForKeyedUnarchiver

Returns the class object. More...
```

**Figure 5-7.** *Properties auto completion and hints*

You can see that the list is sorted alphabetically. A nice hint is the "M" to the left, indicating methods, and also a "P" for properties. Now press the "T" key, as the text property you want to set begins with that. The list will be filtered down to stuff that begins with "T," and Xcode will make a guess about what you want, as "text" is the most common property used that begins with "T." See Figure 5-8.

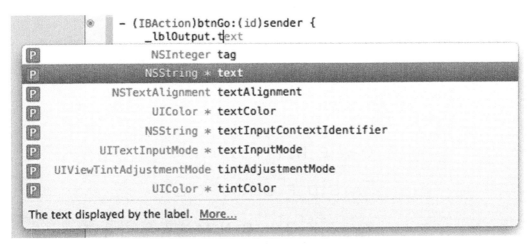

*Figure 5-8. Using the properties editor to pick text*

This is also a really useful way to learn the properties that are available. As you can see, the type of data is also listed; for example, "text" is an NSString type.

Press "tab" again, and the text property will be added.

Continue typing and using the popups until your code looks like this:

```
- (IBAction)btnGo:(id)sender {
    _lblOutput.text = _txtInput.text;
}
```

This code sets the content of the label to be whatever is typed into the text field once the user presses the button. Run it and give it a try. You can see it running in Figure 5-9.

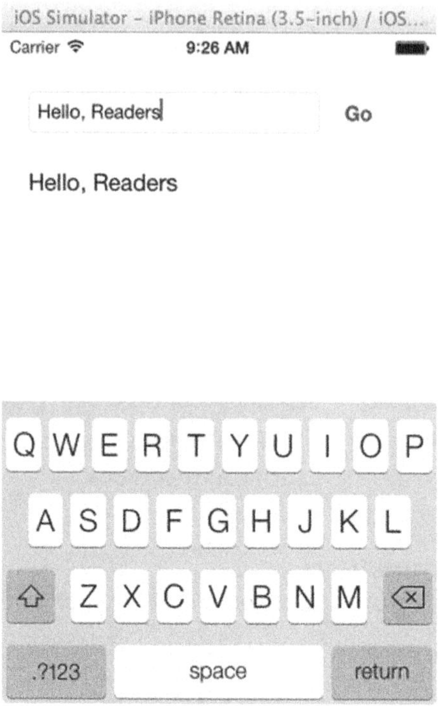

**Figure 5-9.** *Running your app*

As soon as you select text field, the keyboard will appear on the simulator. The behavior is the same on a physical device. If you're running the simulator, you don't need to click on the keys—you can just type on your Mac keyboard and it will be mapped for you. Enter some text and press the button, and you'll see the output.

## Going Deeper into Text Field Behavior

The application you just built runs well, and you get the expected result. But there are two problems.

1. You would *expect* that pressing the "Return" key on the keyboard would give the same behavior. Right now it does nothing.

2. You can't dismiss the keyboard. Once it's there, it's there. iOS apps usually dismiss the keyboard when you're done with it. Clicking the "Go" button or pressing "Return" should give you your iOS display back!

So let's look at solving these issues.

## Using Delegates

This action, while seemingly simple, uncovers some of the programming practices that, to a beginner, are very mysterious. Hopefully, by working through the example it will become a little easier to understand. In order to use the "Return" key, you will be introduced to a new concept in development called *delegates*.

**Tip**    In real life, when you delegate work to somebody else, you are asking them to do something for you. You usually do this in a scenario where it makes sense to do so. Maybe they are more skilled at doing it, maybe you are too busy, or maybe it's just the right thing for the other person to do the work. In programming, it's very similar. An object can delegate work to another object, and this is usually done when it makes sense for the one receiving the work to do it.

## Setting Up the Delegate

Consider an instance where your view (with its code in ViewController.h and ViewController.m, in this case) might have a lot of text field controls on it. It makes sense for there to be one location with the logic for managing the keyboard, such as making it appear and disappear. In this case, if each text field *delegates* control to the view, you can have the view manage the keyboard.

For that to happen, as a programmer you need to do two things.

1.  Tell the view that it's going to get work delegated to it from text fields.

2.  Tell each text field that the view will be the delegate for their work.

To tell the view that it's going to get work delegated to it from text fields, you edit your interface declaration in your ViewController.h file. Right now it looks like this:

```
@interface ViewController : UIViewController
```

To tell it that it's a delegate for something, you append <> to this and list the things that will be delegated to it. In the case of a UITextField, the delegate is simply called UITextFieldDelegate. So, in order to meet the first criterion, telling the view that it's getting delegated to, you would use code like this in ViewController.h:

```
@interface ViewController : UIViewController<UITextFieldDelegate>
```

Next, the text field has to be told who the work is being delegated to. For this you can use the self keyword. At first it's a little confusing when you read code like this:

```
_txtInput.delegate = self;
```

It looks like we're telling the code that its delegate is itself. But *self* refers to the class in which the code is being run, so if we add this code to ViewController.m, we're actually saying that the delegate is ViewController.m. This is the right place for it to be, because we said in ViewController.h that this class will be the delegated class for UITextField.

The best place to put this code is in the viewDidLoad function. This function is called when the class is loaded and ready to go. If you look at your ViewController.m file, it's already created for you, and looks something like this:

```
- (void)viewDidLoad
{
    [super viewDidLoad];
    // Do any additional setup after loading the view, typically from a nib.
}
```

The template already provided a hint—additional setup after loading the view. This is perfect for our needs, so we can edit the code to look like this:

```
- (void)viewDidLoad
{
    [super viewDidLoad];
    // Do any additional setup after loading the view, typically from a nib.
    _txtInput.delegate = self;
}
```

Your ViewController.m is now capable of taking text field delegates, and is configured to be the delegate for txtInput.

## Writing the Delegate Function

Now that the view is a delegate, there are functions available that the view will call when text field events happen. Go right to the bottom of your ViewController.m file, and just above @end, start typing the characters "-te," where "t" and "e" are the first letters in the word "text," and "-" indicates that this is a function.

You'll get a popup that looks something like Figure 5-10.

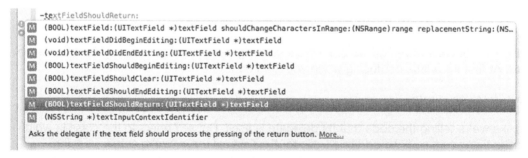

*Figure 5-10. The popup for text field delegation*

This lists everything that you could do as a delegate of functions from the text field. Also, helpfully, the most common one is highlighted, and this is textFieldShouldReturn. Not coincidentally, this is the one that you want!

So press "tab" a few times until the function is created.

Your screen will look something like Figure 5-11 when you're done.

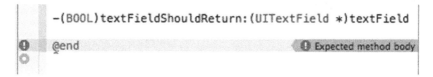

*Figure 5-11. Inserting the delegate function*

There seems to be a problem. This is code that Xcode generated for you, so it can't be wrong, you might think. Thankfully, it isn't—it's just incomplete. But Xcode is still helpful here. Click the little exclamation mark, and the line will be highlighted and will display text telling you the problem. See Figure 5-12.

*Figure 5-12. Xcode tells you what's wrong*

It says it expects a method body. Of course! You haven't written any code yet, and your code always lives within braces—the "{" and "}" characters. So add them and see what happens. Go to the empty line below–(BOOL)—and type the "{" character. You'll see Xcode automatically adds the "}" for you that complements this.

But there's still a red exclamation mark. Click it to see what the problem is now. You can see this in Figure 5-13.

```
-(BOOL)textFieldShouldReturn:(UITextField *)textField
{

}                    ❶ Control reaches end of non-void function
@end
```

*Figure 5-13. Another problem is highlighted by Xcode*

This text might be a little cryptic at first. *Control reaches end of non-void function.* In Chapter 4 we discussed functions and methods and how they are constructed. At the beginning of the function declaration there's a variable type within graphics. In the case of textFieldShouldReturn, we can see that this is BOOL.

This specifies the return type, i.e., this function will always return a BOOL. When the function doesn't return anything, it's called a void function. Now, when we look at the text *Control reaches end of non-void function,* we can parse this as really saying *This function is supposed to return something, in this case a BOOL, but it's not returning anything.*

A BOOL, as we saw earlier, has two values—true and false. So let's make the function return true.

See Figure 5-14, where the code has been added, and the error has gone away.

```
-(BOOL)textFieldShouldReturn:(UITextField *)textField
{
    return true;
}
@end
```

*Figure 5-14. Setting the return value for the function*

Objective-C adds constants YES and NO that equate to true and false, respectively. You'll often see these used in code, so don't worry—it's not something different, it's just Objective-C trying to give you code that's more readable. So, this code will do exactly the same as that in Figure 5-14:

```
-(BOOL)textFieldShouldReturn:(UITextField *)textField
{
    return YES;
}
@end
```

The error might be gone, but the function still needs to be filled out. Use the same code that you did earlier, and when you're done the textFieldShouldReturn function should look like this:

```
-(BOOL)textFieldShouldReturn:(UITextField *)textField
{
    _lblOutput.text = _txtInput.text;
    return YES;
}
```

Run your application, and you should see that when you type in the text field and press "Return" on the virtual keyboard, the label gets updated, but the keyboard isn't dismissed. We'll discuss that later in this chapter.

## Expanding on Delegates

Before going on to showing you how to do that, there's an important concept you should explore first. Note that when you created the delegate function, the signature of the function referred to the text field like this:

```
-(BOOL)textFieldShouldReturn:(UITextField *)textField
```

This isn't our _txtInput field. It also prefixed that with (UITextField *), which is funny-looking syntax. The "*" indicates that this is a *pointer*. So the value being passed into the function, according to this syntax, is a *pointer* to a UITextField, and not an *actual* UITextField. This is good, because we don't have a UITextField called textField; ours is called _txtInput.

Pointers are interesting and difficult concepts to grasp, but with a little practice you'll get it. Try and think of this function definition as follows: I'm working on a UITextField, and it's the one that I'm pointing at. I'm not sure what it's called, so I'll just call it textField.

In the previous section, we ignored this, as we knew the name of the text field that we were using. It was called _txtInput, so our code just looked like this:

```
-(BOOL)textFieldShouldReturn:(UITextField *)textField
{
    _lblOutput.text = _txtInput.text;
    return YES;
}
```

This worked fine, but what if there are lots of text fields on our view? The point of delegates becomes apparent in a situation where we have lots of text fields. Instead of having a piece of code for each one, and probably repeating a lot of code, it's great to have one place to do it all. When you use a delegate, the place to do so is in the view controller.

So we can change our code to this:

```
-(BOOL)textFieldShouldReturn:(UITextField *)textField
{
    _lblOutput.text = textField.text;
    return YES;
}
```

And it will still work! Now when _txtInput delegates action to the view controller, the pointer, called textField, is pointing at _txtInput. Within the function, if you say textField.text, you're telling Objective-C that you want to get the text from the control that you're pointing at.

So now if you were to add several more text fields to your storyboard, and if you were to create outlets for them, and then if you were set their delegates to self in the view controller, no matter which field you type in, and then press "Return," the _lblOutput would be set to whatever text you typed into the field. We'll explore how to fix that in the "Changing the App to Have More Controls" section later in this chapter.

## Dismissing the Keyboard

There's still a small problem—the keyboard doesn't go away when you press the "Return" key. In Objective-C, when the operating system provides something for you, such as the keyboard for typing in text fields, the object that gets it is called the *First Responder*. If you don't want that object to be the first responder any more, you can simply resign the status, and the operating system will know to go away.

So, in the case of the text field becoming first responder, our textFieldShouldReturn has a handy pointer to the text field. So we can say "you know the text field that you're pointing to—resign first responder status on it" using code like this:

```
-(BOOL)textFieldShouldReturn:(UITextField *)textField
{
    _lblOutput.text = textField.text;
    [textField resignFirstResponder];
    return YES;
}
```

Now whenever you run your app, you'll see that pressing the "Return" key will not only set the text of the output label, it'll also make the keyboard go away.

The syntax used here, of square brackets and a space between the object and the command, is a new one. This is what Objective-C calls a *message*. It's very similar to a method, and it's probably the most confusing thing about programming with this language. Sometimes you use a method with the dot syntax (e.g., `object.foo`), and sometimes it's the message syntax (e.g., `[object foo]`).

Picking the right syntax for the right scenario just comes with practice. If you're using objects and classes that are already built for you, then you'll just have to go with however they're implemented and use that, be it a message or a method.

But there's still a problem. We can resign first responder status in the `textFieldShouldReturn` function, but what happens when the user presses the "Go" button? As our view only has one field on it, called `_txtInput`, we could write code like this:

```
- (IBAction)btnGo:(id)sender {
    _lblOutput.text = _txtInput.text;
    [_txtInput resignFirstResponder];
}
```

And it would work. But again, think of the scenario in which there are several text fields. What would happen then? Only the `_txtInput` would have resigned first responder status. If the text is in a different field, the keyboard wouldn't go away when we press the Go button. In this case we don't have the handy pointer passed in, so we'd be stuck.

One solution to this would be to cheat a little bit. We know that we can refer to ViewController.m using the word `self`, and Objective-C will allow you to call functions on it, including resigning first responder status. The iOS operating system is smart enough to understand that if you resign first responder on the view, then any of the objects within that view that have first responder status will lose it.

It's analogous to a room full of people, where one of them is the first responder. If you tell the room to no longer be the first responder, then the person within the room that has that status will resign it.

So you can change your code to this, and it will work for any text field that might be on our view.

```
- (IBAction)btnGo:(id)sender {

    _lblOutput.text = _txtInput.text;
    [self resignFirstResponder];
}
```

This works, but there's one more minor issue, which we'll explore in the next section, and which will be highlighted when we add more "Text Field" controls.

## Changing the App to Have More Controls

In the previous sections you had an app with a single text field, a single label, and a single button. Let's now add a few more text fields.

Open `Main.storyboard` and drag the label with the text "Output Goes Here" about halfway down the design surface. The arrow to the left will give you a rough idea of where it should go. See Figure 5-15.

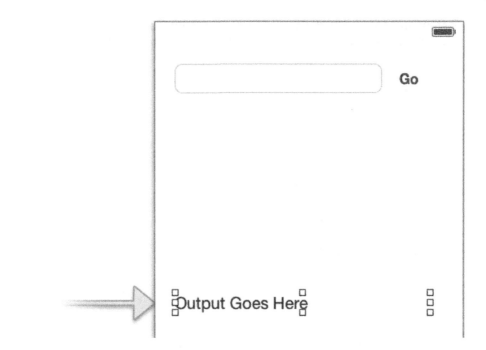

*Figure 5-15.* *Changing the position of the label*

Now drag three new "Text Field" controls onto the surface and make them the same width as the original text field. Space them out evenly so your screen looks like Figure 5-16.

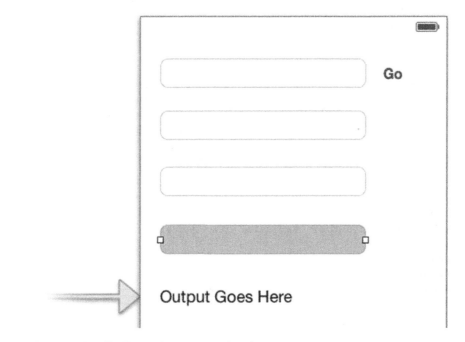

*Figure 5-16.* *Adding more "Text Field" controls to your storyboard*

Now open the assistant, making sure that it's displaying ViewController.h, and CTRL-drag these "Text Field" controls onto it, creating outlets and calling them, from top to bottom, txtInput2, txtInput3, and txtInput4, respectively. Figure 5-17 shows my screen when I'm dragging the last of the controls onto it.

*Figure 5-17.* *Creating the outlets for the new "Text Field" controls*

When you're done, your ViewController.h file should look like this:

```
#import <UIKit/UIKit.h>

@interface ViewController : UIViewController<UITextFieldDelegate>
@property (strong, nonatomic) IBOutlet UITextField *txtInput;
@property (strong, nonatomic) IBOutlet UITextField *txtInput2;
@property (strong, nonatomic) IBOutlet UITextField *txtInput3;
@property (strong, nonatomic) IBOutlet UITextField *txtInput4;

@property (strong, nonatomic) IBOutlet UILabel *lblOutput;
- (IBAction)btnGo:(id)sender;

@end
```

Remember earlier when you were learning about delegates, the first step was to tell the View Controller that it would be the delegate, and the second was to tell each text field that it would use the View Controller to delegate stuff to? To do this we went to the ViewController.m file and added code to the viewDidLoad function for txtInput. We'll need to do the same for the new outlets too.

Here's the code:

```
- (void)viewDidLoad
{
    [super viewDidLoad];
        // Do any additional setup after loading the view, typically from a nib.
    _txtInput.delegate = self;
    _txtInput2.delegate = self;
    _txtInput3.delegate = self;
    _txtInput4.delegate = self;
}
```

Now the whole pointer business in the textFieldShouldReturn function should make more sense. Regardless of which of the text fields is in use when the "Return" key is pressed, the pointer will point to it, and when we do something with the pointer, like reading its text or resigning its first responder, the action will happen on the appropriate text field.

Run the app and give it a try. As soon as you put the cursor into a text field the keyboard will appear, and depending on where you put the label, it might even obscure it. See Figure 5-18.

*Figure 5-18. Running the app*

Pressing the "Return" key will load the text into the label and dismiss the keyboard. This shows how using delegates can be a really nice way to avoid writing a lot of code to do the same thing over and over. While the concept of delegates might seem a little abstract, particularly if you're just beginning programming, consider what you would have had to do in this scenario *without* delegates. Each text field would have to have an action created for it, and each action function would have to set the text of the label and resign first responder status. Your code would get big and complex very quickly.

> **Note**    Programmers often use a concept called DRY, which stands for Don't Repeat Yourself, when writing code. It's a great idea to get into this habit, because if you write the same code more than once, and you have a bug in the code that you need to fix, you need to fix it more than once.

But wait, you might ask—what about the button? The code for the button will only read the original text field and set the label from that. What should we do about it? There are two options: first, we can try to figure out which of the text fields we recently typed our text into and set the output label for that, or second, we can just get rid of the button.

It might seem flippant to remove the button, but when we consider the needs of this app, we realize that we don't really need a button to set the text when the "Return" key on the keyboard does that for us now. When building mobile solutions, particularly phone ones, it's probably best to use as little screen real estate as possible, and to avoid unnecessary controls. So, for this example, we think it's better just to get rid of the button.

Doing this is easy. On the design surface we can just delete it and then resize the text fields to use the newly available width. See Figure 5-19.

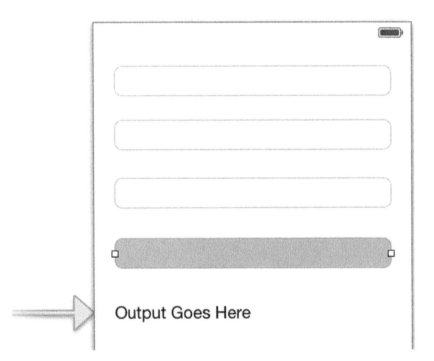

*Figure 5-19. Redesigning the app to not have a button*

Next, since the button is gone, you don't need the action any more. When you CTRL-dragged the button to the header file earlier in this chapter, this code was added to ViewController.h:

```
- (IBAction)btnGo:(id)sender;
```

You can safely delete it.

Next, you can get rid of the btnGo function from ViewController.m. It looked like this:

```
- (IBAction)btnGo:(id)sender {

    // [self changeText:_txtInput];

    _lblOutput.text = _txtInput.text;
    [self resignFirstResponder];
}
```

Go ahead and delete the first line. Run your app, and you'll see that it's more user friendly, as you have more screen real estate for your text, and the keyboard handles the actions for you, as it should. See Figure 5-20.

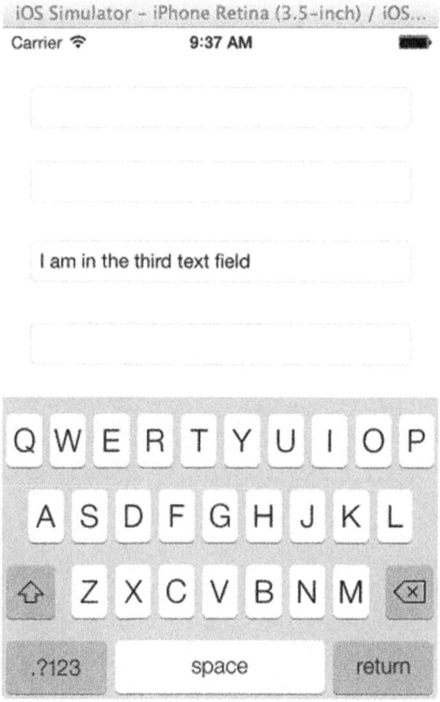

*Figure 5-20.* *The newly redesigned app*

If you've made it this far, congratulations! This is a very simple app, but it demonstrates some of the sophisticated programming patterns, such as delegates and DRY, that you'll need in your toolbox to be a successful developer.

# Summary

In this chapter you learned how to use a text field and how it manages keyboard input. You used this to delve into the concept of delegates, where one object can delegate responsibility to another. You explored an app in which you have multiple text fields. You used delegates to allow the code to handle keyboard input so that these text fields could be managed in a single location. It was a simple scenario and a simple app, but you were able to use it to uncover these complex concepts, and you'll use these concepts extensively in iOS development. Before going further into iOS7 development and learning new controls, APIs, and other good stuff, there's one more thing that you should look at, and that's debugging your application. You'll learn about Xcode's tools for this in Chapter 6.

# Debugging iOS7 Apps

In the previous few chapters you built some basic applications and tested them by running them in the simulator. They didn't really have a whole lot of sophisticated functionality, so playing with them in the simulator was enough. However, as your applications get more complex, you'll need to take a look at them while they are running and inspect what is going on in order to find issues. This process is called *debugging*, in the sense of removing bugs from your applications. In this chapter you'll take a look at the tools that are available to you to do this in Xcode, and while you are doing it, you are going to build a fun little Magic 8-ball app.

## Creating the App

The Magic 8-ball app will be created as a single-view app, in the same way as all the other apps so far in this book.

To create this app, launch Xcode and select "Create a new Xcode Project." When asked to choose a template for your new project, select a "Single View Application" and click "Next."

When asked to "Choose options for your new project" give it the name "magic8" and specify it as an iPhone project. Click "Next." Finally, click "Create" on the next dialog, and the code will be created for you. Xcode will launch and open your project.

## Designing the Magic 8-ball App

In Xcode, click on"Main.storyboard" to open the design surface for your view. Drag a button and drop it on the design surface near the top. Change its caption to "Ask the 8 Ball."Once you've done this, center the button. Use Figure 6-1 as a guideline.

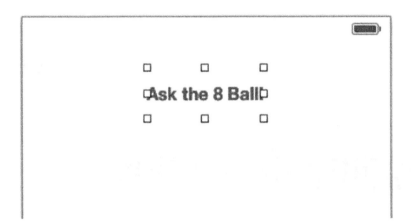

*Figure 6-1.* *Laying out the button for the Magic 8-ball app*

Once you've done this, it's time to add two labels. Double click on the first and change its text to "The answer is:" as shown in Figure 6-2.

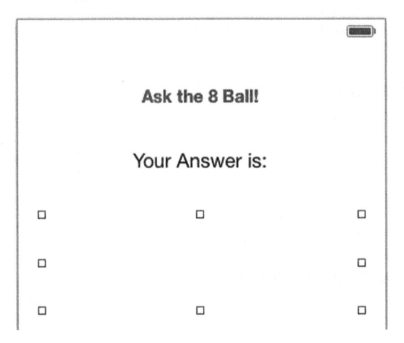

*Figure 6-2.* *Adding the labels*

For the second, double click and delete the text so that it's completely blank.

Use the dots around the border of the label, also known as "sizing handles," to change the location and shape of the label. Use Figure 6-2 as an example of something that looks good, but feel free to experiment on your own.

You now have all the controls that you need. In the next section you'll wire up the controls and begin writing the code that you need for a Magic 8-ball.

# Writing the Code

Before writing any code, you should set up your necessary outlets and actions from the storyboard editor. As you won't be doing anything to the label that reads "Your answer is," you won't need an outlet for it.

You'll need an outlet for the blank label, as that is what will render the answer from the Magic 8-ball. To do this, open the assistant and CTRL-drag the blank label to your "ViewController.h" file. You can access the assistant using the icon that looks like a tuxedo on the upper-right-hand side of the screen. The assistant will open on the right-hand side of your screen, showing some code. At the top of the assistant, you can see the code file that is open. If it isn't ViewController.h, change it to be so.

> **Tip** If this is unfamiliar to you, we recommend you go back to Chapter 2, where you'll be given a step-by-step approach to doing this task.

Once you CTRL-drag the label onto the assistant, a menu like that in Figure 6-3 will pop up. Fill it out to create an outlet, called "lblOutput," as shown in Figure 6-3.

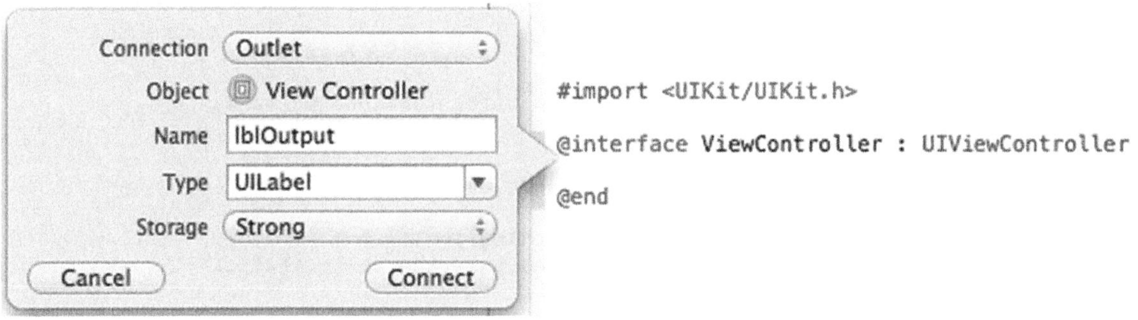

*Figure 6-3.* *Creating the outlet*

Similarly, create an action by CTRL-dragging the button to the header. Call this "btnAsk," as shown in Figure 6-4.

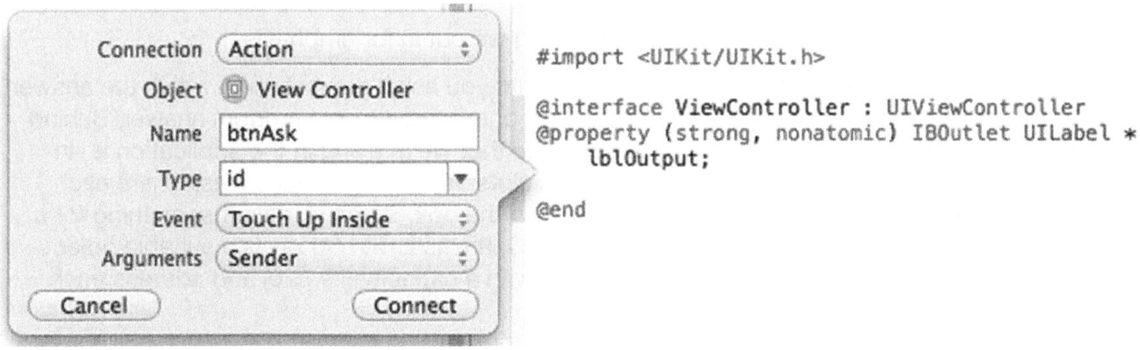

*Figure 6-4.* *Creating the action*

Now you are ready to begin writing the code for your application. Your first task is to create a module-level or class variable. This might sound like a bit of a mouthful, but it's pretty straightforward. Typically in any programming language, when you create a variable it only lives within the function you created it in. So if you have a function called "foo()" and another called "bar()," any variable that you create in foo() cannot be addressed in bar(). When you have a class, such as your "ViewController" class, the same applies. But you *can* create a variable on the class itself, so that every function in that class can use that variable.

To do this, you can declare it by inserting it just above the @implementation line for your class in the "ViewController.m" file. So, open ViewController.m and edit it to add the code NSMutableArray* magicStrings as a class variable. You can see what this looks like in Figure 6-5.

```objc
#import "ViewController.h"

@interface ViewController ()

@end

NSMutableArray* magicStrings;
@implementation ViewController

- (void)viewDidLoad
{
    [super viewDidLoad];
    // Do any additional setup after loading the view,
}

- (void)didReceiveMemoryWarning
{
    [super didReceiveMemoryWarning];
    // Dispose of any resources that can be recreated.
}

- (IBAction)btnAsk:(id)sender {
}
@end
```

*Figure 6-5.* *Placing a class variable*

The code isn't usually highlighted—that's just something we put in for emphasis.

If you've never used a magic 8-ball before, the idea is that you ask it a question to which the answer would usually be "yes" or "no, "then you shake the ball, and it throws up a random answer. Behind the scenes, the ball has 20 answers, so the variable type that we're using in the application is an *array*. An array allows you to store data in addressable slots. It's a lot like mailboxes, where each mailbox has a number (i.e., address), and you put stuff in the box. When you want something for a specific box, you use its number to find it. In Objective-C, the NSMutableArray is a suitable object that allows you to do this. You can initialize this object with a capacity (i.e., 20) and address each element within the array with a square bracket syntax. In software, this is usually zero based, where the first item is number 0, the second is number 1, etc.

Here's Objective-C code (also known as a method) that you can put in your app (put it right above the @end at the bottom), which will initialize the array to have 20 "mailboxes" and will put one of the 20 messages in each.

```
-(void)initializeStrings{
magicStrings = [[NSMutableArrayalloc] initWithCapacity:20];
magicStrings[0]=@"It is certain";
magicStrings[1]=@"It is decidedly so";
magicStrings[2]=@"Without a doubt";
magicStrings[3]=@"Yes, definitely";
magicStrings[4]=@"You may rely on it";
magicStrings[5]=@"As I see it, yes";
magicStrings[6]=@"Most likely";
magicStrings[7]=@"Outlook good";
magicStrings[8]=@"Yes";
magicStrings[9]=@"Signs point to yes";
magicStrings[10]=@"Reply hazy, try again";
magicStrings[11]=@"Ask again later";
magicStrings[12]=@"Better not tell you now";
magicStrings[13]=@"Cannot predict now";
magicStrings[14]=@"Concentrate and ask again";
magicStrings[15]=@"Don't count on it";
magicStrings[16]=@"My reply is no";
magicStrings[17]=@"My sources say no";
magicStrings[18]=@"Outlook not so good";
magicStrings[19]=@"Very doubtful";
}
```

In Objective-C you use an array with NSArray or NSMutableArray, with the difference being that the former is used for arrays that never change, whereas the latter is used for arrays in which you can add and take away elements (i.e., remove some mailboxes or add some others). For an app such as this, it would probably be better to use an NSArray, but we went with the NSMutableArray because it allows us to initialize our array with a fixed size, in this case 20 elements, as seen on this line:

```
magicStrings = [[NSMutableArray alloc] initWithCapacity:20];
```

Now, in our code, if we refer to magicStrings[9], we'll get the string "Signs point to yes" returned to us.

This is great, because that's what we want to display as our answer. Now all you need to do is figure out how to generate a random number. You'll see that, along with your first bug, in the next section.

# Debugging the App

Programs seldom run perfectly the first time you try them. In this section you'll take a look at some of the common causes for errors and the tools that are available for you to fix them. These include the following:

- Handling a coding error. This is when you have written the logic of your code incorrectly, but its syntax is correct. In this case, your application doesn't behave the way you'd expect, but it doesn't crash.

- Handling a runtime error. This is when you've written something wrong in your code, which passes by the compiler, but when you try to run it, the operating system cannot handle it. In this case, your application crashes unexpectedly.

- Handling a compile time error. This is when your code is wrong to the extent that the compiler doesn't understand it at all. In this case, you won't have an app at all, because the compiler isn't able to create it due to the errors.

In the next few sections, you'll introduce errors to the magic 8-ball app in order to demonstrate these concepts and to explore the tools available in Xcode that allow you to find and fix them.

## Handling a Coding Error

The C language, upon which Objective-C is based, has a function called `arc4random_uniform()`, which is perfect for this task. You give it a number—for example, 20—and it will return a random number between 0 and that number minus 1, or in this case between 0 and 19. This is exactly what we need, so go to the `btnAsk` function, which runs when you click the button, and add this line:

```
int r = arc4random_uniform(20);
```

This creates a random number and loads it into a variable of type "int" (meaning integer), which I called "r." So now we can set the label to have the magicStrings at address r using magicStrings[r]. Here's the full `btnAsk` code that achieves this:

```
- (IBAction)btnAsk:(id)sender {
int r = arc4random_uniform(20);
_lblOutput.text = magicStrings[r];
}
```

Now whenever we click the button, we will get a random number from 0 to 19, and we will then use that random number to get the string that we'll load into the `lblOutput`.

Run the app in the simulator. You should see something like Figure 6-6.

**Figure 6-6.** *Running the Magic 8-ball app*

Ask yourself a yes/no question, such as "Is this book awesome?" and click the "Ask the 8 Ball!"button.

You would expect an answer to appear, but nothing happens! Your app didn't crash, you had no warnings or errors when you were compiling and running, but it doesn't work properly. What could be wrong?

In order to figure that out, we need to see what happens when we click the button. To do this we'll use a *breakpoint* in the btnAsk function.

## Using Breakpoints

A breakpoint is an instruction that you add to Xcode telling it to stop executing your code at a specified location. You can then use the debugger to examine it while it's stopped and see what's really going on. You set a breakpoint in Xcode by clicking in the margin of your code window until a little blue arrow like the one in Figure 6-7 appears.

```
- (IBAction)btnAsk:(id)sender {
    int r = arc4random_uniform(20);
    _lblOutput.text = magicStrings[r];
}
```

**Figure 6-7.** *Setting a breakpoint*

If you haven't done so already, stop the application, return to Xcode, and put a breakpoint in the btnAsk function as shown in Figure 6-7.

Now run your application again and click the button. The simulator will stop, and you'll be returned to Xcode, where you will see the line that you put the breakpoint on highlighted in green. This is called hitting the breakpoint. See Figure 6-8.

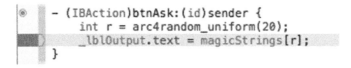

*Figure 6-8.  Hitting the breakpoint*

The app was running in the simulator, but has now frozen, with its internals all wide open for you to inspect to see what's going on. There are a number of great tools that allow you to do this.

First, you have a rollover view of the contents of variables. This line is after the one where r was initialized, so if you hover your mouse over r for a moment, a window will pop up with the contents of r. See Figure 6-9.

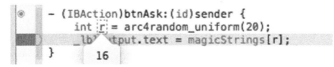

*Figure 6-9.  Inspecting variables in the debugger*

You might see a different number here, because r is generated randomly, but it should always be greater than or equal to 0 and less than20.

In Figure 6-9, you can see that r is 16, which looks valid, and magicStrings[r], according to the initializeStrings function, is set to "My reply is no," which is also good.

But, to double check, hover over magicStrings[r] on the breakpoint line.

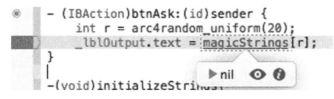

*Figure 6-10.  Inspecting the magicStrings variable*

Now *that* is unusual. It's "nil," which is another word for *nothing* or *empty*. You can click the eyeball icon to the right of nil to see more details. You'll see this in Figure 6-11.

*Figure 6-11. A more detailed inspection of our variable*

We can see that the *entire* array is empty, because its value is all zeros. When we declared magicStrings, we used NSMutableArray* as its type, and if you remember from earlier chapters, when we put a * on a variable name, that means it's a pointer. The pointer itself, if you inspect it, points to the memory location, where the data for the object is stored. When it's all zeros like this, it means that the object hasn't been initialized. Objective-C knows that you want an object, but until you initialize it, it just has an empty (or nil) pointer hanging around waiting for you to do something with it.

Why is that the case? Let's take a look at our code again. We *did* write a function to initialize magicStrings

```
#import "ViewController.h"

@interfaceViewController ()

@end

NSMutableArray* magicStrings;
@implementation ViewController

- (void)viewDidLoad
{
    [superviewDidLoad];
        // Do any additional setup after loading the view, typically from a nib.
}

- (void)didReceiveMemoryWarning
{
    [superdidReceiveMemoryWarning];
// Dispose of any resources that can be recreated.
}

- (IBAction)btnAsk:(id)sender {
int r = arc4random_uniform(20);
_lblOutput.text = magicStrings[r];
}

-(void)initializeStrings{
magicStrings = [[NSMutableArrayalloc] initWithCapacity:20];
magicStrings[0]=@"It is certain";
magicStrings[1]=@"It is decidedly so";
```

```
magicStrings[2]=@"Without a doubt";
magicStrings[3]=@"Yes, definitely";
magicStrings[4]=@"You may rely on it";
magicStrings[5]=@"As I see it, yes";
magicStrings[6]=@"Most likely";
magicStrings[7]=@"Outlook good";
magicStrings[8]=@"Yes";
magicStrings[9]=@"Signs point to yes";
magicStrings[10]=@"Reply hazy, try again";
magicStrings[11]=@"Ask again later";
magicStrings[12]=@"Better not tell you now";
magicStrings[13]=@"Cannot predict now";
magicStrings[14]=@"Concentrate and ask again";
magicStrings[15]=@"Don't count on it";
magicStrings[16]=@"My reply is no";
magicStrings[17]=@"My sources say no";
magicStrings[18]=@"Outlook not so good";
magicStrings[19]=@"Very doubtful";
}

@end
```

Have you spotted the problem yet? Why is magicStrings empty? The answer is that even if we created a function to initialize it, we've never actually *called* that function. Objective-C and iOS7 aren't quite smart enough to figure that out for themselves. So let's call that function when the view loads, as we only need to call it once. Stop your application and update your viewDidLoad function to make the call to initialize the strings.

Here's the code:

```
- (void)viewDidLoad
{
  [superviewDidLoad];
// Do any additional setup after loading the view, typically from a nib.
[self initializeStrings];
}
```

Now run the app and click the button again.

You'll hit the breakpoint once more. Hover over magicStrings and see what happens.

*Figure 6-12. Inspecting magicStrings after we fixed the bug*

Now we can see that magicStrings is no longer empty. There are 20 objects inside it, which is what we'd expect as we loaded it with 20 strings. Remember each string is an object.

Clicking the eyeball to inspect it a little deeper shows us more information. See Figure 6-13.

*Figure 6-13. Deeper inspection of the fixed code*

Now we see that our pointer points to an actual place in memory, in this case address 0x08e22700, so we know at least *something* is working. Objective-C has initialized our NSMutableArray, put 20 strings into it, and told the pointer where in the computer's memory it lives. This is good.

To see if your app works, you want to continue execution past your breakpoint. You might be tempted to think that the way to do this is to run the code again, but it isn't. Whatever you do, make sure that you *don't* hit the "Run" button. This will actually stop your code from running; instead it will compile it and run it again.

Instead, look towards the bottom of the Xcode screen, and you'll see the debug window is open. It looks like Figure 6-14.

*Figure 6-14. The debug window*

To continue execution, click the "Continue" button. It's the third from the left at the top of the bar, and looks like a "Play" button with a vertical line beside it.

Click this, and execution of code returns to the simulator. Take a look to see if your app worked. You can see what happened to us in this session in Figure 6-15.

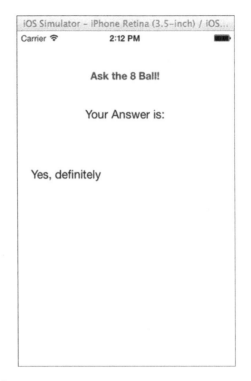

*Figure 6-15.* *The working 8-ball app!*

Now, the debug window had some really nice tools. We should take a look at them. Stop your application and make a new breakpoint on the first line of the initializeStrings function. Your screen should look like Figure 6-16.

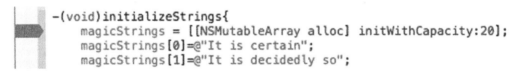

```
-(void)initializeStrings{
    magicStrings = [[NSMutableArray alloc] initWithCapacity:20];
    magicStrings[0]=@"It is certain";
    magicStrings[1]=@"It is decidedly so";
```

*Figure 6-16.* *Setting a new breakpoint*

Run the app again, and you'll hit this breakpoint right away. This is because initializeStrings is called as part of your ViewDidLoad: function, which, as its name suggests, gets called when the view is loaded into memory.

Your debug window will look something like Figure 6-17.

*Figure 6-17.  The debug window when you hit your second breakpoint*

To the right of the "Continue" button that you used earlier, there's a button that looks like an arrow curving over a line. This tells the runtime to move forward by one line of code, in a process typically called *stepping*. Click it once, and a few interesting things will happen.

First, the green highlight over the line of code where you have your breakpoint will step to the next line. See Figure 6-18.

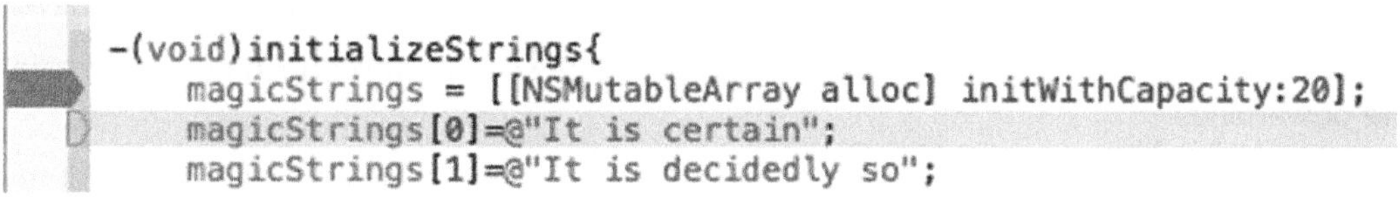

```
-(void)initializeStrings{
    magicStrings = [[NSMutableArray alloc] initWithCapacity:20];
    magicStrings[0]=@"It is certain";
    magicStrings[1]=@"It is decidedly so";
```

*Figure 6-18.  Stepping forward one line*

Additionally, the debug window will update with any new data. If you look at figure 6-17, magicStrings was nil, but the line of code that we stepped over was the one that allocated it and told it to have a capacity of 20 strings. So, look at what happened in the debug window. You can see it in Figure 6-19.

*Figure 6-19.  Inspecting the variables on stepping through the code*

Now it shows us that magicStrings has been initialized, but there's nothing in it yet. Click the "Step" button one more time. You'll see that the green line steps down to the next line, which begins with magicStrings[1]=, having executed the line that says magicStrings[0]=. Thus, one object has been loaded into magicStrings.

Figure 6-20 shows what the debug window will look like at this point.

*Figure 6-20. Inspecting the variables after another step*

As you can see, magicStrings now has one object in it. As you keep stepping, you'll see the result of the commands being executed, which in this case means that magicStrings will keep growing.

When you're satisfied, click the "Continue" button to continue execution, and the app will launch.

Stepping through code like this will prove to be invaluable as you write more and more complex and sophisticated apps. To be able to break open your app and look at the code while it is executing, seeing what the data looks like and comparing it against what you'd expect, is vital to being an iOS developer.

The type of bug that you just hit can be very insidious, because your app doesn't crash or give you any kind of warning.

The app ran perfectly happily—but it didn't do what it was supposed to. It's really important to deal with this type of error, because it can be far more dangerous than one that causes a crash. Consider, for example, an app that would be used in healthcare, where it monitors heart rate. If it doesn't correctly report a dangerous heart rate, but instead continues running without any issues, it could be very damaging for the patient.

# Handling Runtime Errors

In this section, we'll take a look at the type of bug that your app can't handle, leading to what is typically called a *crash*.

Our Magic 8-ball app works well, so let's deliberately introduce a coding error in order to examine a crash.

First, delete the breakpoints that you put in the app in the previous section. To do this, either right click, or hold down "CTRL," while you click on the blue arrow that denotes the breakpoint. You'll see a menu of options popup. One of these is "Delete Breakpoint." See Figure 6-21.

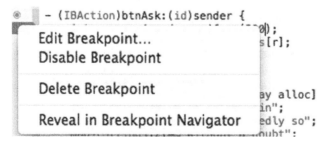

*Figure 6-21. Deleting a breakpoint*

Repeat this for all breakpoints in your app.

Next, we'll introduce a coding error. In the btnAskfunction, we used the arc4random_uniform function, passing it a value of 20, which would return a value between 0 and 19.

```
- (IBAction)btnAsk:(id)sender {
int r = arc4random_uniform(20);
_lblOutput.text = magicStrings[r];
}
```

This was the perfect shape for our magicStrings array.

However, consider what happens if the value passed in to arc4random_uniformis much bigger than 20. If you use 200, then it will return a value between 0 and 199. So, for example, if it returned 147, we could end up assigning _lblOutput.text to magicStrings[147], which doesn't exist.

Update the code to look like this:

```
- (IBAction)btnAsk:(id)sender {
    int r = arc4random_uniform(200);
_lblOutput.text = magicStrings[r];
}
```

Now run your app and click the button. If it works, keep clicking the button until your app crashes. A crash should cause your app to trigger Xcode to reactivate with the file "main.m" opened and the green execution line highlighted. You can see an example of this in Figure 6-22.

```
int main(int argc, char * argv[])
{
    @autoreleasepool {
        return UIApplicationMain(argc, argv, nil, NSStringFromClass([AppDelegate class]));
    }                                                           Thread 1: signal SIGABRT
}
```

*Figure 6-22. Catching a runtime crash*

If you look at the right of Figure 6-22, you'll see that the *signal* (or message) that was sent is SIGABRT, meaning that the operating system has told the app to abort execution. Something has gone wrong, so the app has to die.

If you look at the debug window at the bottom of the screen, on the right-hand side is the output window. A quick look at this might give some hints as to the error. See Figure 6-23.

```
2013-07-28 08:25:11.034 magic8[673:70b] ***
Terminating app due to uncaught exception
'NSRangeException', reason: '*** -[__NSArrayM
objectAtIndex:]: index 106 beyond bounds [0 ..
19]'
*** First throw call stack:
(
    0   CoreFoundation
0x016e4624 __exceptionPreprocess + 180
    1   libobjc.A.dylib
0x014648b6 objc_exception_throw + 44
    2   CoreFoundation
0x016856d6 -[__NSArrayM objectAtIndex:] + 246
    3   CoreFoundation
0x01762b58 -[NSArray objectAtIndexedSubscript:] +
40
    4   magic8
0x00006420 -[ViewController btnAsk:] + 128
    5   libobjc.A.dylib
0x01476874 -[NSObject
performSelector:withObject:withObject:] + 77
    6   UIKit
0x0022faf9 -[UIApplication
sendAction:to:from:forEvent:] + 108
    7   UIKit
0x0022fa85 -[UIApplication
sendAction:toTarget:fromSender:forEvent:] + 61
    8   UIKit
0x0031d7d5 -[UIControl sendAction:to:forEvent:] +
```

All Output ⬍                                        🗑 | ▮▯ ▯▮

*Figure 6-23. The debug output*

The debug output window lists everything that was happening prior to the crash. In other words, the function that called the function that called the function, etc. When you get a crash like this, you can look through it to see if any of your code is in there. And in this case, it is. Look at Line 4 in Figure 6-23, and you'll see that [ViewController btnAsk] is listed. The next item in the stack, in other words, the function that btnAsk called, is in the next line—in this case, Line 5. Your line numbers might be different, and that's fine—it's the content that matters.

> **Note**    You may have heard the term *call stack* being used by developers in debugging their applications. The call stack is the list of code functions that your app calls, in the order in which they are called. You can look through the stack to trace how your app executes. The debug window output here is an example of a call stack.

You can see that the function called was to `performSelector` on an object using another object (`performSelector:withObject:withObject` in the debug window), which looks remarkably like our line `_lblOutput.text = magicStrings[r];` where we are taking an object (`magicStrings`) and performing a selection on it using another object, in this case the integer `r`. This helps us find the line that causes the error, so, a good next step in debugging would be to put a breakpoint on that line and inspect the variables within it.

Do this, and then stop and restart your app.

The first sign that you've at least taken the first step towards finding the bug is that the app doesn't crash when you click the button, and instead stops execution at the breakpoint. See Figure 6-24.

```
- (IBAction)btnAsk:(id)sender {
      int r = arc4random_uniform(200);
      _lblOutput.text = magicStrings[r];                                    Thread 1: breakpoint 1.1
}
```

*Figure 6-24.* *Hitting our breakpoint again*

If you inspect the value of "r," and it is greater than 19, click the "Step Over" button to advance to the next line of code, and you'll see that the exception gets triggered again, telling us that this line is the one that caused the error.

In this case, we cheated a little, because we introduced the error and knew where it was. But hopefully the techniques used to find it make sense to you. They'll be very useful when an error that you did *not* introduce intentionally happens in your apps.

## Handling Compile-time Errors

Both of the error types that we've seen in this chapter are *run time* errors, where the error occurs while the application is running. The first was when the app didn't behave as expected, and the second was when it crashed. The third, and perhaps the most common, form of error you'll encounter is a coding error that prevents your app from compiling. In this section, we'll see how you can fix this type of error.

First of all, let's introduce a few errors to our app code and see what happens when we try to compile.

Change the code of the `btnAsk` function so that it looks like this:

```
- (IBAction)btnAsk:(id)sender {
int r = arc4randoms_uniform(2o);
_lblOutupt.text = magicStrings[r];
}
```

The steps to do this are:

- Change the "20" to "2o" (letter "o" instead of a zero)
- Mistype the name of _lblOutput, so it reads _lblOutupt
- Change the name of the function `arcrandom_uniform` to `arcrandoms_uniform`

You'll see some hints appear to the left of your code to let you know something is wrong. Ignore them for now. Xcode is actually taking a step ahead of you here and testing the validity of your code using the same process the compiler does. It does this while you work on it and lets you know the problems that it sees.

Try to run the application. It will fail to run, and at the top of Xcode you'll see a notification of the errors. See Figure 6-25.

| magic8.xcodeproj — m ViewController.m |
|---|
| Build magic8: **Failed**   Today at 9:42 AM                          △2  ●2 |

*Figure 6-25. Xcode fails to compile your app*

You'll see that the message indicates that your app failed, and on the right you'll see the number of warnings (yellow triangle) and the number of errors (red circle) that the compiler encountered. To get more details, click the tool that represents the issue navigator in the project window at the left, where your files are listed. It is the fourth from the left and looks like an exclamation mark (!) inside a triangle. You can see it selected in Figure 6-26.

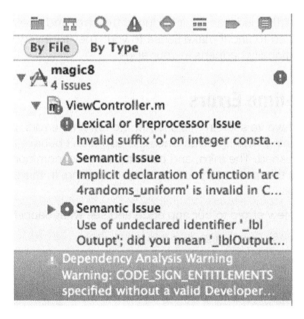

*Figure 6-26. Showing the issue navigator*

Using this navigator, we can see where the errors and warnings occur. In this case, there are three issues detected in ViewController.m—as we'd expect because we introduced three errors. Let's look at these one by one.

The first is a lexical or preprocessor issue. This happened because the compiler had no idea what you meant in your code. Of course the arcrandom_uniform function expects an integer value passed to it, but you typed"2o." Within the navigator, click the "Lexical or Preprocessor Issue" line. The code editor will jump to the line in question, allowing you to fix it. It even points to where it thinks the problem is. See the little triangle under the "o" in Figure 6-27.

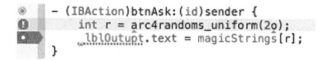

*Figure 6-27.* *Fixing the lexical or preprocessor compiler error*

Change the "o" back to a "0" (zero), and the code will be retested in the background. The error will go away, and your issue navigator should now only have two errors in it. See Figure 6-28.

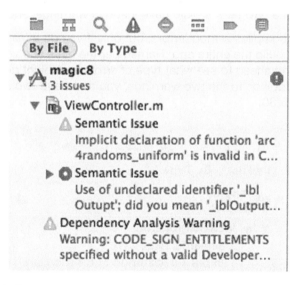

*Figure 6-28.* *Updated issue navigator*

> **Note**   Semantic issues occur when the compiler doesn't understand what you mean. It's smart enough to think it knows what you want, so gives you a hint as to what you might have really meant to type.

These are quite interesting, because the first one is just a warning, and the second is an actual error. This is because the first one is in a function, and the compiler is smart enough to know that sometimes function declarations are implicit. In this case it doesn't think so, but it will let it pass with a warning. The second one is flagged as an error because we are referring to a property on an object called "lblOutupt," which doesn't exist. It's smart enough to find what it *thinks* you are referring to, and in this case it's right.

Click on the second semantic issue, the one with the red circle beside it. You'll be taken to the code, and a little pop-up window will give you the option to fix it the way it thinks it should be fixed. See Figure 6-29.

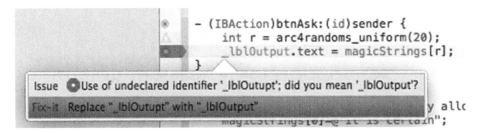

*Figure 6-29. Automatically fixing compiler errors*

If the hint on the blue fix-it line is the right answer, double click the line, and Xcode will fix that line of code for you. Now your issue navigator should have just two warnings, and no errors.

Usually an app will run if it compiles without errors, but only if you do a full compile/link cycle, which is what happens when you build the entire app. Remember the hints you've been getting thus far are from Xcode, which is looking ahead to see what type of errors you might get. When you try to run the app, you'll see that in addition to the two warnings, you now have two additional errors, and your app won't run. See Figure 6-30.

*Figure 6-30. Additional errors when you try to run the app*

Here, the rubber has hit the road, and instead of Xcode looking ahead to try and figure out what the errors might be, it has done a full compile of your app and gotten stuck. Naming the `arc4random_uniform` function incorrectly has caused a serious problem that stops your app from compiling altogether. Go ahead and fix the issue by changing the function name back to `arc4random_uniform` instead of `arc4randoms_uniform`, and you'll be good to continue.

> **Note**  There's another warning shown in many of the screen shots of this chapter, where the CODE_SIGN_ENTITLEMENTS is specified. This error occurs because the code hasn't been signed by the developer. In order to run code on a device (see Chapter 3), some certificates and signatures are needed, but for the emulator they aren't. For ease of development, we generally don't sign apps until we are ready to run and test them in the emulator, so this warning is quite common. It'll go away as you sign your apps for deployment.

## Summary

In this chapter you learned how faults in your app can be found and fixed. You saw how to build a simple app that gives you a Magic 8-ball, and how you can have different types of errors in this application. These include coding errors that stop the app from working, but don't crash it; errors that cause crashes; and errors that prevent the app from compiling at all. You worked through Xcode's tools for each of these errors in order to fix your app completely. Hopefully the skills you've learned in this chapter will help you with any issues you encounter with the apps that we build in the rest of the book!

# Chapter 7

# Exploring UI Controls

In previous chapters of this book, you created some sample apps and used some basic controls like the button, label, image, and text field. In this chapter, you'll broaden your arsenal of controls a little and explore, by building simple apps, how some of these controls work.

This chapter assumes you've worked through the examples in previous chapters and that you know your way around the Xcode interface for creating new apps and editing the UI using the storyboard editor. It also assumes you've practiced creating outlets and actions and that you've done a bit of coding. If you get stuck, refer back to earlier chapters or check out the complementary videos to this book on ios7developer.com.

You'll look at the "segmented" control, which is a horizontal control with multiple segments, each of which acts as a button. You'll see how to use this to create a simple app that changes the background color of your view. From there you'll move onto the "slider" control, which gives you the ability to choose a value by sliding a thumb horizontally. After that, it's the easy but common "switch" control that gives you a consistent on/off switch interface, and finally the "stepper" control, which is similar to the slider in that it gives you the ability to choose a discrete value, but with a different user interface—one that gives you the ability to hit a "+" or a "-" to increment or decrement a value, respectively.

## The Segmented Control

The segmented control, or UISegmentedControl, is a horizontal control made of multiple segments, with each functioning as a discrete button. Using this control gives you a compact means to group together a number of commands that are related.

## UISegmentedControl Example

You can see an example of a UISegmentedControl in the Safari browser. If you don't have an iOS7 device, don't worry—you can still see it in the simulator. Launch the Safari browser, and you'll see something like Figure 7-1.

*Figure 7-1.* *Running Safari in the emulator*

The "Bookmarks/Reading List" icon is the second from the right and looks like an open book. Select it, and you'll be taken to a view that allows you to select between "Bookmarks" and "Reading List." See Figure 7-2.

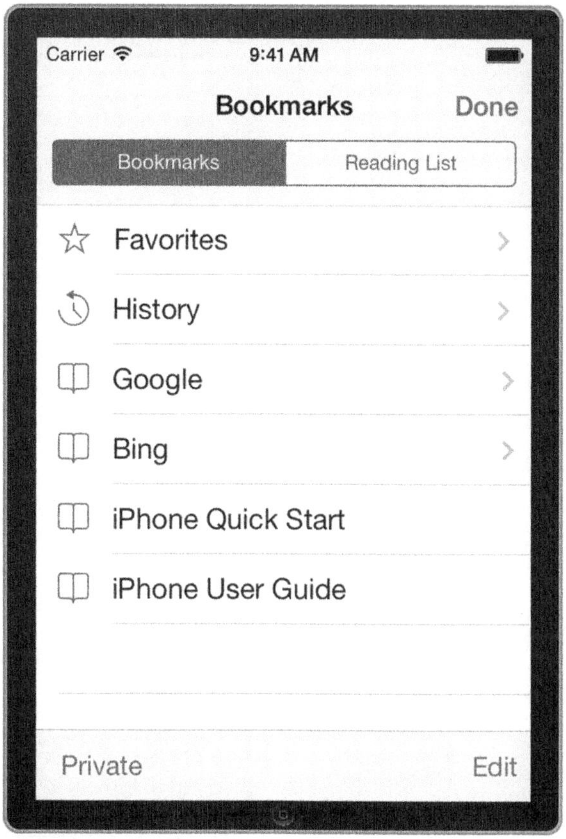

*Figure 7-2. The Bookmarks/Reading view*

At the top of the screen you can see a button with both "Bookmarks" and "Reading List" written on it, and when you touch one or the other, the view changes. This is a UISegmentedControl, so let's take a look at building an app that uses one.

# Building an App with a UISegmentedControl

In this section we'll look at building a simple app that uses a UISegmentedControl with three options on it, and we'll use them to change the color of the current view.

Create a new single view iPhone app and call it "segmentControlDemo." If you're not familiar with doing this, go back to Chapter 2 and take a look at how to create a simple single view app.

When you're done,  select "Main.storyboard" in the project navigator, and the storyboard editor will open. On the left of the storyboard editor, open "View Controller Scene" and make sure that "View Controller" is selected. You'll see a blue border around the design surface when you've done this. See Figure 7-3.

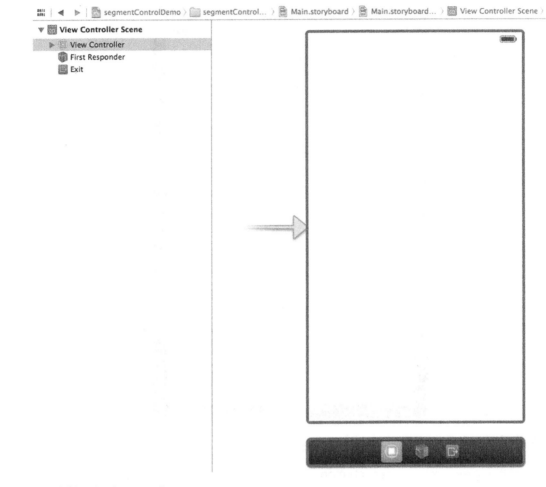

*Figure 7-3. Editing the view controller*

> **Tip** You can also click the black bar under the view controller surface to select it. You can see it in Figure 7-3.

On the right of the screen, near the bottom, you'll see the list of controls. Scroll down until you see the "Segmented Control" item. Alternatively, you can use the search box in this window to speed up selection. See Figure 7-4 to see what the segmented control looks like.

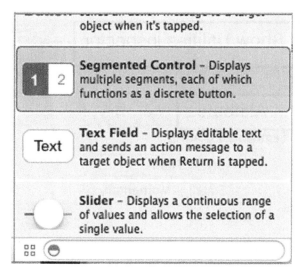

*Figure 7-4.* The segmented control

Drag the control onto the view controller and drop it near the top of the design surface. You can use the sizing handles to make it wider. When you drag it so that it's nearly the full width of the design surface, you'll see blue guidelines appear, indicating the recommended margins. Try to fit the control between them. You'll see that it is created with two segments, called "First" and "Second" by default. See Figure 7-5.

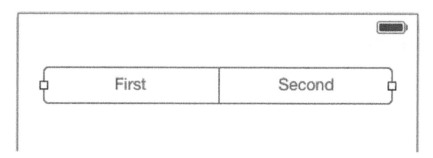

*Figure 7-5.* Placing the segmented control on your view

With the segmented control selected, open the attributes inspector. To do this, ensure that the rightmost icon in the toolbar (a rectangle with a shaded right side) is selected, and that the attributes button, which looks like a down-pointing arrow, is selected on the utilities area. See Figure 7-6.

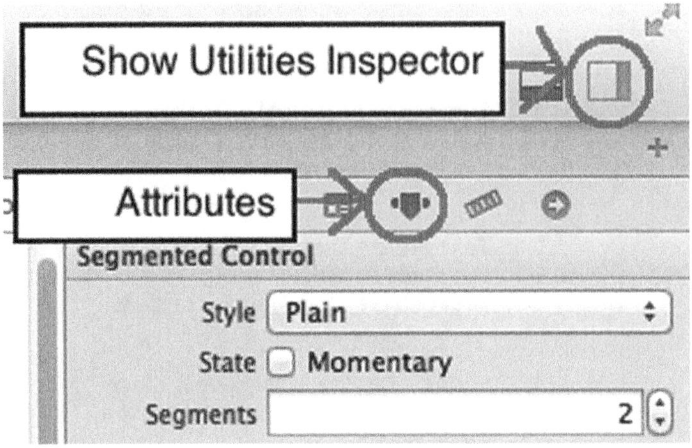

**Show Utilities Inspector**

**Attributes**

**Segmented Control**

Style | Plain

State ☐ Momentary

Segments | 2

*Figure 7-6. Using the attributes inspector*

> **Tip**   You can also access the attributes inspector using Alt-Command-4 keystrokes.

When using a segmented control, the most common attributes you are going to change are the number of segments and the titles for each of these segments. You can see these at the top of the attributes inspector.

First, let's change the number of segments on our control. To the right of the segments entry, you can see a little up/down arrow. Click the up arrow to change the number of segments to three. You'll see that a new, blank segment is created for you on the design surface. See Figure 7-7.

*Figure 7-7. Adding a new segment*

To edit segments, pick the segment from the drop-down list in the segment entry and edit its "Title" setting. So, if you refer to Figure 7-7, you'll see that the segment that is selected is "Segment 0 – First" and its title is "First." As a result, the control shows "First" as its text. Change the title field to "Red," and press the "Enter" key. You'll see that the design updates to "Red," and the segment is now called "Segment 0 – Red." See Figure 7-8.

*Figure 7-8.* *Editing the first segment*

Repeat this for the other segments. From the segment drop-down list, select "Segment 1 – Second," as in Figure 7-9, and edit the title to "Green."

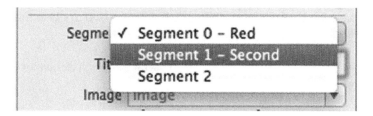

*Figure 7-9.* *Choosing segments*

Finally, choose "Segment 2" and edit the title to "Blue." When you're done, your control should look like Figure 7-10.

*Figure 7-10.* *Your finished segmented control*

You can run your app now, and you will see that when your app starts, the "Red" control will be selected by default. This control always has to have something selected, so iOS will default you at Segment 0.

Now let's wire up our outlets and actions and write some code to see how the segmented control works.

First, close the utilities view and open the assistant editor. To do this, click the same tool that you clicked to open the utilities view (the rectangle with shaded right side in Figure 7-6), and then click the assistant, which is an icon that looks like a tuxedo. If you aren't familiar with this, we strongly recommend referring back to Chapter 2.

Make sure that "ViewController.h" is selected in the assistant view, as in Figure 7-11.

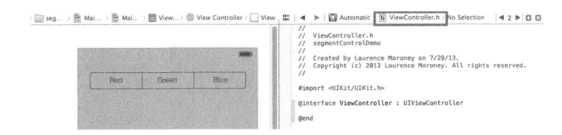

***Figure 7-11.*** *Ensuring the assistant control is editing your ViewController.h file*

Now, select the segmented control on the design surface and CTRL-drag it to ViewController.h. Drop it just below where it says `@interface`, and a helper window will pop up. Use this to create an outlet, and call it "colorChooser." See Figure 7-12.

***Figure 7-12.*** *Insert the colorChooser outlet*

When you're done, click the "Connect" button, and the outlet will be created.

Next, you'll need to create the action. In the same way as before, CTRL-drag the segmented control onto the assistant and drop just below where it says `@interface`.

This time, change the "Connection" setting to "Action," and use the name "colorChosen." The "Event" type should be set to "Value Changed." See Figure 7-13.

***Figure 7-13.*** *Insert the colorChosen action*

Click "Connect," and the action will be created.

> **Note**    It's a personal style, but one we think works well, that outlets should be chosen as nouns that imply that an action can be performed on it, like "colorChooser," which gives the impression that that is what it is used for. Actions should be named as if something has already happened, such as "colorChosen" in this case. It makes it easier to understand your code later, where once the user has chosen a color, the "color chosen" action will run.

You can now close the assistant and open the "ViewController.m" file to edit the code in response to the colorChosen action taking place.

When you created the action, you'll see that a colorChosen function was created in ViewController.m. The code here will execute whenever the user selects a button on your segmented control.

The code should look like this:

```
- (IBAction)colorChosen:(id)sender {
}
```

The outlet that refers to the segmented control was called colorChooser, so we can refer to it in code as _colorChooser. This exposes a property called selectedSegmentIndex, which is an integer containing the index of the selected segment. In our case it will be 0, 1, or 2 as we have three segments. So, if this value is 0, we want red, if it is 1 we want green, and if it is 2, we want blue.

We can check it with code like this:

```
if( _colorChooser.selectedSegmentIndex == 0)
{
    self.view.backgroundColor = [UIColor redColor];
}
```

Remember that self refers to the current view, and it has a property called backgroundColor that can be set to whatever color we like. Objective-C has a number of built-in keywords for colors, such as redColor, blueColor, and greenColor, which we can then use to actually get a color value that we set to be the backgroundColor of the view.

Our finished colorChosen function with all three colors would then look like this:

```
- (IBAction)colorChosen:(id)sender {
    if( _colorChooser.selectedSegmentIndex == 0)
    {
        self.view.backgroundColor = [UIColor redColor];
    }
    if( _colorChooser.selectedSegmentIndex == 1)
    {
        self.view.backgroundColor = [UIColor greenColor];
    }
```

```
    if( _colorChooser.selectedSegmentIndex == 2)
    {
        self.view.backgroundColor = [UIColor blueColor];
    }
}
```

Run the app and you'll see that it works nicely. When you select the different buttons, the background color of the view will change to match them.

But this code is a little untidy and difficult to read. Objective-C has its roots in the C language, which has what is called a case statement functionality that makes code like this clearer.

With a case statement, you have a variable, and based on different potential values for that variable, you have pieces of code that you execute.

To use a case statement for this app, you can change the colorChosen function to look like this:

```
- (IBAction)colorChosen:(id)sender {

    switch(_colorChooser.selectedSegmentIndex)
    {
        case 0:
            self.view.backgroundColor = [UIColor redColor];
            break;
        case 1:
            self.view.backgroundColor = [UIColor greenColor];
            break;
        case 2:
            self.view.backgroundColor = [UIColor blueColor];
            break;
    }

}
```

This is much easier to read, and it executes in the same way. When using a case statement, make sure to always end your clauses with "break," as in the preceding example, or your code will run from one clause to another. If you didn't have a break like this and you selected "red," the code would set the view to red, and then to green, and then to blue!

You can see what the app should look like in Figure 7-14, where "green" has been selected, and the view background color has changed accordingly.

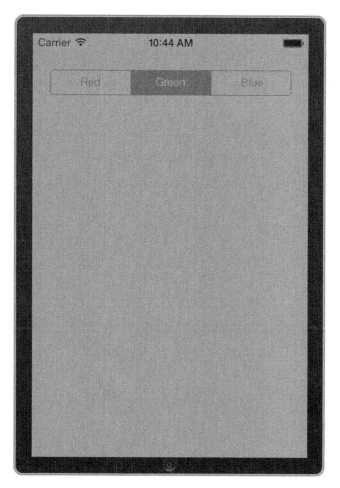

*Figure 7-14.  Using the segmented control*

And that's it for a quick tour of what you can do with this control. As you build apps you'll find it a very useful control for managing user expectations and giving them a quick way to input data. In the next section you'll look at another useful control, the slider.

# The Slider Control

A UI slider control is used to select a single value from a continuous range of values. In iOS7, sliders are always displayed as horizontal bars, with an indicator, also called a thumb, that the user can drag across the range and drop into a new location in order to change the setting.

# Slider Control Example

A great example of a slider control in action is the brightness setting on your iPhone. This isn't available in the simulator, so you need a real device to see it. From your iPhone home screen, select the "Settings" app, and then select "Brightness and Wallpaper." You'll see the setting screen, which looks like Figure 7-15.

*Figure 7-15.* *The slider control in the Settings app*

Right at the top of the screen, you'll see the slider, where, if you slide the thumb to the right, the screen gets brighter, and if you slide it to the left, the screen gets darker. This is a common UI paradigm for changing values like this, and it's quite an easy control to implement.

Let's build an app that uses a slider like this.

# Building an App with a Slider

As before, create a new single view application and call it "sliderControlDemo." Open the "Main.storyboard" file and find the slider control in the controls list. It should look like Figure 7-16.

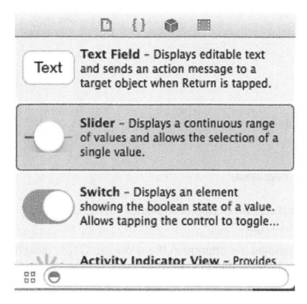

*Figure 7-16. Choosing the slider control*

Drag and drop it onto the design surface of your view controller.

Use the sizing handles to make the control almost as wide as the screen. As you resize, you'll see blue guidelines giving you a recommended margin size. It's good practice to use them. See Figure 7-17 for a good width for the control.

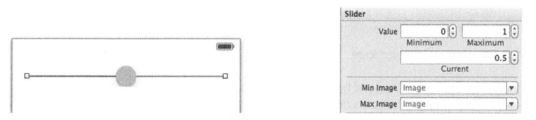

*Figure 7-17. Putting the slider on the view*

By default the slider gives you what is called a *normalized* value, where the setting is between 0 and 1. You can change this by changing the minimum and maximum settings on the inspector. If you can't see the inspector, go back to the previous example of the segmented control, and you'll see how to open it up.

In Figure 7-17 you can see this normalized value, and you can see that the current value is 0.5, which is halfway between 0 and 1—the thumb is at the halfway point of the line.

To see the slider in action, add a label to the design surface for your view controller. Make it the same width as the slider, and position it a little below the slider. See Figure 7-18.

*Figure 7-18. Adding a label to the slider sample*

Next, open the inspector and add an outlet for the label. CTRL-drag it to your ViewController.h and add an outlet called "lblOutput."

You'll need an action that handles the change in the slider, so CTRL-drag the slider onto your ViewController.h and add an action called "sliderChanged" for the "Value Changed" event. See Figure 7-19.

| Connection | Action |
|---|---|
| Object | View Controller |
| Name | sliderChanged |
| Type | id |
| Event | Value Changed |
| Arguments | Sender |

Cancel    Connect

```
#import <UIKit/UIKit.h>

@interface ViewController : UIViewController
@property (strong, nonatomic) IBOutlet UILabel *lblOutput;

@end
```

*Figure 7-19. Adding the sliderChanged action*

Click "Connect," and the action will be created, along with a function to handle it in ViewController.m. Finally, you'll also need an outlet for the slider, as you need to inspect its value in code, which is easier to do with a named outlet. So CTRL-drag the slider to ViewController.h again and create an outlet called "valueSlider." See Figure 7-20.

| Connection | Outlet |
|---|---|
| Object | View Controller |
| Name | valueSlider |
| Type | UISlider |
| Storage | Strong |

Cancel    Connect

```
#import <UIKit/UIKit.h>

@interface ViewController : UIViewController
@property (strong, nonatomic) IBOutlet UILabel *lblOutput;
- (IBAction)sliderChanged:(id)sender;

@end
```

*Figure 7-20. Creating an outlet for the slider*

Now, open ViewController.m, where you'll see the action code that was created for you. It should be right at the bottom of your code window and will look like this:

```
- (IBAction)sliderChanged:(id)sender {
}
```

In this function, you're going to read the value of the slider whenever it changes and assign that value to the label, so we can see what value the user has set.

You can get the value of the slider with its value property. This returns a floating point number, represented by a float. A floating point number is a number with portions of the number represented by a decimal point. So, for example, while 10 is an integer, 10.0 or 10.012103 are floats. You'll need to convert the float into a string in order to use it as the text for the label. To do this, the NSString type conveniently has a constructor function that allows you to construct a string based on a format. The "%f" format corresponds to a float, so if you construct your string using it, the value of the float will be loaded into the string.

> **Tip**   The "%f" code instructs the parser to treat the float as a string and print it that way. There are lots of different formats, and you can find a reference for how to use them at bit.ly/stringformats.

Here's the code:

```
NSString *value = [NSString stringWithFormat:@"%f", _valueSlider.value];
```

The entire function is here:

```
- (IBAction)sliderChanged:(id)sender {
    NSString *value = [NSString stringWithFormat:@"%f", _valueSlider.value];
    _lblOutput.text = value;

}
```

Now you can run your app and experiment with the slider. See Figure 7-21.

*Figure 7-21. The slider sample*

As you drag the thumb around, you'll see that you can get very granular results. Indeed, the screenshot in Figure 7-21 shows the value to six decimal places.

There's more customization that you can do to the slider, such as setting custom minimum and maximum images in order to get the effect of images on either side of the track line, as in Figure 7-15, so experiment and have fun!

# The Switch Control

The switch control is a very basic but powerful UI control that allows you to set a value to be on or off. They're used extensively in iOS, such as in the "Photos & Camera" settings screen. See Figure 7-22.

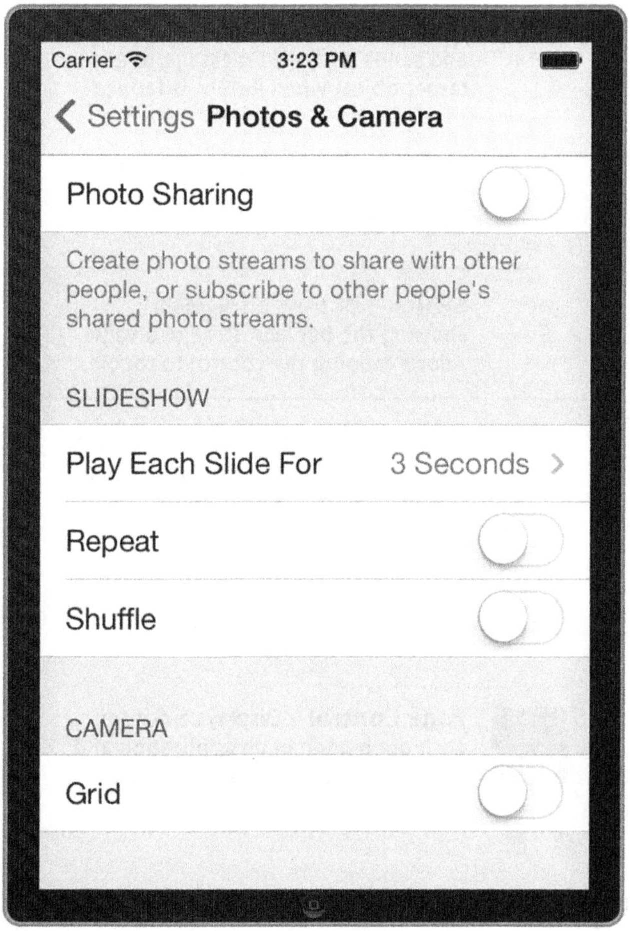

*Figure 7-22.* *The UI switch control in iOS7*

To examine how it works, create a new single view app called "switchControlTest" and open its storyboard in the designer.

On the controls list, select the "Switch" control from the controls list. You can see it in Figure 7-23.

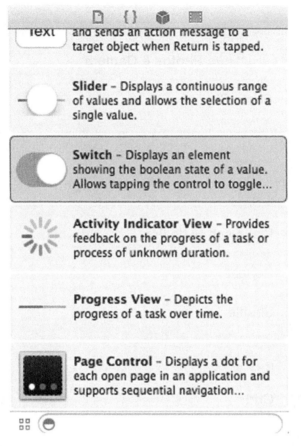

*Figure 7-23. Picking the switch control*

Drag and drop it to the design surface for your view controller and place it towards the right-hand side. You'll notice that the control is just the switch—there is no label. See Figure 7-24.

*Figure 7-24. The switch control*

It's a good idea to put a label control beside it as a hint as to what the switch does. Go ahead and do that now, and also drop another label beneath the first that we'll use for the output. Give the labels the text "This is my first switch" and "My first switch is on," as in Figure 7-25. Make sure that the width of the label will hold all the text.

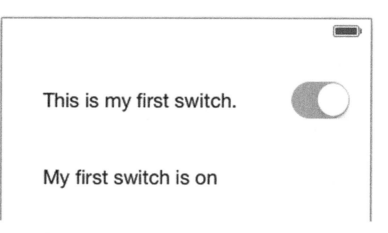

*Figure 7-25. Adding labels to the switch*

Open the assistant editor and CTRL-drag the switch onto ViewController.h. Create an outlet called "firstSwitch."

CTRL-drag the switch again and create an action called "switchChanged." This should be mapped to the "Value Changed" event. If you're not familiar with this, go back through the earlier examples in this chapter for other controls—the process is identical.

Finally, CTRL-drag the "My first switch is on" label to ViewController.h and create an outlet called "lblOutput."

Now you can write some code. Close the assistant editor and then open ViewController.m. Find the action function. It should look like this:

```
- (IBAction)switchChanged:(id)sender {
}
```

The UISwitch provides a BOOLEAN property called "on," which will be true if the switch is on, and false if not. So, in our switchChanged function, we can set the text of the lblOutput based on this value. Here's the code:

```
- (IBAction)switchChanged:(id)sender {
    if(_firstSwitch.on)
    {
        _lblOutput.text = @"My first switch is on";
    }
    else
    {
        _lblOutput.text = @"My first switch is off";
    }
}
```

Now you can run the app, and the output label will change as you flip the switch. See Figure 7-26.

*Figure 7-26. Testing the switch*

A very simple demo for a very simple control. But as you can see, as you build up your skills with each control, you're learning more and more of what goes into an iOS7 user interface. In the next section you'll learn how to use the stepper control, a simple control that gives you a user interface for incrementing or decrementing a value.

# The Stepper Control

The stepper control provides a user interface for quickly incrementing or decrementing a control by a fixed amount. It defaults to having a range of 0 to 100 in steps of 1, but you can easily override this functionality in the attributes inspector.

To explore how the stepper control works, create a new app called "stepperControlDemo." Open Main.storyboard and, from the controls list, find the "Stepper" control. You can see it in Figure 7-27.

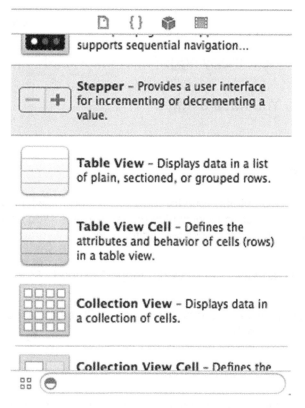

*Figure 7-27. The stepper control*

Place it on the upper-right-hand side of the design surface for your view controller. Your screen should look something like Figure 7-28 when done.

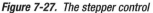

*Figure 7-28. Adding the stepper control*

Add a couple of label controls to the design surface. The first should read "How many eggs?"; the second should read "You have 0 eggs." See Figure 7-29 for how they should be arranged.

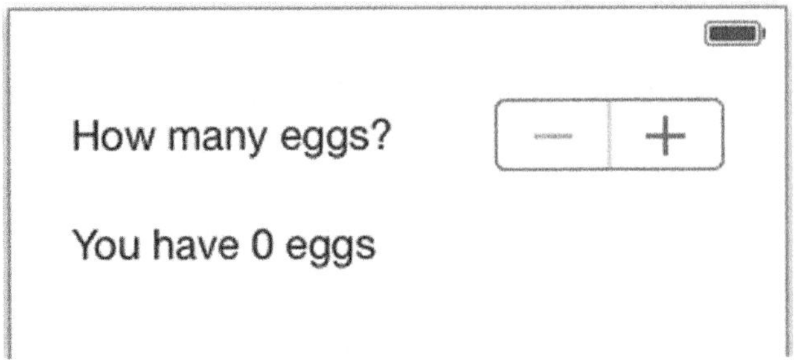

*Figure 7-29. Adding the text labels*

Now you are going to need two outlets—one for the stepper control, which you should call "eggCounter," and one for the second label (which presently reads "You have 0 eggs"), which you should call "lblOutput." Do this with the assistant editor using CTRL-drag, as you've done with all other examples.

When you're done with that, add an action called "stepperChanged." Make sure that its event is the "Value Changed" event.

Now you can take a look at your ViewController.m code. You'll see the action function has been created for you. It should look like this:

```
- (IBAction)stepperChanged:(id)sender {
}
```

The UIStepper returns a numeric value. In order to read it, you can use code like:

```
int numberOfEggs = _eggCounter.value;
```

Earlier in this chapter, in the slider section, you saw that you can create a string from a float value by using the format "%f" within the string. Now we're going to do the same, but with an int, which can be represented by "%d." This will render the number with zero decimal places.

Thus, we can set our label text like this:

```
_lblOutput.text = [NSString stringWithFormat:@"You have %d eggs", numberOfEggs];
```

The entire stepperChanged function should look like this:

```
- (IBAction)stepperChanged:(id)sender {
    int numberOfEggs = _eggCounter.value;
    _lblOutput.text = [NSString stringWithFormat:@"You have %d eggs", numberOfEggs];

}
```

You can now run the app and try changing the settings on the stepper. See Figure 7-30.

Figure 7-30. *Using the stepper control*

You might notice that iOS is smart enough to realize that your range is from 0 to 100, so if you keep clicking the "-" until you have 0 eggs, it will disable the "-" button so that you can't go further!

Changing the range and the step size is simple. It can be done from the attributes inspector, where you have four boxes (each with a stepper control of their own!) that allow you to set the minimum, maximum, current, and step sizes. See Figure 7-31.

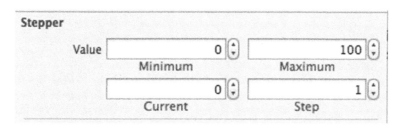

Figure 7-31. *Changing the stepper time values*

And it's as simple as that. You've gotten pretty much all the basic controls down now! As you build more-complex apps you'll be using these controls, as well as a couple of bigger, more sophisticated ones, which you'll look at over the next few chapters, including date and time controls, mapping controls, and table views.

# Summary

In this chapter you took a look at a few new controls that are commonly used in iOS applications and built simple applications that use them in order to get a feel for how they work.

You looked at the UISegmentedControl, which gives you a horizontal, ordered list of buttons that allow you to make a selection from a fixed group. This control is commonly used in Apple-built iOS applications, so now you know how to do the same yourself! You explored the UISlider control, which allows you to specify a value by dragging a thumb along a track, as is commonly used for scenarios such as that in the brightness settings dialog for your iPhone, or perhaps something like audio volume. You then looked at a simple switch control, which is very commonly used in settings apps for an on/off scenario, and finally you saw the UIStepper control, which allows your users to enter a value from a discrete range with a discrete step size. Now, when you look at your iPhone or iPad and see other people's apps, you'll see these controls in action and can feel confident that you know how to use them for yourself!

In the next chapter, you'll take a look at two much bigger controls for data entry, the "Picker View," which gives you a spinning wheel motif for a range of values, and the "Date Picker," which allows your users to easily enter a date and time.

# Chapter 8

# Picker Controls

In Chapter 7, you looked at a number of basic controls that allow your user to input data to your app. Ultimately, controls are all about either putting data in or rendering data out. In this chapter, you'll explore some more sophisticated data entry controls in which the user is given the ability to enter complex information by choosing it from a list. This process, in iOS generally called "picking," presents the user with a list of information from which the user picks what they want. A common form of picking is to choose a date using separate spinners for day, month, and year, instead of having the user type them in. Xcode provides a control for that, which you'll look at first. You'll then learn how to use the generic "UIPicker" control to create your own set of input options, rendered in the same way, and how to catch the user's input from it.

## Date Input with the Date Picker

The date picker is a common user interface component for entering date and/or time information. You can see an example of a date picker in the "Contacts" app on your iPhone when you try to add a new contact and set their birthday. See Figure 8-1.

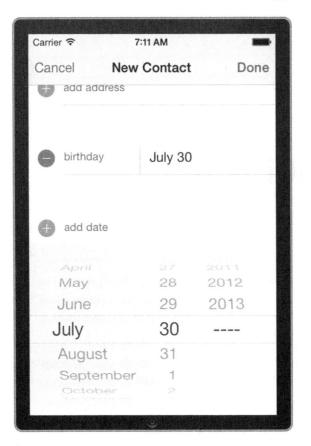

*Figure 8-1.* *The date picker in action*

Depending on where the user places their finger, they can spin the month, day, and year columns independently, making it very easy, and very quick, to choose a specific date.

The same control is used when you want to pick a specific time. For example, in the "Alarms" app that ships with your device, you can set the time that you want an alarm to go off. You can see this in Figure 8-2.

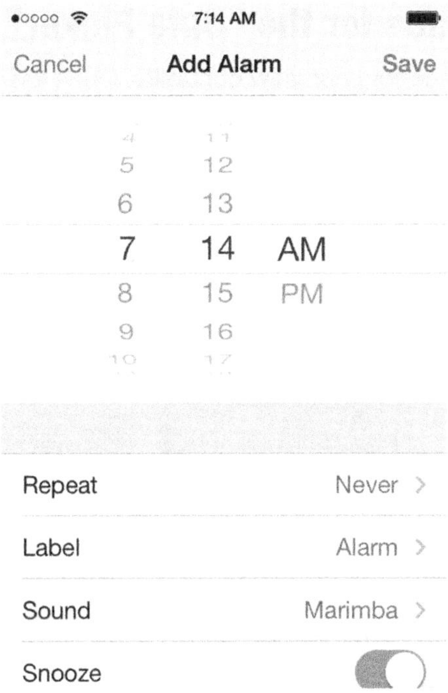

*Figure 8-2.  Using the date picker for a time*

As you can see, the UI paradigm is very similar—there are separate spinners for the hour, minute, and AM/PM settings, which allow the user to enter a time value very quickly.

Creating this interface is very simple thanks to the "UIDatePicker" control. You'll see how to do that in the next section.

# Using UIDatePicker in an App

To get started, create a new single view app and called it "datePickerDemo." If you're not familiar with this process, go back to Chapter 2 and review how to create a simple app, including how to do actions and outlets. You'll be using those techniques extensively throughout this chapter.

# Create the User Interface for the "Date Picker" App

You'll be editing the design surface for your view controller. Open `Main.storyboard`, and you'll get this (see Figure 8-3):

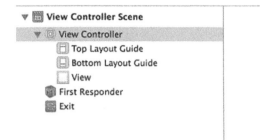

*Figure 8-3. Selecting the view controller*

On the right of your Xcode window, near the bottom, you'll see the list of controls. Scroll through this list until you see "Date Picker." It should look like Figure 8-4. You can take a shortcut by typing "Picker" in the search box at the bottom, and Xcode will show you all controls with the word "Picker" in their name.

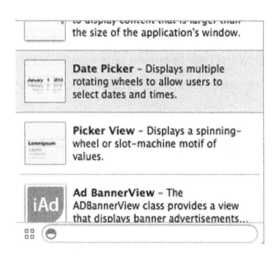

*Figure 8-4. The date picker control*

Drag the control and drop it on your design surface near the top. It will fit across the entire width of the iPhone screen. See Figure 8-5 for an example.

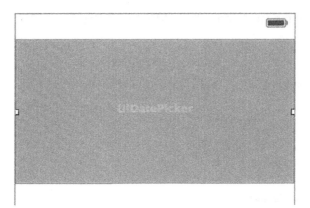

*Figure 8-5. Adding the UIDatePicker*

Next, find the "Label" control and drag and drop a label beneath the "UIDatePicker" control. You will use this to render whatever date the user picks in the UIDatePicker. Stretch the label to the full width of the design surface.

Switch to the assistant view and CTRL-drag a connection from the UIDatePicker to your "ViewController.h" file to create an action called "dateChosen." Make sure that the event setting is "Value Changed." See Figure 8-6.

*Figure 8-6. Click "Connect" to insert the action*

Next, CTRL-drag the UIDatePicker to ViewController.h to create an outlet called "dateChooser." See Figure 8-7.

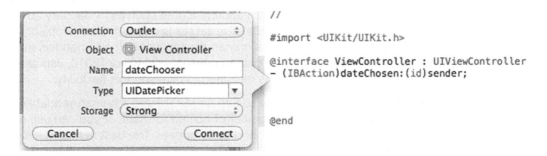

*Figure 8-7. Adding the outlet for the UIDatePicker*

Finally, create an outlet for the label and call it "lblOutput." See Figure 8-8.

**Figure 8-8.** *Adding an outlet for the UILabel*

Now that your user interface is wired up, you're ready to start coding.

## Write the Code for Your "Date Picker" App

Close the assistant and open your "ViewController.m" file. Because you created an action called dateChosen, you'll see the following function near the bottom of the file:

```
- (IBAction)dateChosen:(id)sender {
}
```

This function will get called whenever the value of the picker changes. Fortunately, this will only happen once any of the spinning wheels stops moving. So, for example, with the date picker, you'll notice on your device that you can slide your finger over the day value, and the values will spin like a slot machine. The change event doesn't happen while it is spinning. When it stops and settles on a date, the event will fire.

You can get the value of the date picker at this point using its date property, which is of type NSDate.

Here's the code:

```
NSDate *chosenDate = _dateChooser.date;
```

Dates are one of the most complex data types in software, because there are so many rules around them. Think about how many days there are in a month, or which years are leap years, or even the difficulties in keeping track of what day a particular date has. As a result, the NSDate object has a lot of complex functionality and isn't just a simple representation of a date such as "1 January 2010." To get the representation, a helper object called an NSDateFormatter is needed. It's this object's job to take the complex date information and render it in a human-readable way. It also handles turning the date into different formats. You might prefer your date to read "1-1-2010" or "2010, January 1," or one of many other options. The NSDateFormatter is designed to give you this flexibility.

The NSDateFormatter provides two main ways for you to turn an NSDate into a human-readable string. You can either use a *style*, which is one of a number of built-in formats, or you can use a *format,* which is a string that defines how you want your date to appear. The best resource we've found for this string format is Microsoft's developer site for C# developers, MSDN, which you can find here: http://msdn.microsoft.com/en-us/library/az4se3k1.aspx, or by searching the web for "Standard Date and Time Format Strings."

The format string takes specifiers to determine how it should look, so for example you could specify a format string of "dd/MM/yyyy" to get a British-style date or "MM/dd/yyyy" to get an American-style one.

Objective-C also has a number of built-in styles that you can use with the NSDateFormatter to get common date formats. For the sake of simplicity in this app, we're going to use these.

First, you'll need to create, allocate, and initialize your NSDateFormatter.

```
NSDateFormatter *dateFormat = [[NSDateFormatter alloc]init];
```

Once you've done this, you can specify your desired style using the setDateStyle message.

```
[dateFormat setDateStyle:NSDateFormatterFullStyle];
```

You'll see as you type the code that there are a number of NSDateFormatter styles available to you. These are documented for you at https://developer.apple.com/library/mac/#documentation/ Cocoa/Reference/Foundation/Classes/NSDateFormatter_Class/Reference/Reference.html, and you can see from this documentation that if you choose the NSDateFormatterFullStyle, your date will look like "Tuesday, April 12, 1952AD."

Now that we have our formatter set up, all we have to do is use that to format our chosen date and then assign the value to our label.

Here's the code:

```
_lblOutput.text = [dateFormat stringFromDate:chosenDate];
```

And that's everything you need for the action. Here's the full code for it:

```
- (IBAction)dateChosen:(id)sender {
    NSDate *chosenDate = _dateChooser.date;
    NSDateFormatter *dateFormat = [[NSDateFormatter alloc]init];
    [dateFormat setDateStyle:NSDateFormatterFullStyle];
    _lblOutput.text = [dateFormat stringFromDate:chosenDate];

}
```

So now you can run your app and choose a date. The date will be rendered in the label. See Figure 8-9.

*Figure 8-9. Your "Date Picker" app*

But wait, there's a problem. Your "Date Picker" app is different from the one in the "Calendar" app. It's picking both date *and* time. And when you render the result, you only get the date and not the time! So let's fix this to turn it into a date-only picker.

## Exploring Options on the UIDatePicker

Stop your app and go back to Main.storyboard. Open the attributes inspector and you'll see that there's a "Mode" setting, which by default is set to "Date and Time." See Figure 8-10.

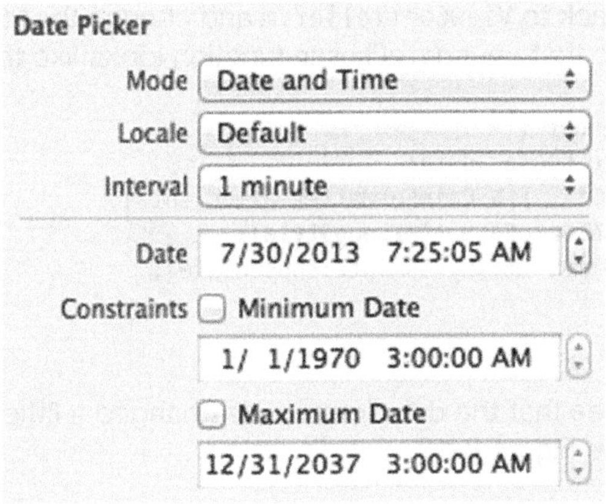

**Figure 8-10.** *Date picker options*

Change the mode to "Date" and re-run your app. You'll see that now you just have date entry, and that the label is correct. See Figure 8-11.

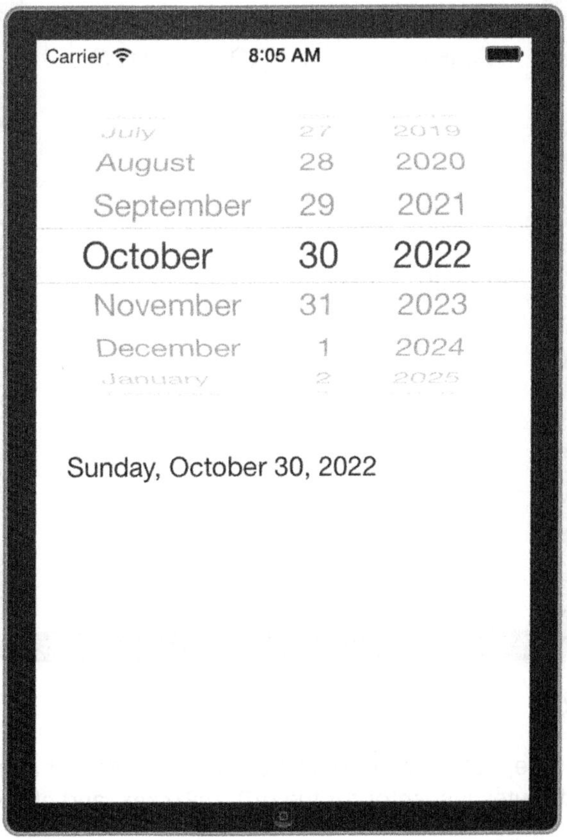

**Figure 8-11.** *The date picker in "Date" mode*

Stop your app and then go back to ViewController.m and change the NSDateFormatter to use NSDateFormatterLongStyle so that your dateChosen function looks like this:

```
- (IBAction)dateChosen:(id)sender {
    NSDate *chosenDate = _dateChooser.date;
    NSDateFormatter *dateFormat = [[NSDateFormatter alloc]init];
    [dateFormat setDateStyle:NSDateFormatterLongStyle];
    _lblOutput.text = [dateFormat stringFromDate:chosenDate];

}
```

Now re-run your app. You'll see that the date format has changed a little—it no longer shows the day of the week, just the date. See Figure 8-12.

*Figure 8-12. The reformatted output*

This shows us a separate date, but what about just using the picker for a time? To do this, stop the app, go back to the attributes inspector for the UIDatePicker, and change the mode setting to "Time." See Figure 8-13.

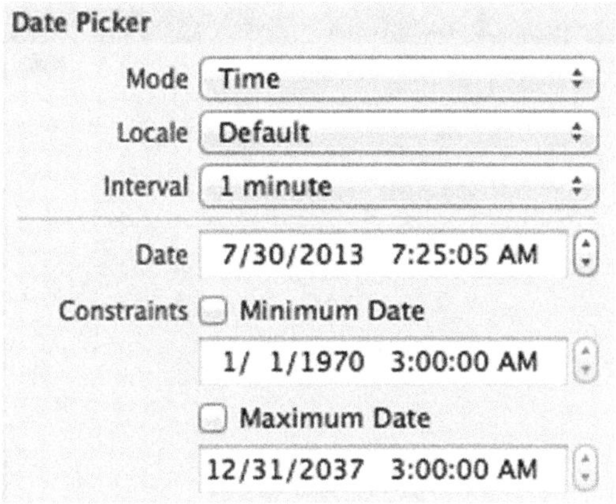

*Figure 8-13. Setting the UIDatePicker mode to "Time"*

Now you'll need to let your NSDateFormatter know that you're interested in showing a time, but not a date. You can do this by setting the date style to "NSDateFormatterNoStyle" to indicate that you don't want anything. You then need to tell it how to render a time, which you do with the setTimeStyle message. Here's the full code:

```
- (IBAction)dateChosen:(id)sender {
    NSDate *chosenDate = _dateChooser.date;
    NSDateFormatter *dateFormat = [[NSDateFormatter alloc]init];
    [dateFormat setDateStyle:NSDateFormatterNoStyle];
    [dateFormat setTimeStyle:NSDateFormatterLongStyle];
    _lblOutput.text = [dateFormat stringFromDate:chosenDate];

}
```

Now re-run the app, and you'll see that your picker is now a time picker like that in the alarm app, and that your output text format is correct. See Figure 8-14.

*Figure 8-14. The time picker*

By experimenting with the settings in the attributes inspector, you can tweak the UIDatePicker to suit your app's needs, including setting time and date constraints and the granularity of the interval you can change.

Now you might have noticed the same type of user interface on other types of picker, but using much more flexible data, such as city names. You'll see how to build one of those in the next section.

# Using the UIPicker Control

In this chapter you've seen how to use the UIDatePicker to have a user experience that allows your users to input date and/or time values easily. The same user interface experience can be made available for any data, and in this section you'll learn how to do that. This section is going to use delegates, and if you aren't familiar with this technique, you should look back to Chapter 5 to review patterns and delegates.

## Creating a UIPicker App

Create a new single view application with Xcode and call it "uipickerDemo." Open Main.storyboard and find the "Picker View" control, as seen in Figure 8-15.

*Figure 8-15.  The UIPicker control, called "Picker View"*

Drag and drop it onto the design surface of your view controller. It will get populated with some sample data, but this is only for design time to show you the dimensions of the control. When you run the app, this data will be blank; having the data at design time is useful to help you place controls around it. See Figure 8-16.

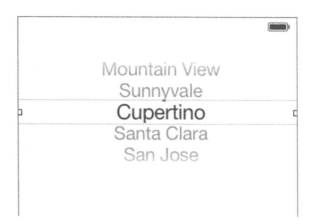

*Figure 8-16.* *The UIPicker control with dummy data at design time*

Before we start coding, there are just a couple more things you should do to the user interface. First, drag a label and place it below the "UIPicker" control. Make sure it's full width. See Figure 8-17.

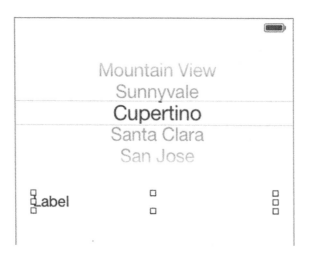

*Figure 8-17.* *Adding an output label*

Next you should create an outlet for the label, called "lblOutput," and an outlet for the UIPicker, called "myPicker."

In order to use custom data in a UIPicker, your app needs to be able to handle delegated functionality from the control, so your view should also have a data source for the control. To do this you use the same syntax as a delegate. So, edit your ViewController.h to add the delegate and the data source like this:

```
#import <UIKit/UIKit.h>

@interface ViewController : UIViewController<UIPickerViewDelegate, UIPickerViewDataSource>

@end
```

Now your `ViewController.m` can create the data for the `UIPickerView`, *and* it can accept events for the `UIPickerView`.

# Creating the Data Source

Now that you've configured your view controller to be a data source, you can add code to `ViewController.m` to set up how your `UIPicker` will look. To do this, you'll create an `NSArray` and load it with a number of data items, which in this case will be the names of soccer teams.

Open ViewController.m and, right under the line that reads `@implementation`, declare your `NSArray`.

It should look like this:

```
@implementation ViewController
NSArray *teamNames;
```

This will make the "teamNames" array available to all functions in ViewController.m, which is perfect for our needs. Let's initialize it with some data. We can do this in the `viewDidLoad` function.

You can initialize an `NSArray` using the `initWithObjects` message and passing it a list of objects, in this case strings, with a nil at the end. Here's an example:

```
teamNames = [[NSArray alloc] initWithObjects:@"Liverpool",
                @"Manchester United",
                @"Manchester City",
                @"Cardiff City",
                @"Arsenal",
                @"Chelsea",
                @"Spurs", nil];
```

Also, in your viewDidLoad function, tell the picker that it's going to use this view (a.k.a. self) as its delegate and data source. Here's the full `viewDidLoad` function:

```
- (void)viewDidLoad
{
    [super viewDidLoad];
        // Do any additional setup after loading the view, typically from a nib.
    teamNames = [[NSArray alloc] initWithObjects:@"Liverpool",
                @"Manchester United",
                @"Manchester City",
                @"Cardiff City",
                @"Arsenal",
                @"Chelsea",
                @"Spurs", nil];
    _myPicker.delegate = self;
    _myPicker.dataSource = self;
}
```

When you configure a view as a data source, there are three functions that you need to implement in your view, otherwise your app won't know how to set up your view. These are to set up the number of columns or components that the control will display, to set up the number of rows per component, and to set up the data to be rendered in a particular row within a component.

## Setting the Number of Components

The first of these is to configure the number of components in the picker. This is the number of columns of data that the control will display. So, if you look back at the date picker, there were three columns—one for the day, one for the month, and one for the year. Similarly, the time picker had three columns—one for the hours, one for the minutes, and one for AM/PM.

When a view controller is a data-source delegate, it will call the numberOfComponentsInPickerView method automatically when it loads. You'll need to implement it so it returns the number of components that you want. Fortunately Xcode makes it easy for you to do this.

Near the bottom of your code window, above @end, start typing -(NSInteger)n. You'll notice that a hint pops up, prompting that you might want to insert the numberOfComponentsInPickerView function.

> **Note** Sometimes Xcode doesn't give you the popups as shown in Figure 8-18. If you encounter this, try closing and reopening Xcode.

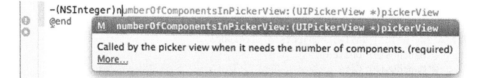

**Figure 8-18.** *Configuring the number of components*

Press the "tab" key and the rest of the line will be written for you. All you have to do now is type the braces (the curly brackets that look like { and } ), and the code, to return 1, like this:

```
-(NSInteger)numberOfComponentsInPickerView:(UIPickerView *)pickerView
{
    return 1;
}
```

If you want more than one column, you can just return a different number. But as our sample only has one column, which allows us to pick a soccer team, we'll return a 1 here. In the next section, you'll see how to specify the number of rows.

## Setting the Number of Rows

Next, your UIPicker needs to know how many rows of data it should render. If you look back to where we created the data, we created seven items in the array, so we want the UIPicker to give us seven items to choose from. Similar to the number of rows, there's a function we need to write that tells the view how many rows we'll have. This function is called numberOfRowsInComponent. This is because each component (a.k.a. column) will have a number of items, and not every column will have the same number. Consider, for example, the time picker. The hours component will have twelve items, the minutes will have sixty, and the AM/PM will have two. Thus, each will need to be configured separately, and when a `UIPicker` has more than one component, the function `numberOfRowsInComponent` will be called multiple times—once for each component.

You'll typically check the component number and return a value for the number of rows in that component. As we only have one component, it's a little easier for us—we just need to return the length of our `NSArray` of teams.

To create the function, type –(NSInteger)p and the hint should pop up. See Figure 8-19.

```
-(NSInteger)pickerView:(UIPickerView *)pickerView numberOfRowsInComponent:(NSInteger)component
@end    M  pickerView:(UIPickerView *)pickerView numberOfRowsInComponent:(NSInteger)component

        Called by the picker view when it needs the number of rows for a specified component. (required) More...
```

*Figure 8-19.  The numberOfRowsInComponent function*

Press the "tab" key and the function will be written for you. Now all you need to do is create the return value. We have seven items in our array, so we could return "7," but it's a bit nicer to return the count of items of the array. That way if we change the array later, we don't need to know how many items are in it. To do this, you can edit the method to return the count of your array.

Here's the code:

```
-(NSInteger)pickerView:(UIPickerView *)pickerView numberOfRowsInComponent:(NSInteger)component
{
    return [teamNames count];

}
```

Now you've told your picker how many columns and how many rows, so the next and final step in setting it up is telling it what data should go in each item. You'll see that in the next section.

## Setting the Values for Rows and Components

Each component (or column) in your `UIPicker` has a number of rows. You specified the number of columns and the number of rows per column in the previous sections. To set the text for the row title, you use the `titleForRow` function. As your view loads, this function will be called for every row in every component. You'd typically have to check the number of the component and the number of the row and return a string for what should data should go into that particular row and component.

As we only have one component, it's a bit easier for us; we just need to return element X on our team names array for row X on our `UIPicker`.

To write the function, start typing -(NSString *)p, and the hint will pop up for this function. See Figure 8-20.

```
-(NSString *)pickerView:(UIPickerView *)pickerView titleForRow:(NSInteger)row
    forCo
@end    M  pickerView:(UIPickerView *)pickerView titleForRow:(NSInteger)row forComponent:(NSInteger)component

        Called by the picker view when it needs the title to use for a given row in a given component. More...
```

*Figure 8-20.  Setting the titleForRow function*

As before, press the "tab" key, and the function will be filled out for you.

This function passes in a parameter *row,* which is the number of the row we want to fill data out for. Our NSArray object allows us to pull a string out of the array using the objectAtIndex message. So, if we pass that the row value, we can get that element on our array. Thus, row 0 on the picker will be element 0 on the array, row 1 on the picker, row 1 on the array, and so on.

To do this in code, we just use the following message:

```
-(NSString *)pickerView:(UIPickerView *)pickerView titleForRow:(NSInteger)row
forComponent:(NSInteger)component
{
    return [teamNames objectAtIndex:row];
}
```

And that's everything needed to set up the data source for the picker. Now, all we need to do is determine whatever the user picked. As the UIPicker control delegated to the view controller, we need to write a method to catch the event.

## Handling Delegated Events on the UIPicker

Now that you've created the data, your UIPicker will render your data for you. But we also want to make the control useful, so that we know what the user has selected. To do this, you have to write the didSelectRow function. When the user selects an item, this function will be called by the delegate, and it will tell the function which row and which component were picked.

To implement it, start typing -(void)p, and a hint will appear. There are a few void functions that begin with the letter "p," but Xcode is smart enough to figure out that you probably want didSelectRow. See Figure 8-21.

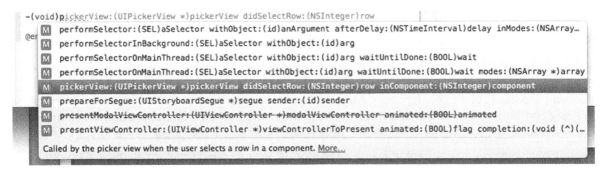

*Figure 8-21. The didSelectRow function hint*

Press "tab" a couple of times and the code will be filled out for you. The function knows the row that will be selected, and, if you remember from the previous section, we set it up so that row X in the picker has the data from element X in the array. So, to set the output label to the name of the team that was picked, you just need to use code like this:

```
-(void)pickerView:(UIPickerView *)pickerView didSelectRow:(NSInteger)row inComponent:(NSInteger)
component
{
    _lblOutput.text = [teamNames objectAtIndex:row];
}
```

Before running the app, just double check that you have ViewController.h looking like this:

```
#import <UIKit/UIKit.h>

@interface ViewController : UIViewController<UIPickerViewDelegate, UIPickerViewDataSource>

@property (strong, nonatomic) IBOutlet UIPickerView *myPicker;
@property (strong, nonatomic) IBOutlet UILabel *lblOutput;

@end
```

ViewController.m should look like this:

```
#import "ViewController.h"

@interface ViewController ()

@end

@implementation ViewController
NSArray *teamNames;

- (void)viewDidLoad
{
    [super viewDidLoad];
        // Do any additional setup after loading the view, typically from a nib.
    teamNames = [[NSArray alloc] initWithObjects:@"Liverpool",
                @"Manchester United",
                @"Manchester City",
                @"Cardiff City",
                @"Arsenal",
                @"Chelsea",
```

```
                        @"Spurs", nil];
    _myPicker.delegate = self;
    _myPicker.dataSource = self;
}

- (void)didReceiveMemoryWarning
{
    [super didReceiveMemoryWarning];
    // Dispose of any resources that can be recreated.
}

-(NSInteger)numberOfComponentsInPickerView:(UIPickerView *)pickerView
{
    return 1;
}

-(NSInteger)pickerView:(UIPickerView *)pickerView numberOfRowsInComponent:(NSInteger)component
{
    return [teamNames count];
}

-(NSString *)pickerView:(UIPickerView *)pickerView titleForRow:(NSInteger)row
forComponent:(NSInteger)component
{
    return [teamNames objectAtIndex:row];
}

-(void)pickerView:(UIPickerView *)pickerView didSelectRow:(NSInteger)row inComponent:(NSInteger)
component
{
    _lblOutput.text = [teamNames objectAtIndex:row];
}
@end
```

If you're all good, run the app, and you should see something like Figure 8-22.

*Figure 8-22. Running the custom UI picker*

When the user selects an item, the label is set to the team for that item.

This was a simple case with a single column. In the next section you'll see how to edit the picker for multiple components.

# Using a Multi-component UIPicker

In the previous sections you built a custom UIPicker with a single column that allowed you to pick a data item that you specified. In this section you'll take that to the next level, making a multi-column picker.

## Adding Another Data Source

For multiple columns, you will have multiple items of data. Earlier, we created an NSArray of teamNames, with seven teams in it. Now let's create another one, containing predicted outcomes for teams at the end of the season.

Under the declaration of teamNames, add a new one for teamPredictions, like this:

```
@implementation ViewController
NSArray *teamNames;
NSArray *teamPredictions;
```

Then, in viewDidLoad, set up the array of predictions, like this:

```
teamPredictions = [[NSArray alloc] initWithObjects:@"will be champions.",
                    @"will qualify for Europe",
                    @"will win the FA Cup",
                    @"will be relegated", nil];
```

There are only four entries here, and the teams array has seven entries, so we can demonstrate components of different size in the numberOfRowsInComponent function later.

Here's the entire viewDidLoad function:

```
- (void)viewDidLoad
{
    [super viewDidLoad];
        // Do any additional setup after loading the view, typically from a nib.
    teamNames = [[NSArray alloc] initWithObjects:@"Liverpool",
                @"Manchester United",
                @"Manchester City",
                @"Cardiff City",
                @"Arsenal",
                @"Chelsea",
                @"Spurs", nil];

    teamPredictions = [[NSArray alloc] initWithObjects:@"will be champions.",
                    @"will qualify for Europe",
                    @"will win the FA Cup",
                    @"will be relegated", nil];

    _myPicker.delegate = self;
    _myPicker.dataSource = self;
}
```

Next you'll have to update the number of components, because we'll have two columns, one for the team and one for the predictions.

## Updating the Number of Components

Earlier we had only one component in our UIPicker, the list of teams, so our function returned the value 1. Now we have two, one for the teams and one for the predictions, so we need to update the numberOfComponentsInPickerView method to return a value of 2 instead.

Here's the code:

```
-(NSInteger)numberOfComponentsInPickerView:(UIPickerView *)pickerView
{
    return 2;
}
```

And now the app will know that the UIPicker will be created with two columns.

## Updating the Number of Rows per Column

The numberOfRowsInComponent function takes in a parameter component for the current component. So, when we create a UIPicker with two components (or more), this function will be called once for each component. You saw in the last section that we returned 2, so the numberOfRowsInComponent method is going to be called twice, once with the component value of 0 and once with the component value of 1. Depending on this value, we can then return the correct number of rows. When the component parameter is 0, we have one row for each of the team names, and when it is 1, we have one row for each of the predictions, which we can do in code, like this:

```
-(NSInteger)pickerView:(UIPickerView *)pickerView numberOfRowsInComponent:(NSInteger)component
{
    int numberOfRows;
    switch(component)
    {
        case 0:
            numberOfRows = [teamNames count];
            break;
        case 1:
            numberOfRows = [teamPredictions count];
            break;
    }
    return numberOfRows;
}
```

We create an integer called numberOfRows and then set it to the count of either teamNames or teamPredictions based on the component parameter.

## Updating the Titles per Row

The titleForRow function is called once for each row in every component, and it expects you to return the string that will be put in that row for that component. It gives you parameters row and column that you can use to determine which data you want to use. We can use this to return the teamNames when the column is 0 and the teamPredictions when the column is 1.

Here's the code:

```
-(NSString *)pickerView:(UIPickerView *)pickerView titleForRow:(NSInteger)row
forComponent:(NSInteger)component
{
    NSString *title;
    switch(component)
    {
        case 0:
            title = [teamNames objectAtIndex:row];
            break;
        case 1:
            title = [teamPredictions objectAtIndex:row];
            break;
    }
    return title;
}
```

## Catching the Selection

Before going further, add another label to Main.storyboard and create an outlet for it called "lblOutput2."

Now you can update the didSelectRow function to update one label when the "teams" component is picked and the other when the "predictions" component has a selection. Here's the code:

```
-(void)pickerView:(UIPickerView *)pickerView didSelectRow:(NSInteger)row inComponent:(NSInteger)
component
{
    switch(component)
    {
        case 0:
            _lblOutput.text = [teamNames objectAtIndex:row];
            break;
        case 1:
            _lblOutput2.text = [teamPredictions objectAtIndex:row];
            break;
    }

}
```

Now when you run your app, you'll see that the picker has two components, and based on what you select, the user interface will be updated. See Figure 8-23.

*Figure 8-23. The multi-column picker*

This isn't the friendliest, because the text is heavily cropped. The UIPicker delegate offers a function called viewForRow that allows you to override the view that is used to render each text "cell," which is a pretty advanced technique. As this is a beginners' book, we won't go into the details, but if you want to tidy up the UI for this application, you can do so with the following code:

```
-(UIView *)pickerView:(UIPickerView *)pickerView viewForRow:(NSInteger)row forComponent:(NSInteger)
component reusingView:(UIView *)view
{
    UILabel* tView = (UILabel*)view;
    if(view==nil)
    {
        tView = [[UILabel alloc] initWithFrame:CGRectZero];
        switch(component)
        {
            case 0:
                tView.text = [teamNames objectAtIndex:row];
                break;
            case 1:
                tView.text = [teamPredictions objectAtIndex:row];
```

```
                break;
        }
        [tView setTextAlignment:NSTextAlignmentCenter];
        tView.adjustsFontSizeToFitWidth = YES;
    }
    return tView;
}
```

Using this, if you run the app, you'll see that the text is automatically sized to fit the available space. You can see this in Figure 8-24.

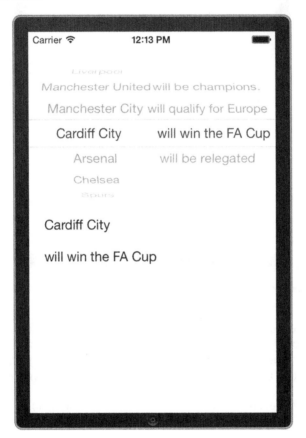

*Figure 8-24. The tidied-up UIPicker*

For the sake of completeness, here's the code for ViewController.h with the multi-component UIPicker:

```
#import <UIKit/UIKit.h>

@interface ViewController : UIViewController<UIPickerViewDelegate, UIPickerViewDataSource>

@property (strong, nonatomic) IBOutlet UIPickerView *myPicker;
@property (strong, nonatomic) IBOutlet UILabel *lblOutput;
@property (strong, nonatomic) IBOutlet UILabel *lblOutput2;

@end
```

Here's ViewController.m:

```objc
#import "ViewController.h"

@interface ViewController ()

@end

@implementation ViewController
NSArray *teamNames;
NSArray *teamPredictions;

- (void)viewDidLoad
{
    [super viewDidLoad];
        // Do any additional setup after loading the view, typically from a nib.
    teamNames = [[NSArray alloc] initWithObjects:@"Liverpool",
                @"Manchester United",
                @"Manchester City",
                @"Cardiff City",
                @"Arsenal",
                @"Chelsea",
                @"Spurs", nil];

    teamPredictions = [[NSArray alloc] initWithObjects:@"will be champions.",
                    @"will qualify for Europe",
                    @"will win the FA Cup",
                    @"will be relegated", nil];

    _myPicker.delegate = self;
    _myPicker.dataSource = self;
}

- (void)didReceiveMemoryWarning
{
    [super didReceiveMemoryWarning];
    // Dispose of any resources that can be recreated.
}

-(NSInteger)numberOfComponentsInPickerView:(UIPickerView *)pickerView
{
    return 2;
}

-(NSInteger)pickerView:(UIPickerView *)pickerView numberOfRowsInComponent:(NSInteger)component
{
    int numberOfRows;
    switch(component)
    {
        case 0:
            numberOfRows = [teamNames count];
            break;
```

```
                case 1:
                    numberOfRows = [teamPredictions count];
                    break;
        }
        return numberOfRows;
}

-(NSString *)pickerView:(UIPickerView *)pickerView titleForRow:(NSInteger)row
forComponent:(NSInteger)component
{
    NSString *title;
    switch(component)
    {
        case 0:
            title = [teamNames objectAtIndex:row];
            break;
        case 1:
            title = [teamPredictions objectAtIndex:row];
            break;
    }
    return title;
}

-(void)pickerView:(UIPickerView *)pickerView didSelectRow:(NSInteger)row inComponent:(NSInteger)
component
{
    switch(component)
    {
        case 0:
            _lblOutput.text = [teamNames objectAtIndex:row];
            break;
        case 1:
            _lblOutput2.text = [teamPredictions objectAtIndex:row];
            break;
    }

}

-(UIView *)pickerView:(UIPickerView *)pickerView viewForRow:(NSInteger)row forComponent:(NSInteger)
component reusingView:(UIView *)view
{
    UILabel* tView = (UILabel*)view;
    if(view==nil)
    {
        tView = [[UILabel alloc] initWithFrame:CGRectZero];
        switch(component)
        {
            case 0:
                tView.text = [teamNames objectAtIndex:row];
                break;
            case 1:
                tView.text = [teamPredictions objectAtIndex:row];
```

```
                break;
        }
        [tView setTextAlignment:NSTextAlignmentCenter];
        tView.adjustsFontSizeToFitWidth = YES;
    }
    return tView;
}
```

@end

Hopefully you've been able to keep up, because you are getting into some complex stuff. Not bad for a beginner!

## Summary

In this chapter you learned about pickers and how to use the date picker to do date and time selection. You explored a custom picker, using the delegate and data source to put custom data in the picker and capture user input. You saw how you can easily extend this for multiple components and how to capture data back from it.

In the next chapter, you'll look at what is perhaps the most common component used in iOS applications—the table view.

# Chapter 9

# Using Table Views

Perhaps the most common user interface control that you'll see when using iOS apps is the table view. This control is a means for displaying and editing hierarchic information. Tables are typically lists of information that are used to select an item or navigate to another item. Tables can have sections for visual style, and the items within a table can be configured in a number of different styles.

In this chapter you'll get an introduction to the table view, and you'll see how to use delegates and data sources to configure it. You'll also see how you can configure the table with different sections for data and different views for the table cells.

## Examples of the Table View

The table view is used so heavily on the iPhone that it's very easy to find examples of it, and the examples show the versatility of the control. In this section you're going to look at some of these examples, and as you learn how to use the table view you'll understand more about them.

## Custom Cells in a Table View

An example of a basic table view, albeit one that still has some custom cell settings, is on the About screen in General Settings. You can see it in the iPhone simulator. See Figure 9-1.

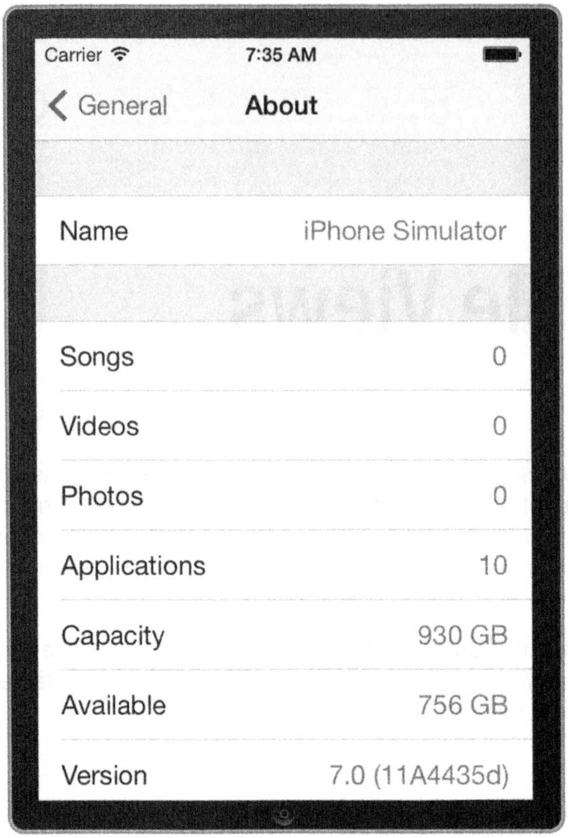

*Figure 9-1.* *The About settings table view*

This instance uses two sections: the name of the device and a list of its attributes. Each cell has been overridden from a simple text label to have two text labels, one on the left with the description and one on the right with the data.

## Navigation in a Table View

This is another example of a table view, this time having multiple sections and being tied to a navigation controller so that it may be used to navigate to other views. See Figure 9-2.

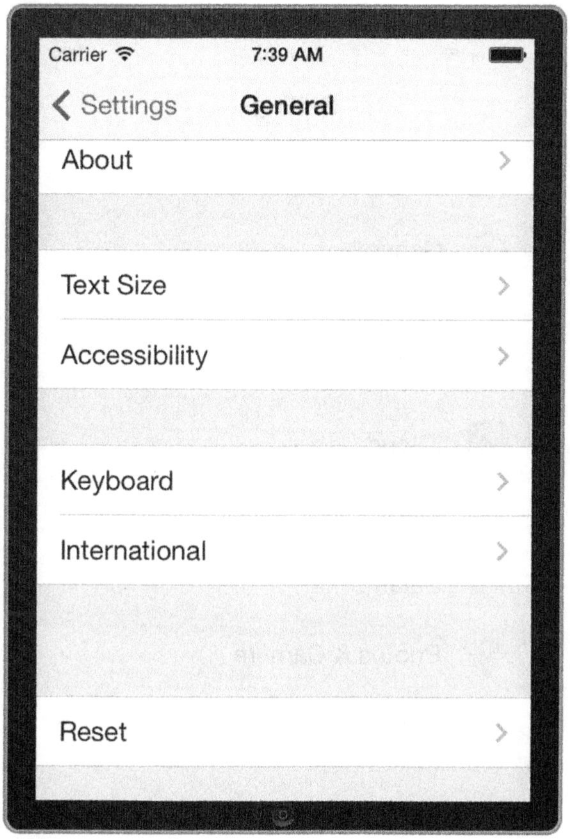

*Figure 9-2.* *The General Settings showing navigation*

As you can see, this table has multiple sections, with some having only a single cell (the Reset section). Additionally, when cells are configured for navigation, iOS provides an arrow on their right-hand side to inform the user that selecting them will perform an action.

## Graphical Subviews for Table View Cells

Another great example of the versatility of the table view is that the cells can be configured with graphics as their subviews, as in the Settings app. See Figure 9-3.

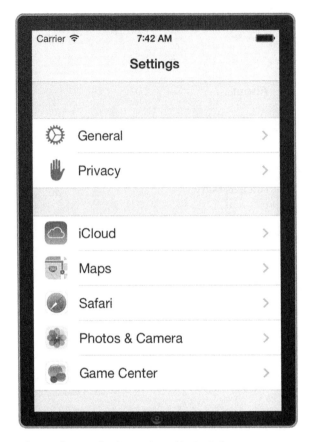

*Figure 9-3.* *The Settings app showing sections, navigation, and graphical subviews*

As well as the graphics, we see further customization, such as the sections and navigation arrows (as shown in the previous section).

## Controls Within Table View Cells

Another great example of how customizable the table view is comes in the Location settings screen. Here you can see that the background has been customized with help hints, and the cells, as well as having graphics in them, also have controls, such as the switches seen in Figure 9-4.

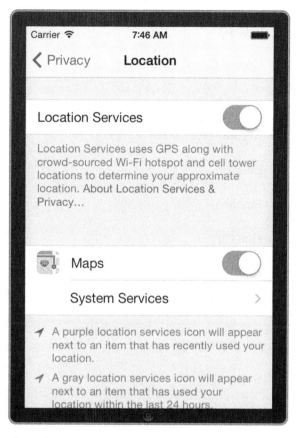

*Figure 9-4. Controls within table view cells*

The Maps cell shown in Figure 9-4 is particularly interesting—you can see that it has a graphical subview like with the Settings app in the previous section, as well as a switch.

These are just a few examples of the versatility of the table view. For the rest of this chapter you're going to go hands-on in constructing your own table views.

# Your First Table View App

The best way to get started with understanding how the table view works is to roll up your sleeves and get building. For this example, you're going to create a very simple table view app for the iPhone that renders a number of cells and allows you to scroll up and down the list.

Figure 9-5 shows the app in action.

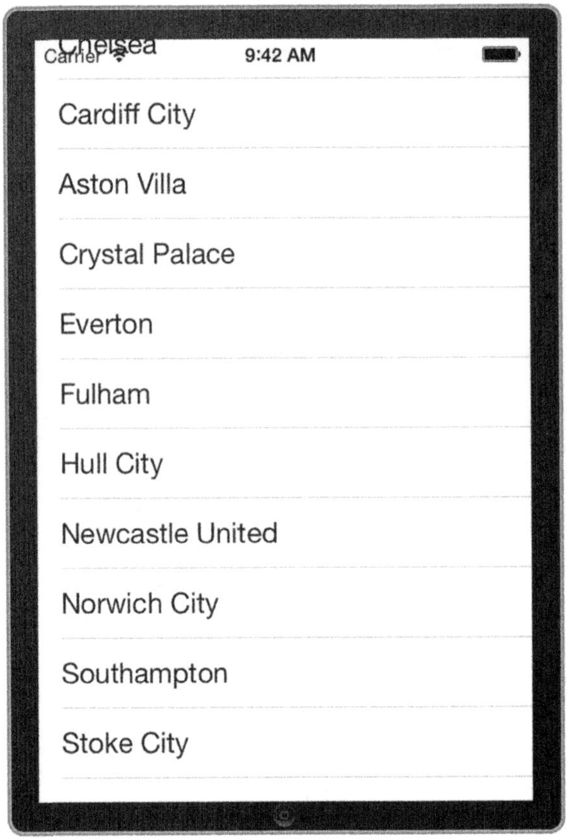

*Figure 9-5. Your first table view app*

To build this, create a new single view application and call it "tableViewDemo."

> **Note** If you've just jumped into this chapter, we're going to go over some concepts that were covered in previous chapters. It's a good idea to go back to Chapter 2 if you haven't done any development at all, where you'll learn how to create a simple app and understand concepts like outlets and actions. You'll probably also want to look at Chapter 5, where we talk about patterns and delegates, which will be used heavily in the table view. Finally, you'll want to also first read Chapter 8, where we built a custom picker control, which uses many of the same techniques as the table view, but in a more basic manner.

Open the "Main.storyboard" file and find the "Table View" control. Note that on the control list there is also a Table View Controller, which you do *not* want. The "Table View" control will look something like that on Figure 9-6.

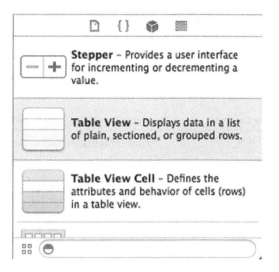

*Figure 9-6.* *The "Table View" control*

Drag and drop this onto your view controller. By default it will snap to fill the entire view. That's fine. When you're done, your screen should look like Figure 9-7.

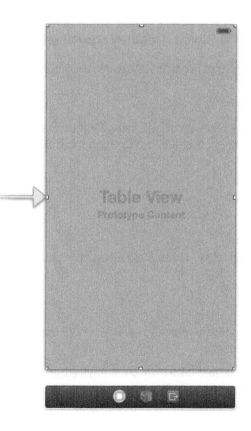

*Figure 9-7.* *Adding the table view*

Next, you should open the assistant and make sure that it is showing "ViewController.h."
CTRL-drag a connection from the table view to ViewController.h and drop it just below where
it says @interface. Use this to create an outlet called "teamsTable." See Figure 9-8.

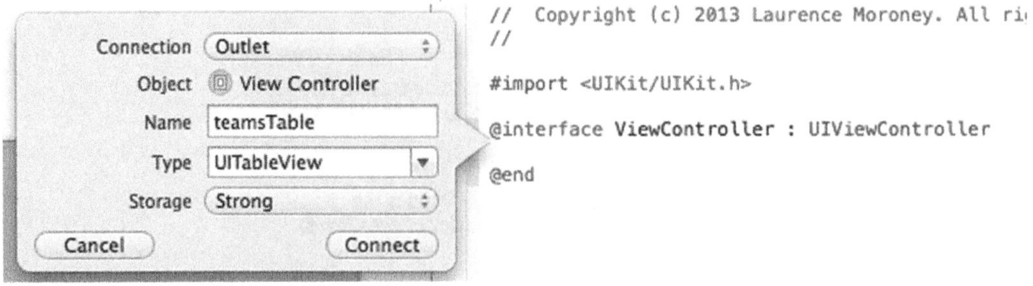

*Figure 9-8.* *Creating the "teamsTable" outlet*

This will add an @property line to your ViewController.h. In addition to this, the view controller
needs to handle delegate functions (see Chapter 5) and data source functions (see Chapter 8)
for the table view. This is done by adding the UITableViewDelegate and UITableViewDataSource
to the interface. To do this, you update the ViewController.h like this:

```
#import <UIKit/UIKit.h>

@interface ViewController : UIViewController<UITableViewDelegate, UITableViewDataSource>

@property (strong, nonatomic) IBOutlet UITableView *teamsTable;

@end
```

Next, you'll need to edit your ViewController.m file. First off, in the viewDidLoad function, you should
let the ViewController.m file know that it is going to be the delegate and the data source for the
teamTable control.

Here's the code:

```
- (void)viewDidLoad
{
    [super viewDidLoad];
    // Do any additional setup after loading the view, typically from a nib.
    _teamsTable.dataSource = self;
    _teamsTable.delegate = self;
}
```

Now you're ready to add data to the table. To do this, you'll use an NSArray to hold the data, and the
table will read its values from that.

At the top of ViewController.m, just below where it says @implementation, add a declaration of an
NSArray called "teamsData."

```
@implementation ViewController
NSArray *teamsArray;
```

Now, in `viewDidLoad`, you can add data to the `teamsArray`. This is done with the `initWithObjects` message that allows you to specify a list of objects, which in this case are strings.

```
teamsArray = [[NSArray alloc]initWithObjects:
                @"Manchester United",
                @"Manchester City",
                @"Arsenal",
                @"Liverpool",
                @"Chelsea",
                @"Cardiff City",
                @"Aston Villa",
                @"Crystal Palace",
                @"Everton",
                @"Fulham",
                @"Hull City",
                @"Newcastle United",
                @"Norwich City",
                @"Southampton",
                @"Stoke City",
                @"Sunderland",
                @"Swansea City",
                @"Tottenham Hotspur",
                @"West Bromwich Albion",
                @"West Ham United", nil];
```

You are now ready to build the table. To do this, there are functions that you have to implement because the view controller is set up as a `UITableViewDelegate`. These are functions that will be called by iOS when it creates the view, and if you implement them you can use them to set up the data.

In fact, if you look at Xcode, you'll see a warning on your `@implementation` pointing out that you haven't implemented these yet. It's a useful feature that Xcode has to remind you of what you need to do! See Figure 9-9.

```
@implementation ViewController          Method 'tableView:numberOfRowsInSection:' in protocol not implemented
NSArray *teamsArray;                     Method 'tableView:cellForRowAtIndexPath:' in protocol not implemented
```

*Figure 9-9. Warnings about non-implemented functions*

The warnings are that you haven't implemented `tableView:numberOfRowsInSection`, the function by which iOS will ask your app how many rows of data should be in each section. In this case we only have one section, and the number of rows that the table should have is the number of teams in the `teamsArray`. The `tableView:cellForRowAtIndexPath` is called whenever iOS is constructing each cell in the table. You use this to put the contents into each cell, such as text or graphics.

So let's implement these next.

First, the `tableView:numberOfRowsInSection`. To do this, go to the bottom of the `ViewController.m` file, just above `@end`, start typing `-(NSInteger)t`, and you'll see the hint for the function pop up. See Figure 9-10.

```
-(NSInteger)tableView:(UITableView *)tableView numberOfRowsInSection:(NSInteger)section
@end
        M   tableView:(UITableView *)tableView indentationLevelForRowAtIndexPath:(NSIndexPath *)indexPath
        M   tableView:(UITableView *)tableView numberOfRowsInSection:(NSInteger)section
        M   tableView:(UITableView *)tableView sectionForSectionIndexTitle:(NSString *)title atIndex:(NSInteger)index

        Tells the data source to return the number of rows in a given section of a table view. (required) More...
```

*Figure 9-10.  Adding the numberOfRowsInSection function*

---

**Tip**    If you don't get the popup as shown in Figure 9-10, don't worry. This appears to be a bug in Xcode. Simply close and restart Xcode and it should go away. Failing that, double check all your code to make sure that it's correct.

---

Press the "tab" key a couple of times to fill out the function and then update it to return the number of teams in the teamsArray, like this:

```
-(NSInteger)tableView:(UITableView *)tableView numberOfRowsInSection:(NSInteger)section
{
    return [teamsArray count];

}
```

The tableView:cellForRowAtIndexPath function is a bit more complex. This function is called by iOS for every cell, and it expects you to return a UITableViewCell object. Thus, in the function you'll need to create this cell.

---

**Note**    This section is quite complex. Don't worry if you don't get it all right away. Just focus on working through the code and getting a working app. Over time, as you repeat these steps in building table views, it will become more natural.

---

But first things first: let's create the method. Just above the @end line at the bottom of ViewController.m, start typing -(UITableViewCell *)t, and Xcode will pop up a menu for you. See Figure 9-11.

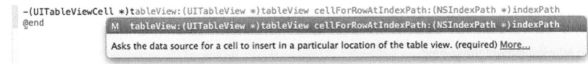

```
-(UITableViewCell *)tableView:(UITableView *)tableView cellForRowAtIndexPath:(NSIndexPath *)indexPath
@end
            M   tableView:(UITableView *)tableView cellForRowAtIndexPath:(NSIndexPath *)indexPath

            Asks the data source for a cell to insert in a particular location of the table view. (required) More...
```

*Figure 9-11.  Adding the cellForRowAtIndexPath function*

Press the "tab" key a couple of times to fill out the function and add some braces to complete it so that the function looks like this:

```
-(UITableViewCell *)tableView:(UITableView *)tableView cellForRowAtIndexPath:(NSIndexPath
*)indexPath
{

}
```

First of all, some of the methods that are available on the tableView need you to have an identifier type for the cells. When a view has multiple tableView controls, identifier types are necessary to prevent confusion between the cells, where cell 0 on one table is very different from cell 0 on another. This string is called an "identifier."

So let's create a string called "simpleTableIdentifier" and give it some text to use as an identifier.

```
static NSString *simpleTableIdentifier = @"TeamCell";
```

Using "static" in front of the declaration tells iOS that you're going to use the same string across lots of different calls to this function. It's a nice way to save memory in a circumstance like this.

Next we want to call the dequeueReusableCellWithIdentifier function on the table view to see if this cell has already been created. You do that with this code:

```
UITableViewCell *thisCell = [tableView dequeueReusableCellWithIdentifier:simpleTableIdentifier];
```

This creates a UITableViewCell called "thisCell." If the cell already exists on the table, then thisCell will be a reference to that. If it isn't, we'll need to create a new one. The best way to tell is if thisCell is nil, which it will be if the cell doesn't already exist:

```
if(thisCell==nil)
{
}
```

So if it doesn't already exist, we'll need to allocate a new cell within the braces.. When we allocate it, we can initialize the cell in a particular style and specify what its identifier should be. There are a number of different cell styles, but we'll just use the default one. Here's the code:

```
if(thisCell==nil)
{
   thisCell = [[UITableViewCell alloc] initWithStyle:UITableViewCellStyleDefault
                             reuseIdentifier:simpleTableIdentifier];

}
```

Later on as we customize cells, you'll look at different style types. But for now, just use this code. At this point, we know that we have a cell. Either we had one already, or we have the one that we just initialized. Every cell has a textLabel for its text, and this hasn't been set yet. Next you'll specify the text for this particular row. If you look at the signature for the function, no row has been passed in, but an indexPath has. When we have a table with multiple sections, the indexPath is the index of the particular section that is being called for now. In this case, we only have one section, so we can get the row for the current call with indexPath.row.

Thus, we can specify the text for this cell using the following:

```
thisCell.textLabel.text  = [teamsArray objectAtIndex:indexPath.row];
```

Now all you have to do is return thisCell, and the function is complete. Here's the code:

```
-(UITableViewCell *)tableView:(UITableView *)tableView cellForRowAtIndexPath:(NSIndexPath
*)indexPath
{

    static NSString *simpleTableIdentifier = @"TeamCell";

    UITableViewCell *thisCell = [tableView
        dequeueReusableCellWithIdentifier:simpleTableIdentifier];
    if(thisCell==nil)
    {
      thisCell = [[UITableViewCell alloc] initWithStyle:UITableViewCellStyleDefault
        reuseIdentifier:simpleTableIdentifier];

    }
    thisCell.textLabel.text  = [teamsArray objectAtIndex:indexPath.row];
    return thisCell;
}
```

Now your table view is complete, so you can run the app, and you'll see the list of soccer teams!
See Figure 9-12.

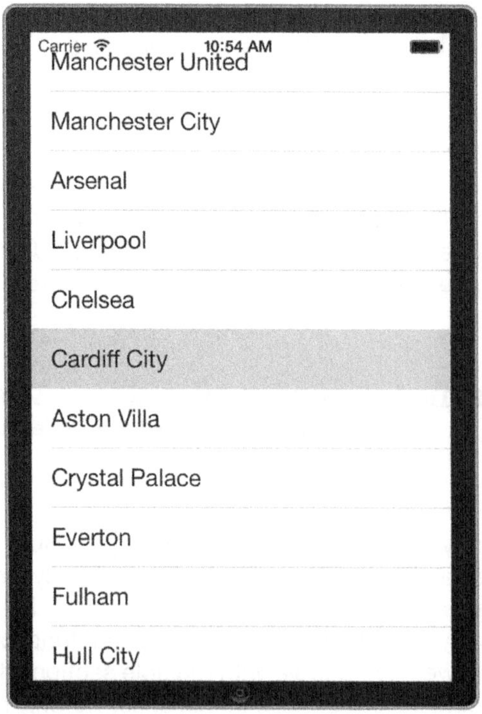

*Figure 9-12. Running your first table view app*

And that's it! You've just created your first table view app. In the next section you'll take a look at how to edit this app to capture whatever the user selected on the table.

# Capturing User Selection

In the previous section you built your first table view application. It allowed you to scroll through a list of items, and you could highlight one of them. However, even though it was highlighted, there was no way for you to catch the user selection. In this section you'll edit the code to handle user selection.

First, resize the table view on your Main.storyboard so that you can add a label. Make it about half the height of the screen, using the arrow as a guide, and drag a "Label" control underneath it. Resize the label to fit the width of the screen. You might see vertical blue lines marking out a recommended margin for the control. See Figure 9-13 for a good placement of the label.

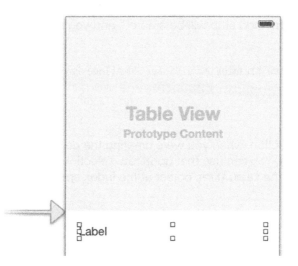

*Figure 9-13.* *Resizing the table view and adding a label*

Create an outlet for the label and call it "lblOutput."

Now, typically when you want to run code in response to an event, you would create an action using the assistant, but, unfortunately, that isn't supported on the table view, so you need to do it yourself in code. Fortunately, it's easy enough to do. In a similar vein to the functions that you wrote to set up the table, you can write a method to capture user input.

The method is called tableView:didSelectRowAtIndexPath, and Xcode will assist you in creating it. At the bottom of ViewController.m, above the @end, start typing -(void)t, and the assistant will give you a window of potential options. See Figure 9-14.

*Figure 9-14. Adding the tableView event function*

You can see that there are lots of potential events here, but you'll want the `didSelectRowAtIndexPath` one. You can get this by using your cursor keys to move the highlight down to that method, and press the "Enter" key. The method stub will be created, and you should add some braces to open and close the method too.

```
-(void)tableView:(UITableView *)tableView didSelectRowAtIndexPath:(NSIndexPath *)indexPath
{

}
```

If you recall the previous section, when you were creating the cells, you used `indexPath.row` to tell you what the current row is. You can use that upon row selection too, so you can specify that the `lblOutput.text` should be the `teamsArray` object at the index specified by `indexPath.row`. You can see the code here:

```
-(void)tableView:(UITableView *)tableView didSelectRowAtIndexPath:(NSIndexPath *)indexPath
{
    _lblOutput.text = [teamsArray objectAtIndex:indexPath.row];
}
```

Now if you run your application, and select any item, you'll see the name of the team that you selected loaded into the label. See Figure 9-15.

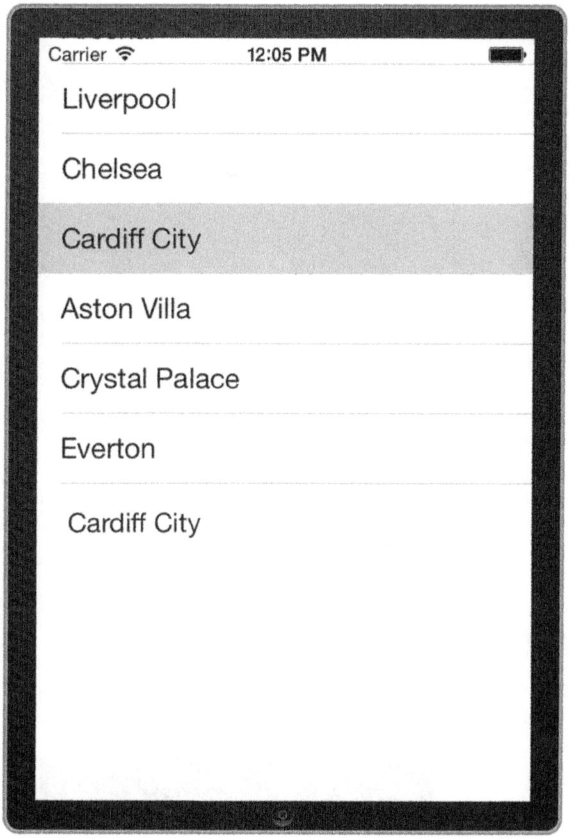

*Figure 9-15. Running your app and handling a selection*

Now that you've done this, in the next section you'll take a look at creating tables with multiple sections.

# Creating a Multi-Selection Table View

Creating a multi-selection table view is very similar to a single-selection one. You need to make a few tweaks to the control properties and to your code, but they're pretty straightforward.

## Designing the Interface

To get started, create a new single view app and call it "tableViewMultiSegmentDemo." Drag and drop a table view component to the design surface. Size it so you have a little space at the top and room for a label underneath. Drag and drop a "Label" control to that space and make it wide enough to hold some text. When done, your design surface should look something like Figure 9-16.

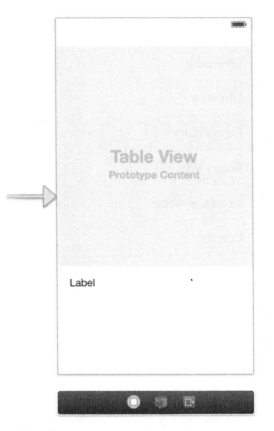

*Figure 9-16. Designing the multi-selection table*

With the table view selected, take a look at the attributes inspector and make sure that the style property is set to "Grouped," and the separator property is set to "Single Line." See Figure 9-17.

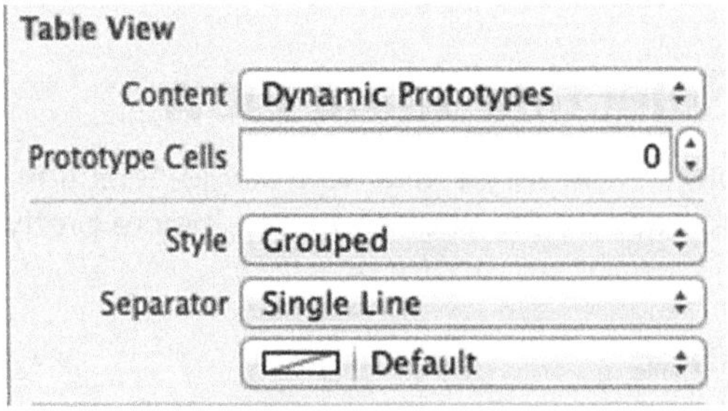

*Figure 9-17. Setting the table view properties*

## Editing the Headers

As in the previous example, create an outlet for the table view and call it "teamsTable." Also create an outlet for the label and call it "lblOutput." Finally, make sure that you specify that this view controller will implement the UITableViewDataSource and UITableViewDelegate.

Your ViewController.h should look like this when you're done:

```
#import <UIKit/UIKit.h>

@interface ViewController : UIViewController<UITableViewDataSource, UITableViewDelegate>
@property (strong, nonatomic) IBOutlet UITableView *teamsTable;
@property (strong, nonatomic) IBOutlet UILabel *lblOutput;

@end
```

## Creating the Data

Earlier you had an NSArray with the data for the single-sectioned table. It makes sense that if you are having more than one section, you can have more than one array in which to store the data. So, in this case we'll create a table with two sections, one for countries and one for sports.

Thus, we'll need two NSArray objects, one for each. Declare them below @implementation as before.

```
@implementation ViewController
NSArray *countriesArray;
NSArray *sportsArray;
```

Next, in your viewDidLoad function, initialize these and add data to them.

```
countriesArray = [[NSArray alloc] initWithObjects:
    @"USA",
    @"Canada",
    @"Mexico",
    nil];

sportsArray = [[NSArray alloc] initWithObjects:
    @"Baseball",
    @"Football",
    @"Hockey",
    @"Soccer",
    @"Basketball",
    nil];
```

## Setting the Delegate and Data Source

While you're editing viewDidLoad, you should put the code in to have the view controller be the delegate and dataSource for teamsTable.

```
_teamsTable.delegate = self;
_teamsTable.dataSource = self;
```

## Setting the Number of Sections

Next up, you need to specify the number of sections in the table view. Naturally, there's a function for that, and it's called (unsurprisingly) `numberOfSectionsInTableView`. Implement that function and have it return 2, because we want two sections.

Here's the code:

```
-(NSInteger) numberOfSectionsInTableView:(UITableView *)tableView
{
    return 2;
}
```

As before, if you don't want to type out the whole thing, you can start typing `-(NSInteger) n`, and Xcode will give you hints to help.

## Setting the Number of Rows per Section

In the earlier example, there was only one section in the table, so you could just return the amount of data as the number of rows. However, now we have two sections, so we want one section to have the number of elements in our array of countries, and the other to have the number of elements in our array of sports.

You use the `numberOfRowsInSection` function as before, but this time you can inspect the `section` parameter that is passed in. This is zero based, so the first section is number 0, the second is number 1, etc.

Here's the code:

```
-(NSInteger)tableView:(UITableView *)tableView numberOfRowsInSection:(NSInteger)section
{
    if(section==0)
    {
        return [countriesArray count];

    }
    else
    {
        return [sportsArray count];
    }
}
```

As you can see, it's very straightforward. You just check which section is passed in and return the appropriate array size.

## Creating the Table Cells

Similarly, when you create a cell in the `cellForRowAtIndexPath`, you do pretty much the same work as you did for a single-section table. The only big difference is that you have to check which section is selected so you can pick the appropriate text. The parameter that is passed in to the function, indexPath, has a property called "section" that you can check. Thus, based on the value of this property, you can set the text of the cell using the indexPath.row property.

Here's the code, with the differences between this and the single-section table highlighted:

```
-(UITableViewCell *)tableView:(UITableView *)tableView cellForRowAtIndexPath:(NSIndexPath
*)indexPath
{
    static NSString *simpleTableIdentifier = @"MyCell";
    UITableViewCell *thisCell = [tableView dequeueReusableCellWithIdentifier:simpleTableIdentifier];
    if(thisCell==nil)
    {
        thisCell = [[UITableViewCell alloc] initWithStyle:UITableViewCellStyleDefault
reuseIdentifier:simpleTableIdentifier];

    }
    if(indexPath.section==0)
    {
        thisCell.textLabel.text  = [countriesArray objectAtIndex:indexPath.row];

    }
    else
    {
        thisCell.textLabel.text  = [sportsArray objectAtIndex:indexPath.row];

    }
    return thisCell;

}
```

You've now done everything to create the multi-selection table. There's one more task—catching the user's selection.

## Getting the User's Selection

As with the previous functions, the indexPath parameter is available to didSelectRowAtIndexPath, and this has a section property. So, in order to know which text was most recently selected, we can take a look at the section property, and then, based on that selection, we know which NSArray to use. And, as before, we can take the correct text using the indexPath.row property, and apply it to the correct array.

Here's the code:

```
-(void)tableView:(UITableView *)tableView didSelectRowAtIndexPath:(NSIndexPath *)indexPath
{
    if(indexPath.section==0)
    {
        _lblOutlet.text = [countriesArray objectAtIndex:indexPath.row];

    }
```

```
        else
        {
            _lblOutlet.text = [sportsArray objectAtIndex:indexPath.row];
        }
}
```

# Running the App

For your convenience, here's the complete ViewController.m code:

```
#import "ViewController.h"

@interface ViewController ()

@end

@implementation ViewController
NSArray *countriesArray;
NSArray *sportsArray;

- (void)viewDidLoad
{
    [super viewDidLoad];
        // Do any additional setup after loading the view, typically from a nib.
    _teamsTable.delegate = self;
    _teamsTable.dataSource = self;

    countriesArray = [[NSArray alloc] initWithObjects:@"USA", @"Canada", @"Mexico", nil];
    sportsArray = [[NSArray alloc] initWithObjects:@"Baseball", @"Football", @"Hockey", @"Soccer",
@"Basketball", nil];
}

- (void)didReceiveMemoryWarning
{
    [super didReceiveMemoryWarning];
    // Dispose of any resources that can be recreated.
}

-(NSInteger) numberOfSectionsInTableView:(UITableView *)tableView
{
    return 2;
}

-(NSInteger)tableView:(UITableView *)tableView numberOfRowsInSection:(NSInteger)section
{
    if(section==0)
    {
        return [countriesArray count];
    }
```

```
        else
        {
            return [sportsArray count];
        }
}

-(UITableViewCell *)tableView:(UITableView *)tableView cellForRowAtIndexPath:(NSIndexPath
*)indexPath
{
    static NSString *simpleTableIdentifier = @"MyCell";
    UITableViewCell *thisCell = [tableView dequeueReusableCellWithIdentifier:simpleTableIdentifier];
    if(thisCell==nil)
    {
        thisCell = [[UITableViewCell alloc] initWithStyle:UITableViewCellStyleDefault
reuseIdentifier:simpleTableIdentifier];

    }
    if(indexPath.section==0)
    {
        thisCell.textLabel.text  = [countriesArray objectAtIndex:indexPath.row];

    }
    else
    {
        thisCell.textLabel.text  = [sportsArray objectAtIndex:indexPath.row];

    }
    return thisCell;

}

-(void)tableView:(UITableView *)tableView didSelectRowAtIndexPath:(NSIndexPath *)indexPath
{
    if(indexPath.section==0)
    {
        _lblOutlet.text = [countriesArray objectAtIndex:indexPath.row];

    }
    else
    {
        _lblOutlet.text = [sportsArray objectAtIndex:indexPath.row];
    }
}

@end
```

That's everything you need, so run the app and take a look. You can see it running in Figure 9-18.

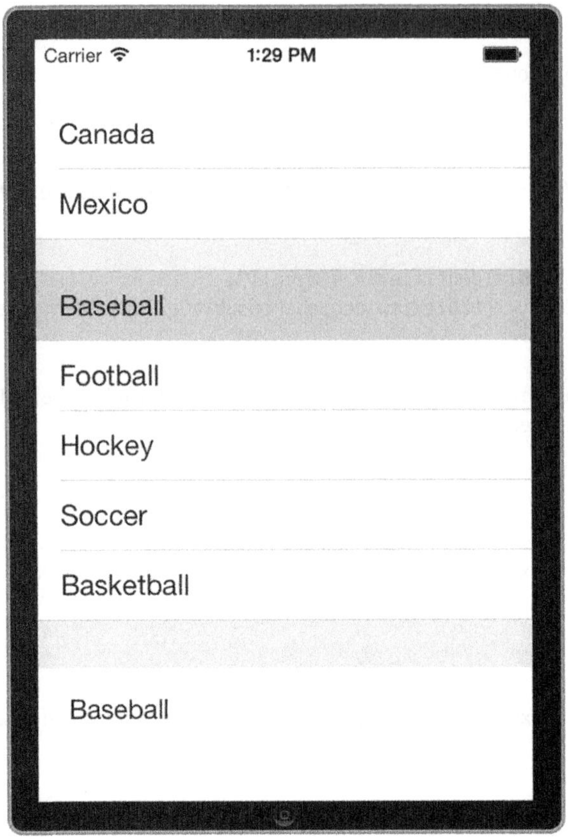

*Figure 9-18. Your multi-selection table*

> **Note**   There's a lot more customization that you can experiment with on the attributes inspector for the table. For example, you'll notice as you run it that you can only have one selection, even though you have multiple sections. To change this, use the selection property on the attribute inspector and set it to "Multiple Selection."

# Using Table Views for Navigation

In many of the examples you saw earlier in this chapter, the "Table View" control was used for navigation as opposed to selection. A visual cue of a small, right-pointing arrow was present in the cells to denote this. In this section, you'll learn how to create a simple app that provides table view–based navigation in the same way.

> **Note**   While this book is for absolute beginners, many of the concepts presented here are more suitable for intermediate level developers. If you've held your own this far into the book, you're doing brilliantly, but don't worry if some of it goes over your head for the time being. Just keep experimenting and learning, and you'll understand it in no time at all!

## Creating the App

As you work through this section, you'll create a table navigation app that looks like the one in Figure 9-19. This app presents a table view with three options, and when you select an option, it will navigate to a different view, passing some data as it goes.

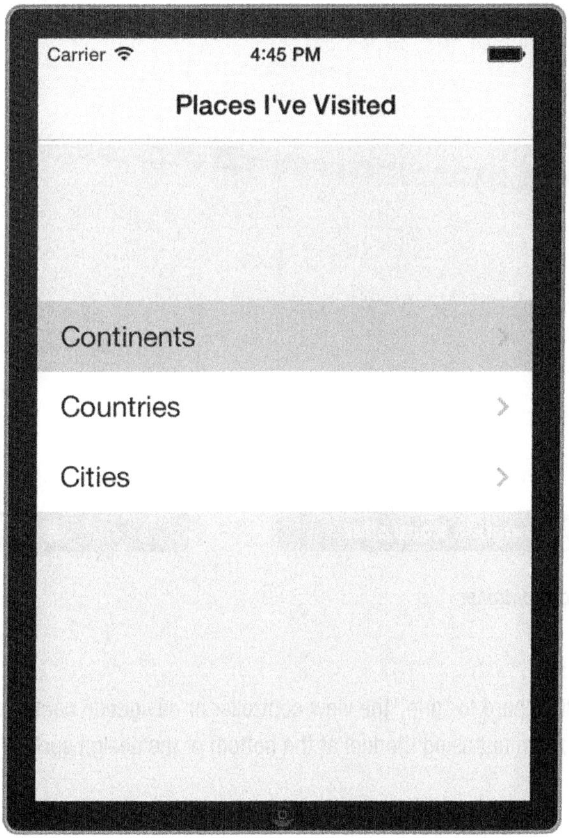

*Figure 9-19.*  *The navigation app*

As you create this app, we'll touch upon some more details of how storyboards work, as well as of how to use navigational controllers and segues. If these are all new concepts to you, don't worry—the best way to learn is by doing!

First, create a new single view application and call it "`tableViewNavDemo`."

Before going any further, you're going to add a navigation controller to your app. To do this, open `Main.Storyboard`, select the view controller, and then go to the "Editor" menu at the top of your screen. Select "Embed In" and then select "Navigation Controller."

You'll see that a new navigation controller gets added to your design surface. It might be partially obscuring your original view controller. If so, drag things around until you can see them all. Your screen should look like Figure 9-20.

*Figure 9-20. Adding the navigation controller*

> **Note**    Sometimes it's a little hard to "grip" the view controller or navigation controller to move them around. If this is the case, simply zoom out using the tool at the bottom of the design surface, move them around, and then zoom back in.

Next, you can add a table view to the view controller screen on the right. Do not add it to the navigation controller. Place it so that it is below the grey bar at the top of the view controller. Size it so that it's about half the height of your view. See Figure 9-21 for an example.

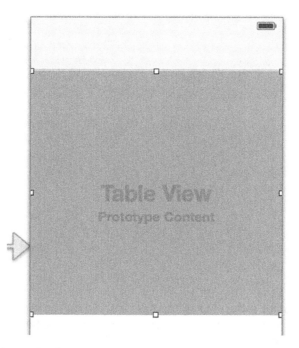

*Figure 9-21.* *Placing the table view on the view controller*

With the table view selected, on the attributes inspector, make sure that the "Content" field is set to "Dynamic Prototypes" and change the "Prototype Cells" setting to "1." See Figure 9-22.

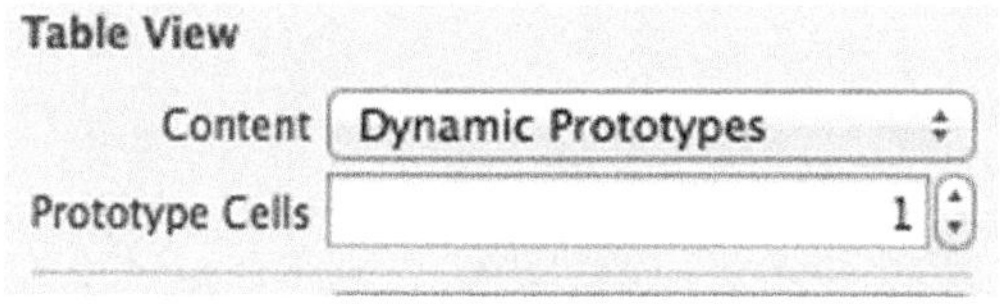

**Table View**

| | |
|---|---|
| Content | Dynamic Prototypes ⇕ |
| Prototype Cells | 1 ⇕ |

*Figure 9-22.* *Configuring the table view for prototype cells*

You'll notice that once you've done this, the design surface changes, giving a space near the top. This is a "Table View Cell" control that you can select and configure. See Figure 9-23.

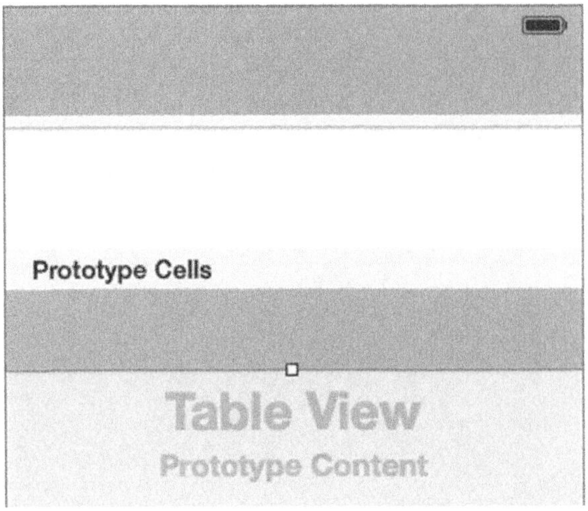

*Figure 9-23. The prototype cell*

Select it, and you'll see that it has a set of properties that you can configure in the attributes inspector. A prototype cell is simply a template for how you want the table cells to appear. Having the cell contain an arrow that hints at navigation is configured using the "Accessory" property. You can see this in the attributes inspector if the cell is selected. See Figure 9-24, where we've changed the "Accessory" property to "Disclosure Indicator." You'll notice that the little arrow appears on the prototype. Also set the "Identifier" text to "navCell."

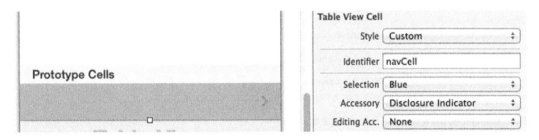

*Figure 9-24. Setting the accessory type for the cell*

Next, create an outlet for the table view and call it "placesTable." Make sure that it's the table that you CTRL-drag onto the assistant, and not the cell. If you do it right you should see the UITableView in the "Type" field for the dialog. See Figure 9-25.

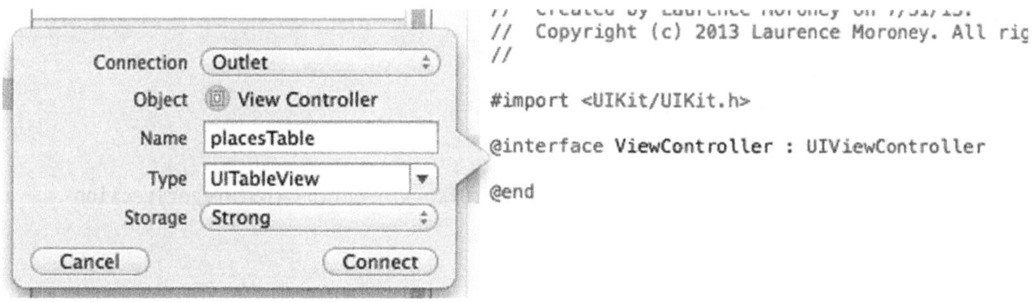

*Figure 9-25.* *Creating the outlet for the table view*

While you have the ViewController.h file open, add the interfaces to make the view controller the data source and the delegate for a UITableView.

Here's the finished code for ViewController.h:

```
#import <UIKit/UIKit.h>

@interface ViewController : UIViewController<UITableViewDataSource, UITableViewDelegate>

@property (strong, nonatomic) IBOutlet UITableView *placesTable;

@end
```

In ViewController.m, you'll need to set up the data for the table, as well as set up the cells of the table and their contents. If you need help with this, go back to the earlier examples in this chapter. Instead of going through all of them step by step here, we're just going to give the code for ViewController.m. Again, if this isn't familiar, go back and work through the earlier examples.

Here's the code:

```
#import "ViewController.h"

@interface ViewController ()

@end

@implementation ViewController
NSArray *navItems;
- (void)viewDidLoad
{
    [super viewDidLoad];
        // Do any additional setup after loading the view, typically from a nib.
    _placesTable.dataSource = self;
    _placesTable.delegate = self;
    navItems = [[NSArray alloc]initWithObjects:@"Continents",
        @"Countries", @"Cities", nil];
}
```

```
- (void)didReceiveMemoryWarning
{
    [super didReceiveMemoryWarning];
    // Dispose of any resources that can be recreated.
}

- (NSInteger)tableView:(UITableView *)tableView numberOfRowsInSection:(NSInteger)section
{
    return [navItems count];
}

- (UITableViewCell *)tableView:(UITableView *)tableView cellForRowAtIndexPath:(NSIndexPath
*)indexPath
{
    static NSString *simpleTableIdentifier = @"navCell";

    UITableViewCell *cell = [tableView dequeueReusableCellWithIdentifier:simpleTableIdentifier];

    if (cell == nil) {
        cell = [[UITableViewCell alloc] initWithStyle:UITableViewCellStyleDefault
reuseIdentifier:simpleTableIdentifier];
    }

    cell.textLabel.text = [navItems objectAtIndex:indexPath.row];
    return cell;
}

@end
```

Do take note that the simpleTableIdentifier text should match what you configured in the prototype cell back in Figure 9-24, which was, in this case, "navCell."

Now, if you run the app, you should see your table view with three cells, but you can't do much. Earlier you added the navigation controller. In the next section you'll see how it works.

## Using a Navigation Controller

A navigation controller, as its name suggests, manages navigation between different views. Think of it like a traffic cop who controls everything when a traffic light is out. The navigation controller is in charge of keeping tabs on who is where, and, when you move forwards or backwards in navigation, that the right views get displayed.

Go to your storyboard, and, on the "Controls" list, find the view controller. It should look something like Figure 9-26.

*Figure 9-26.* *The view controller control*

Drag this and drop it to the right of the existing view controller. Then, pick the prototype cell that you created earlier and CTRL-drag it to the new view controller that you just dropped.

A menu with a number of options will pop up. See Figure 9-27.

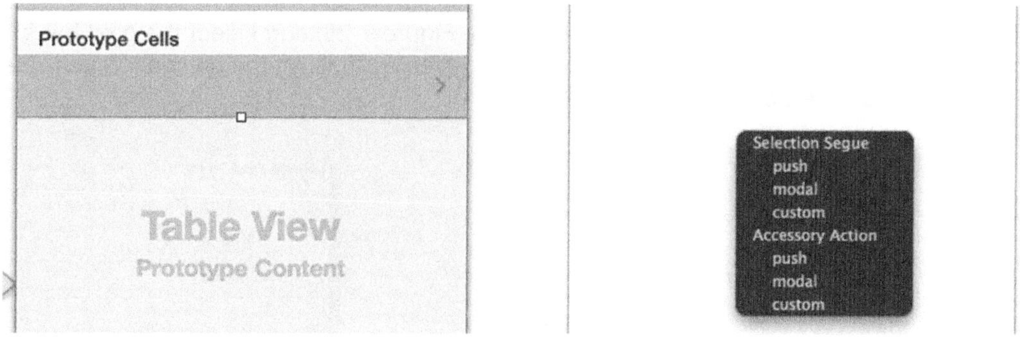

*Figure 9-27.* *Configuring the segue*

Under "Selection Segue," select "push." When you're done, you should see a connector between the views, and your Main.storyboard should look something like Figure 9-28.

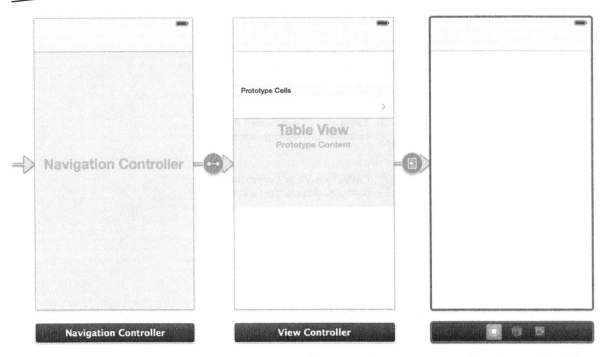

*Figure 9-28. Navigation controller storyboard*

Select the main view controller (the one in the middle in Figure 9-28) and select the grey bar at the top. Open the attributes inspector, and you'll be able to create a title for the navigation item. Set the "Title" field to "Places I've Been." See Figure 9-29.

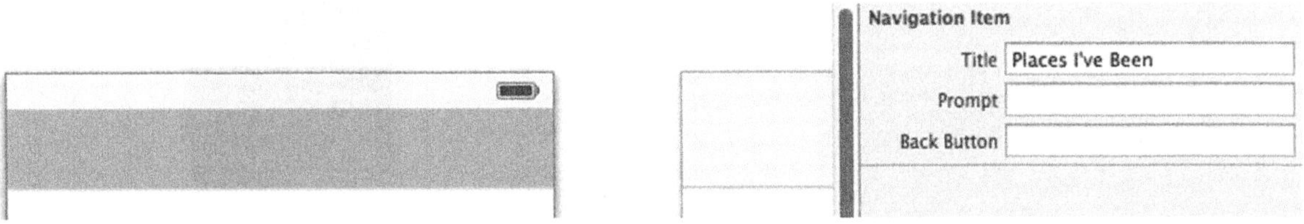

*Figure 9-29. Setting navigation item title*

Select the view controller on the right and do the same, then set the title to "Details." When you're done, the designer should look something like Figure 9-30.

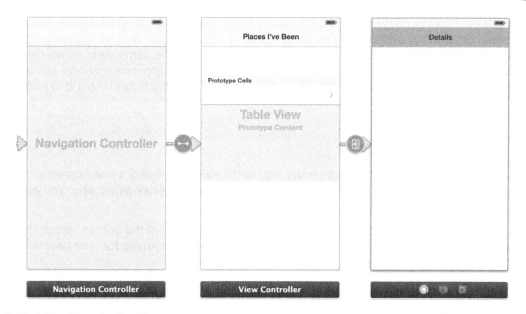

*Figure 9-30.* *Adding the navigation titles*

Now, if you run your app and select one of the items in the menu, you'll see that the screen will navigate to the details screen, and a button labeled "<Back" will appear at the top of the screen, allowing you to return to the menu. See Figure 9-31.

*Figure 9-31.* *Running the app*

Congratulations if you've made it this far! This was your first foray into using navigation across multiple views. In the next section, you're going to take it a little deeper, and we will show how you can pass data to a view. In this case, all three menu items point to the same view, so we need to distinguish each view somehow. If you are sharing a view across different navigational items, which is perfectly fine, you'll just need to tell the view which item called it, so it can respond in kind. You'll see that in the next section.

## Passing Data to a View

In every example you've worked through so far, you had a single view and a class called ViewController that had the code and the data for that view. For the navigation app, you added a second view, but that view doesn't have a class behind it.

So, let's go and create that class now. From the File menu at the top of the screen, select "New" and then select "File." You'll see a dialog that asks you to select a template for your new file. See Figure 9-32.

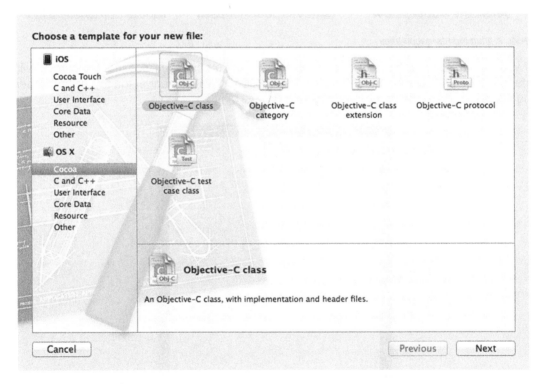

*Figure 9-32.  Creating a new file*

Select "Objective-C "class as in Figure 9-32, and select "Next." On the next screen, give your class the name "TravelDetailsViewController" and make sure that it is a subclass of UIViewController, as shown in Figure 9-33. Make sure also that "With XIB for user interface" is unchecked, if you can see it.

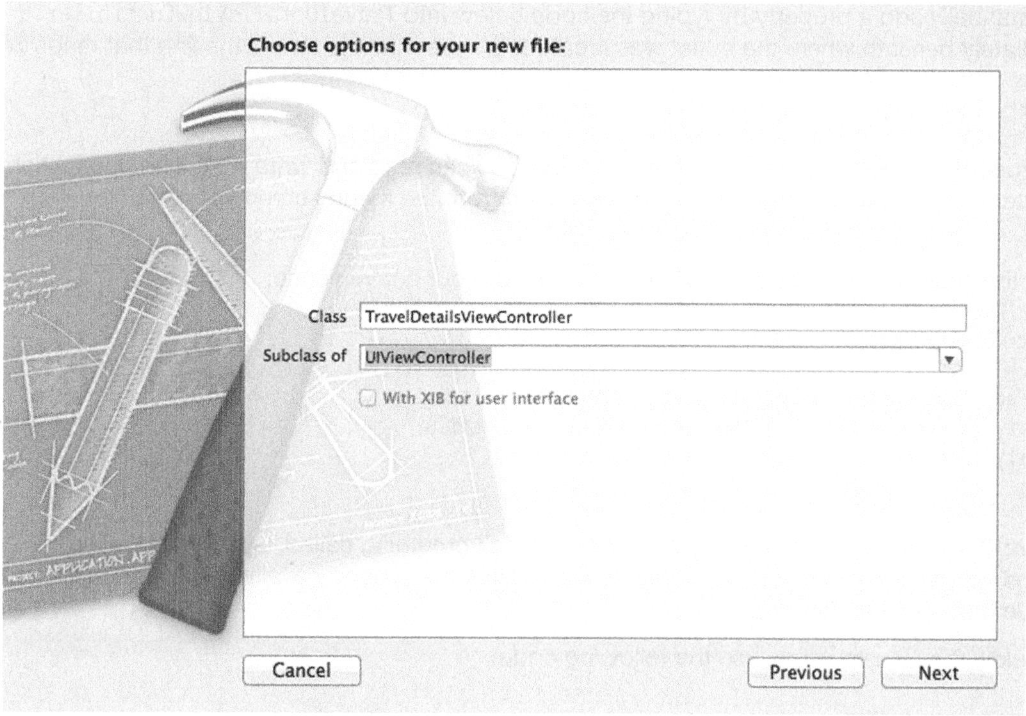

*Figure 9-33. Adding the class for the details screen*

Click "Next" and then click "Create" to create the class. Now return to Main.storyboard and select the details view controller. It should be the one on the right. On the inspector window, select the third icon from the left to open the identity inspector. There, change the "Class" setting to read "TravelDetailsViewController." If you can't see "TravelDetailsViewController" on the list, make sure that the view controller, and not the view, is selected on storyboard view. You should see a bold blue outline around it, like in Figure 9-34.

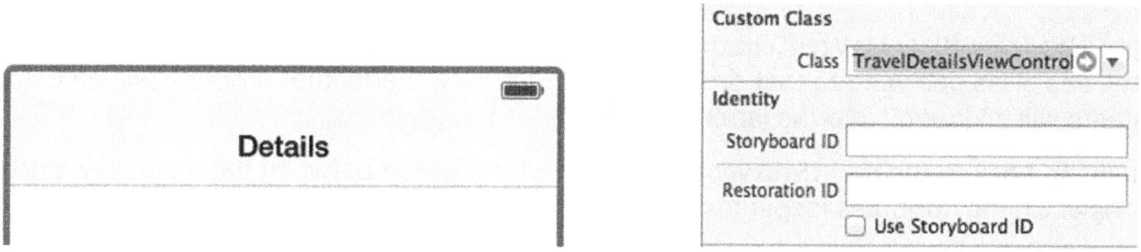

*Figure 9-34. Setting the custom class for the details view*

Now, add a label to the details view and make it large enough to hold some text. Make it the width of the screen (less some sensible margins as guided by the storyboard editor) and tall enough to hold three to four lines of text. Create an outlet for the label and call it "lblOutput." When you create the outlet, make sure that you are dragging to TravelDetailsViewController.h and *not* ViewController.h.

Next, manually add a property by typing the code below into `TravelDetailsViewController.h` immediately beneath where the outlet was created. Ensure that it is above the line that reads @end.

```
@property (nonatomic, strong) NSString *navItemName;
```

This property will be a piece of data that other classes can read and write to. It'll be used when we navigate to the details view, and the navigation item from the menu screen will set it. You'll see that shortly.

Here's the entire `TravelDetailsViewController.h`, for your convenience:

```
#import <UIKit/UIKit.h>

@interface TravelDetailsViewController : UIViewController
@property (strong, nonatomic) IBOutlet UILabel *lblDetails;
@property (nonatomic, strong) NSString *navItemName;
@end
```

In `TravelDetailsViewController.m`, you'll need to do something called "synthesizing" the `navItemName` property that you just created. This makes the property available for getting and setting its value from outside this class.

Just below @implementation, use the following code:

```
@synthesize navItemName;
```

Finally, you'll need to set the contents of the label to this property when the view loads. Here's the code:

```
-(void)viewDidLoad
{
    [super viewDidLoad];

    _lblOutput.text = navItemName;
}
```

To recap: The `TravelDetailsViewController` now exposes a property called `navItemName`. Any code that uses this class can write to that property. When the view loads, that property will be read, and its contents will be loaded into the label.

To do this, go back to the `Main.Storyboard` and select the segue between the table view and the details view. On the attributes inspector, you'll see settings for "Storyboard Segue." See Figure 9-35.

*Figure 9-35. Naming the segue*

Give the segue the name "showDetail," as shown in Figure 9-35.

In ViewController.m, there are a couple of things you'll need to do.

First, as you are going to be using the TravelDetailsViewController class that you created earlier, you need to tell ViewController.m about it. This is done using the #import function, which you point at TravelDetailsViewController.h and place at the top of the file, above where it says @interface.

```
#import "TravelDetailsViewController.h"
```

Next, you'll need to implement the prepareForSegue method. This gets called as iOS does the transition to the next screen in the navigation. It's the ideal place for us to set our data.

Here's the code:

```
-(void)prepareForSegue:(UIStoryboardSegue *)segue sender:(id)sender
{
    if([segue.identifier isEqualToString:@"showDetail"])
    {
        NSIndexPath *indexPath = [_placesTable indexPathForSelectedRow];
        TravelDetailsViewController *deetsController = segue.destinationViewController;
        deetsController.navItemName = [navItems objectAtIndex:indexPath.row];
    }
}
```

Your app may have many segues, so the one that triggered this function is passed into the function with a pointer called "segue." This has a property called "identifier," which, if it is set to "showDetail," we'll know that it's the segue that links to the detail view. Look back to Figure 9-35 where you named the segue.

Once we have the right segue, we can get our indexPath by looking at what the indexPath is for the selected row. This is the same type of indexPath that you used when setting up the table view, and it contains information about the section and row of the presently selected item.

We then create an instance of the TravelDetailsViewController class that we call deetsController. We can set its navItemName property to the item from our navItems array that corresponds to the currently selected item. And as you saw in the viewDidLoad function for TravelDetailsViewController, when this property is set it will load its contents into the label and render them.

Run the app and you'll see this. See Figure 9-36, where "Continents" was selected to trigger the detail view for continents.

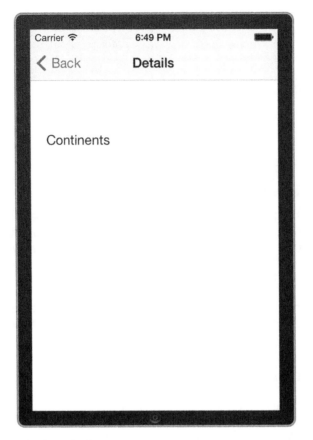

*Figure 9-36.  Navigating to the details view with data*

Typically items that are grouped in the same section of a table will have similar views, but the view itself handles rendering the appropriate data. An example like this one shows how to pass the data, and the view itself is simple. In real-world apps, this might be used to trigger a data query for different data sets that would be rendered on the view, but, for learning purposes, hopefully this has been a good demonstration of what's possible!

# Summary

In this chapter you were introduced to the table view control. You saw a number of scenarios where it can be used, before going rolling up your sleeves and building three sample apps that use the table view. The first rendered a simple list, the second a multi-sectioned list, and the third showed how to use the table view for navigation, as many settings screens on your iOS device do.

You've barely scratched the surface of what's possible with this very powerful and very complex control, but hopefully it was enough to whet your appetite and get you building some more!

In the next chapter we're going to have a small change of pace and take a look at the map control that puts maps into applications!

# Chapter 10

# Mapping in iOS

A very common scenario for application developers in iOS is to add mapping to an application. Apple launched a new mapping service in 2012, and there's a really useful toolkit that's available to integrate this into your apps. In this chapter you'll learn how to use the mapping control, as well as the MapKit libraries, to build a simple mapping app that shows you the basics of how it works!

## Creating a Mapping App with the Map View

Let's roll our sleeves up and get started with creating a new app that uses mapping. If you aren't familiar with creating new apps, it's a good idea to go back to Chapter 2 and Chapter 4 for a quick getting-started guide.

Create a new single view app and call it "mapControlDemo." When this is done, open the "Main.storyboard" file and find the "Map View" control. You can see this in Figure 10-1.

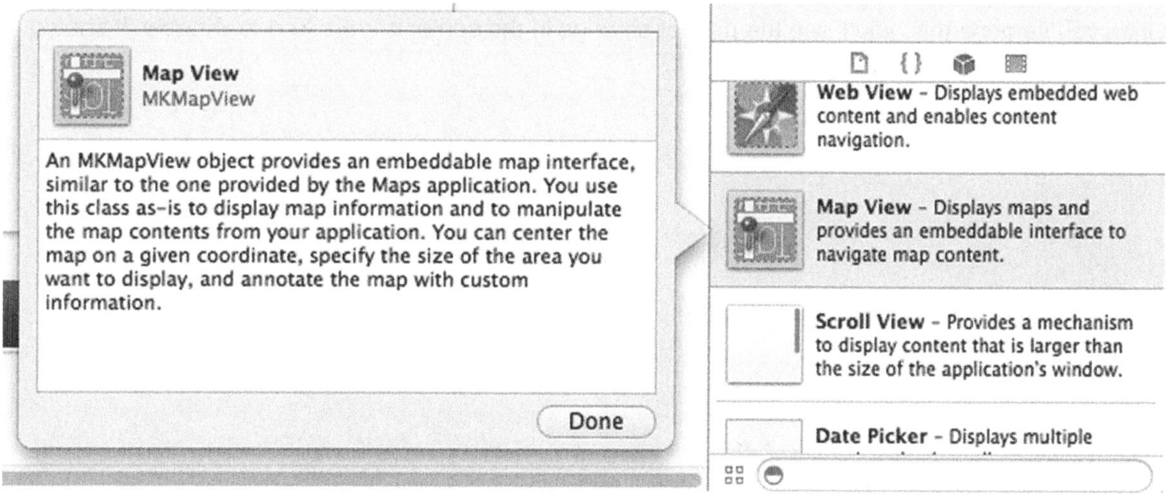

**Map View**
MKMapView

An MKMapView object provides an embeddable map interface, similar to the one provided by the Maps application. You use this class as-is to display map information and to manipulate the map contents from your application. You can center the map on a given coordinate, specify the size of the area you want to display, and annotate the map with custom information.

Done

**Web View** – Displays embedded web content and enables content navigation.

**Map View** – Displays maps and provides an embeddable interface to navigate map content.

**Scroll View** – Provides a mechanism to display content that is larger than the size of the application's window.

**Date Picker** – Displays multiple

*Figure 10-1. The "Map View" control*

Drag and drop the "Map View" control, and it will snap to fill the full screen area. If you try to run the app at this point it will fail because you haven't included the necessary libraries for the MapKit. This is a common scenario in iOS development, and while this is the first time you've hit something like this, it won't be the last!

It's easy to do though, so let's take a look at how you add new libraries to your app.

First, in the project navigator, make sure that you've selected just the project file and none of the source files. It will be the entry at the top with the blue Xcode icon. See Figure 10-2.

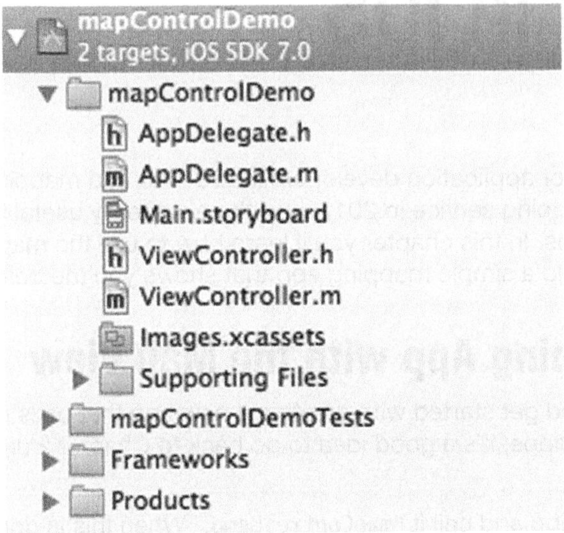

Figure 10-2. Selecting the project file

Once you've done this, you'll see the project settings in the center of your Xcode window. It should look something like Figure 10-3.

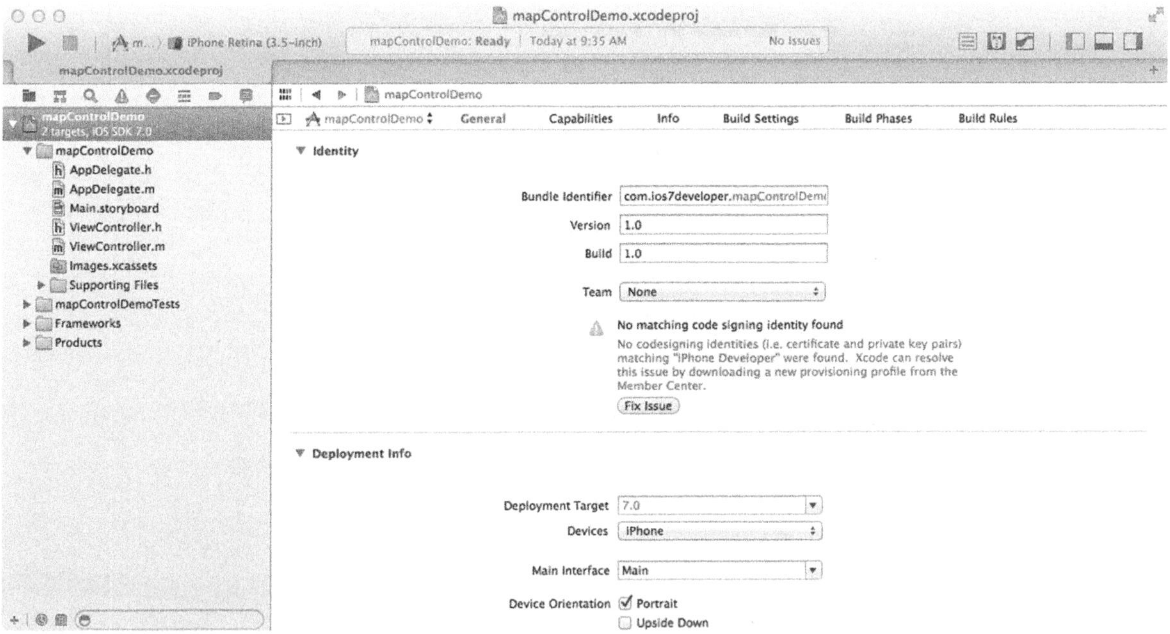

*Figure 10-3.* *Xcode project editor settings*

Across the top of the screen you'll see a number of tabs. Select the one called "General." You'll see a section called "Linked Frameworks and Libraries," which you should open. You'll see that CoreGraphics, UIKit, and Foundation are the specified linked libraries. See Figure 10-4.

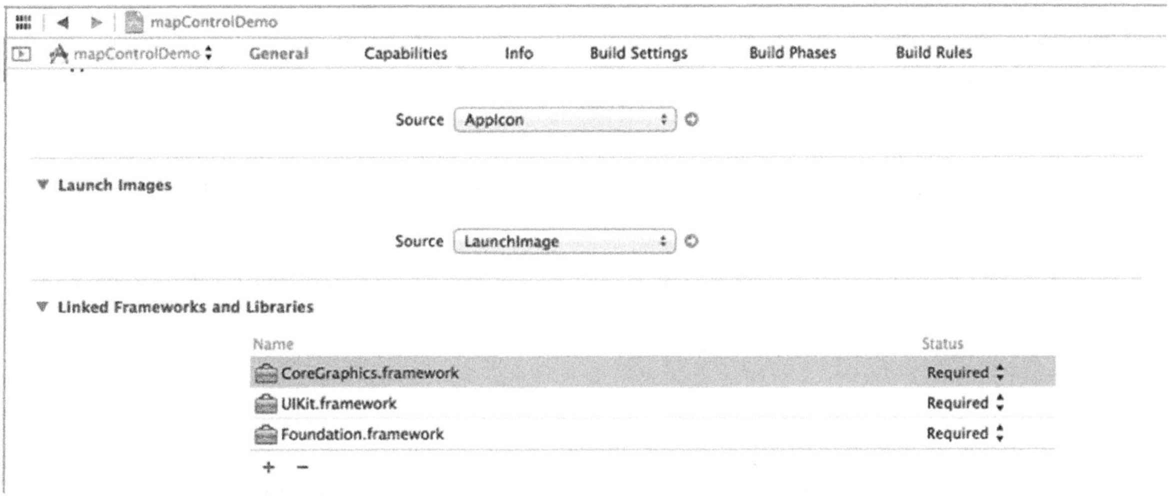

*Figure 10-4.* *Linking with libraries*

Click the "+" button at the bottom of the list, and you'll be presented with a list of frameworks and libraries that you can add. See Figure 10-5.

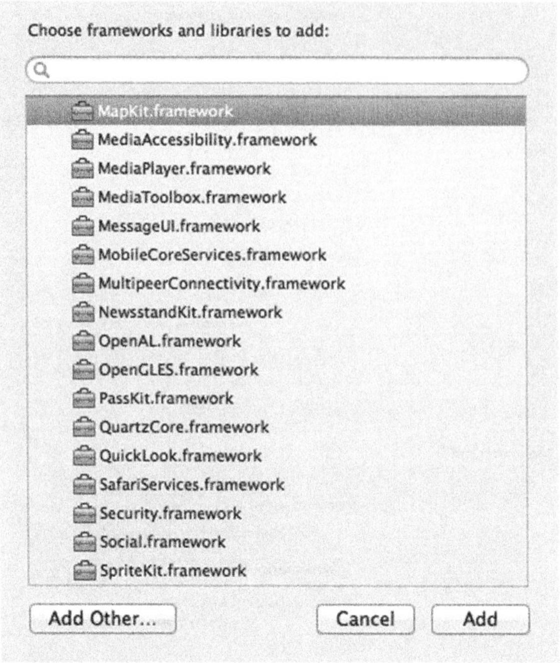

*Figure 10-5.* *Choosing your framework*

Pick the MapKit framework as shown in Figure 10-5 and click "Add." Now you can launch your app, and it should run happily.

**Tip** You can search for frameworks instead of scrolling through the entire list. Simply type into the search box, and Xcode will filter the list based on your criteria.

The app will fill your screen, including the area behind the clock and battery meter at the top. See Figure 10-6.

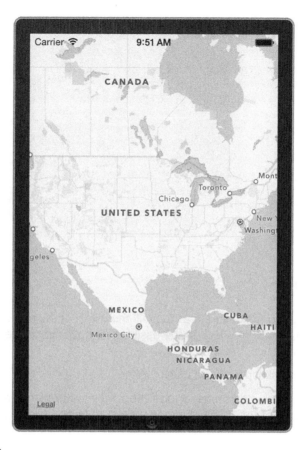

*Figure 10-6.  Running your app*

You can now pan around the app and simulate multi-touch to zoom in and out of the app by holding the "Option" key on your keyboard as you drag.

# Detecting Map Location

In the previous section you saw how to add a "Map View" control to your app. It filled the screen and allowed you to explore it, but other than that there was no interactivity. In this section you'll amend the app so that whenever the user moves the map, it will report back on the location of the center of the map in latitude and longitude.

If the app is running, stop it and go back to your Main.storyboard file. Resize the "MKMapView" control so that it fills the top half of the screen. Sometimes it's a little tricky to do this, so we find the best thing to do is drag the control off the view, resize it using a corner, and then drag it back on and resize further.

You can see it filling the top half of the View in Figure 10-7.

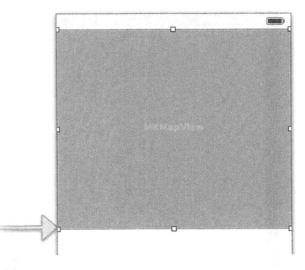

*Figure 10-7. Resizing the MKMapView*

Add two labels below this, and make sure that they fill the width of the screen. When you're done, CTRL-drag them to ViewController.h in the assistant window to create two outlets called "lblLatitude" and "lblLongitude," respectively.

Also, create an outlet for the MKMapView and call it "myMap."

Mapping works using delegates, so you need to tell your view controller that you'll be using them. This is done in the "ViewController.h" file. First, you need to import the header files for the MapKit at the top of the file:

```
#import <MapKit/MapKit.h>
```

Then you'll need to implement the interface to have your view controller be an MKMapViewDelegate. Here's the code:

```
@interface ViewController : UIViewController<MKMapViewDelegate>
```

Here's the complete code for your ViewController.h file:

```
#import <UIKit/UIKit.h>
#import <MapKit/MapKit.h>
@interface ViewController : UIViewController<MKMapViewDelegate>
@property (strong, nonatomic) IBOutlet UILabel *lblLatitude;
@property (strong, nonatomic) IBOutlet UILabel *lblLongitude;
@property (strong, nonatomic) IBOutlet MKMapView *myMap;

@end
```

Now, go to the "ViewController.m" file and make the edits. Start with your viewDidLoad function, where you'll inform iOS that this view controller is the delegate for your map control, which you called myMap. Here's the code:

```
- (void)viewDidLoad
{
    [super viewDidLoad];
        // Do any additional setup after loading the view, typically from a nib.
    _myMap.delegate = self;
}
```

The control supports lots of different methods, and the one you're going to use in this example is the regionDidChangeAnimated function. This function will get called whenever the user changes the location of the map by panning or zooming. Start typing -(void)m, and you'll see a hint pop up with a list of all the functions that are available, because you've set this view up as an MKMapViewDelegate. See Figure 10-8.

```
-(void)mapView:(MKMapView *)mapView regionDidChangeAnimated:(BOOL)animated
 [M]  mapView:(MKMapView *)mapView didFailToLocateUserWithError:(NSError *)error
 [M]  mapView:(MKMapView *)mapView didSelectAnnotationView:(MKAnnotationView *)view
 [M]  mapView:(MKMapView *)mapView didUpdateUserLocation:(MKUserLocation *)userLocation
 [M]  mapView:(MKMapView *)mapView regionDidChangeAnimated:(BOOL)animated
 [M]  mapView:(MKMapView *)mapView regionWillChangeAnimated:(BOOL)animated
 [M]  mapViewDidFailLoadingMap:(MKMapView *)mapView withError:(NSError *)error
 [M]  mapViewDidFinishLoadingMap:(MKMapView *)mapView
 [M]  mapViewDidFinishRenderingMap:(MKMapView *)mapView fullyRendered:(BOOL)fullyRendered
 Tells the delegate that the region displayed by the map view just changed. More...
```

*Figure 10-8. Choosing the mapping function*

Select the regionDidChangeAnimated function and create braces for the function. Your code should look like this:

```
-(void)mapView:(MKMapView *)mapView regionDidChangeAnimated:(BOOL)animated
{

}
```

The map control has a property called region, which has a property called center, which defines the coordinates of the center of the map. This includes a latitude and a longitude value for the center of the map. Each is a floating point number, and you can get the string for the latitude like this:

```
NSString *lat = [[NSString alloc]
    initWithFormat:@"%f",_myMap.region.center.latitude];
```

Similarly, the longitude can be loaded into a string like this:

```
NSString *longt = [[NSString alloc]
    initWithFormat:@"%f",_myMap.region.center.longitude];
```

These can be assigned to the labels via their outlets. Here's the complete function:

```
-(void)mapView:(MKMapView *)mapView regionDidChangeAnimated:(BOOL)animated
{
    NSString *lat = [[NSString alloc] initWithFormat:@"%f",_myMap.region.center.latitude];
    _lblLatitude.text = lat;

    NSString *longt = [[NSString alloc] initWithFormat:@"%f",_myMap.region.center.longitude];
    _lblLongitude.text = longt;

}
```

Now if you run your app and move the map around, you'll see the longitude and latitude of the current map center. See Figure 10-9.

*Figure 10-9. Viewing the latitude and longitude of the center of the map*

As you zoom and pan around the map, you'll see the labels update with the current center coordinates. In Figure 10-9, you can see where we've set the map location to be a neighborhood on the east side of Seattle.

# Adding Pins to a Map

Another common scenario for mapping applications is adding pins to a map to denote a particular area. This can be done using annotations. In this section, you'll see how to update the simple app to allow you to drop pins on the center of the map.

Before starting, you'll need to create a custom class that represents your pin. Right click on the mapControlTest folder in project navigator, and select "New File." See Figure 10-10.

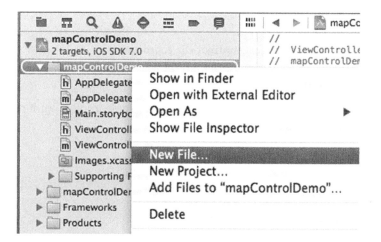

*Figure 10-10. Adding a new file to a project*

You'll see a dialog that asks you to choose a template for your new file. Pick "Objective-C Class" and click "Next."

The next dialog asks you to name the class and specify its subclass. Give it the name "myPin" and set the subclass field to "NSObject." Click "Finish" and then click "Create." The class will be added to your project.

This class will be a map annotation, which needs to implement the MKAnnotation interface. To do this, open your "myPin.h" file and add an import to the MapKit headers.

```
#import <MapKit/MapKit.h>
```

Next you have to specify that your class implements the MKAnnotation interface. Here's the code, with the changes in bold:

```
@interface myPin : NSObject<MKAnnotation>
```

Finally, your annotation class should implement properties that an annotation needs, with—at the very minimum—a coordinate, which is a CLLocationCoordinate2D type, and a title, which is an NSString type. You *must* use these names, or the interface won't work. The concept of interfaces in object-oriented programming means that if you build an object that implements an interface, its data classes should be the same as those in the class it is using. As such, you must use these names.

Here's the complete myPin.h code:

```
#import <Foundation/Foundation.h>
#import <MapKit/MapKit.h>

@interface myPin : NSObject<MKAnnotation>
{
    CLLocationCoordinate2D coordinate;
    NSString *title;
}

@property (nonatomic,copy) NSString *title;
@property (nonatomic, assign) CLLocationCoordinate2D coordinate;

@end
```

Now your class's implementation file "myPin.m" has a very simple implementation—you just need to synthesize the properties that you created on myPin.h.

Here's the full code for myPin.m:

```
#import "myPin.h"

@implementation myPin
@synthesize coordinate,title;

@end
```

Now let's edit the user interface to add a button. Open Main.storyboard, drag a "Button" control to the view, and edit its title to read "Drop Pin." See Figure 10-11.

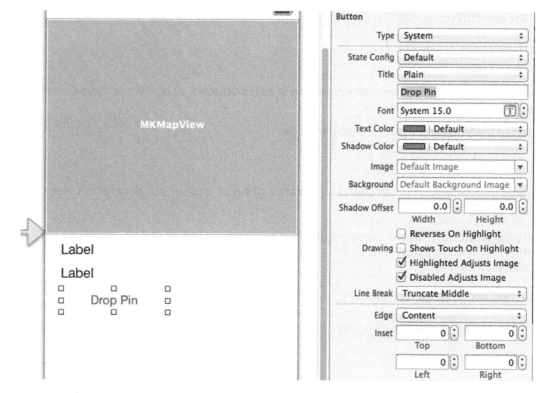

*Figure 10-11. Adding a button to the app*

Using the assistant, create an action by CTRL-dragging the button to `ViewController.h`. Give it the name "`dropPin`," and make sure the "Event" field reads "Touch Up Inside." Click "Connect" to create the function. See Figure 10-12.

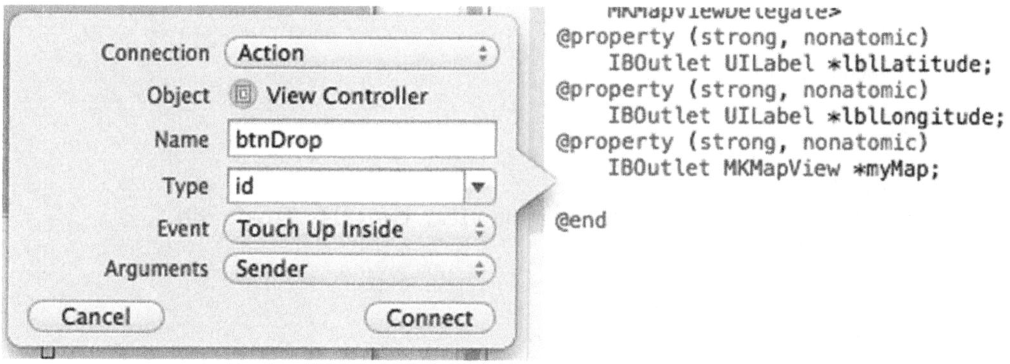

*Figure 10-12. Creating the button action*

In your ViewController.m, you'll see a btnDrop function is created for you. It looks like this:

```
- (IBAction)dropPin:(id)sender {
}
```

Before you can code this function, which will use a myPin object, you have to tell ViewController.m about myPin by importing its header.

At the top of the ViewController.m, add this code:

```
#import "myPin.h"
```

Now, within this method, you can create an instance of myPin and set its coordinate value from the map center, like this:

```
CLLocationCoordinate2D center = _myMap.region.center;
myPin *thePin = [[myPin alloc] init];
thePin.coordinate = center;
```

You can then assign a title to it, like this:

```
thePin.title = @"Map Center";
```

Then add it to the map, like this:

```
[_myMap addAnnotation:thePin];
```

For your convenience, here's the entire ViewController.m code:

```
#import "ViewController.h"
#import "myPin.h"
@interface ViewController ()

@end

@implementation ViewController

- (void)viewDidLoad
{
    [super viewDidLoad];
        // Do any additional setup after loading the view, typically from a nib.
    _myMap.delegate = self;
}

- (void)didReceiveMemoryWarning
{
    [super didReceiveMemoryWarning];
    // Dispose of any resources that can be recreated.
}
```

```
-(void)mapView:(MKMapView *)mapView regionDidChangeAnimated:(BOOL)animated
{
    NSString *lat = [[NSString alloc] initWithFormat:@"%f",_myMap.region.center.latitude];
    _lblLatitude.text = lat;

    NSString *longt = [[NSString alloc] initWithFormat:@"%f",_myMap.region.center.longitude];
    _lblLongitude.text = longt;

}

- (IBAction)dropPin:(id)sender {
    CLLocationCoordinate2D center = _myMap.region.center;
    myPin *thePin = [[myPin alloc] init];
    thePin.coordinate = center;
    thePin.title = @"Map Center";

    [_myMap addAnnotation:thePin];
}
@end
```

Run the app, and when you press the button, a pin will be dropped in the center of the map. You can also touch the pin to see the string. As you pan the map around and drop new pins, the old ones will stay in their previous locations. See Figure 10-13.

*Figure 10-13. Using pins on a map*

Now that you've seen how to add annotations, let's next look at changing the map type between a standard map and satellite imagery.

# Changing the Map Mode

In order to change the map mode, you use the `mapType` property of the map view, which takes the values `MKMapTypeStandard`, `MKMapTypeSatellite`, or `MKMapTypeHybrid`, which correspond to a standard map, a satellite view, and a mixed map with both styles, respectively.

If the app is presently running, stop it and open Main.storyboard.

In Chapter 7 you learned about the "segmented" control, which allows you to have multiple commands across a horizontal space. On Main.storyboard, drop a segmented control onto the design surface of your view controller. Using the attributes inspector add a new segment by setting the "segments" value to 3. Give the segments the names "Map," "Satellite," and "Hybrid," respectively.

See Figure 10-14.

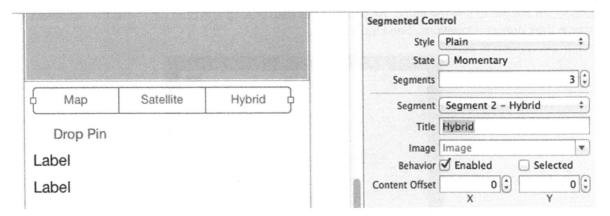

*Figure 10-14.  Adding a segmented control*

Create an outlet for the segmented control, called "`styleChosen`," and create an action for it called "`btnChoose`."

Now, in your `ViewController.m`, you'll have a function called `btnChoose` that looks like this:

```
-(IBAction)btnChoose:(id)sender {
}
```

As you created an outlet called "`styleChosen`" for the segmented button, you can find out which segment was touched by the user with its `selectedSegmentIndex` property. The following code will change the `mapType` based on what the user touched.

```
- (IBAction)btnChoose:(id)sender {
    switch(_styleChosen.selectedSegmentIndex)
    {
```

```
        case 0:
            _myMap.mapType = MKMapTypeStandard;
            break;
        case 1:
            _myMap.mapType = MKMapTypeSatellite;
            break;
        case 2:
            _myMap.mapType = MKMapTypeHybrid;
    }
}
```

You can now run the app and change the map type using the segmented control.

Figure 10-15 shows the app with the map in satellite mode.

*Figure 10-15.  Map in satellite mode*

Selecting the hybrid mode will give you satellite imagery overlaid with titles such as street names, park names, and metadata like one-way streets. See Figure 10-16.

*Figure 10-16.  Seeing the map in hybrid mode*

Hopefully these were good examples that will teach you the basics of mapping. There is a lot more great information about how to use MapKit on Apple's developer site at: http://developer.apple.com/library/ios/#documentation/MapKit/Reference/MapKit_Framework_Reference/_index.html.

# Summary

In this chapter, you were introduced to mapping in iOS. You saw how to use the "Map View" control and the Map Kit libraries to add a map to your application and to query that map for its location. You also saw how to add annotation pins to the map, as well as how to change the map mode to different styles, such as a basic map, a satellite image, or a hybrid of the two. Mapping is an integral part of many iOS applications, and this was an introduction on how to use it!

Chapter **11**

# Web Views and Connections

It's hard to find an app that doesn't rely on networking in some way. It might need to get updated data, connect with online leaderboards, or just receive a news feed of some sort. In Chapter 10 you used online data within the Map View, and you'll build on that experience in this chapter. You'll enlist a "Web View" control to provide embedded browsing functionality and learn to use the underlying networking APIs to build an app that pulls data off the Internet.

## The Web View Control

As its name suggests, the "Web View" control is used to provide a view of web content. It's basically the Safari browser from your iOS device, but without all the functionality for controlling it, such as back buttons, bookmark management, and so on. You can use this control to get a view of HTML data embedded in your app. This is useful when that's the type of data that you want to render, because managing HTML for yourself within your app, including layout, styling, JavaScript, and all of the other bits and pieces that go into a web page, is a very complex task.

You can see where the "Web View" control is in Safari in Figure 11-1.

*Figure 11-1. The "Web View" control in Safari*

The rest of the browser app is typically called the "chrome," and it includes the address bar, buttons, other screens such as bookmark management, and more. Incidentally, this is what inspired the name for Google's browser, as its aim was to reduce the amount of chrome that was visible on the screen, for a clean, elegant look. In the next section you'll take a look at how to build a very basic browser—one with a lot less chrome than the Safari one, using the "Web View" control.

# Build a Web View App

This chapter will gloss over many of the basic concepts of building an app, such as what is in the project and where. We'll mostly be asking you to create outlets and actions without showing you how. If you're not familiar with any of the concepts, go back, and at least read Chapter 2 and Chapter 4, where you'll see how to create applications and how to use the storyboard editor to add controls to your view controller, as well as how to wire them up with outlets and actions.

# Designing the App

To begin, create a single view application and call it "webViewDemo." When you're done, open its "Main.storyboard" file.

On the controls list at the bottom right of the screen, scroll until you see the "Web View" control. It should look like Figure 11-2.

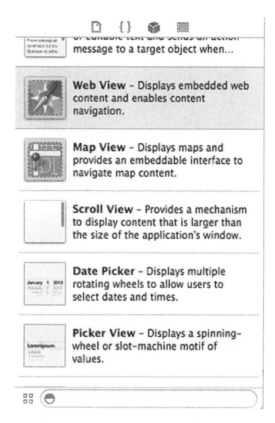

*Figure 11-2. Finding the web view*

Drag and drop the "Web View" control onto your view on the storyboard. It will automatically size itself to take up the full size of the window. You do *not* want to do this, and the simple trick to avoid it is to drop it somewhere other than directly on the window. See Figure 11-3, where I've dropped it off to the side a little.

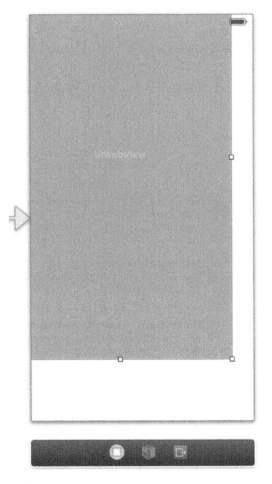

*Figure 11-3. Dropping the web view to the side*

Once you do this, you get sizing handles that you can use to size and place the web view where you want it. Put it where it fills the bottom of the view, leaving a small space at the top, as shown in Figure 11-4.

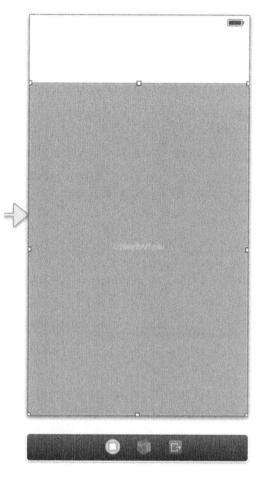

*Figure 11-4. Placing the web view for our app*

Now that you've placed it, add a text field and a button at the top of the view and change the button's title to "Go."

When you're done, the designer should look something like Figure 11-5.

*Figure 11-5. Adding the text field and the button*

# Outlets, Actions, and Delegate Declarations

Now you need to set up some outlets and actions. All of this should be done with the assistant using CTRL-dragging of the relevant controls and dropping them onto ViewController.h.

For the web view, create an outlet called "webView."

For the text field, create an outlet called "txtAddress" and create an action for the "Editing did End" event that you call "AddressChanged."

For the button, create an action called "GoPressed" that works for the "Touch Up Inside" event.

Finally, while you're editing ViewController.h, add a <UITextFieldDelegate> delegate to the interface. When you're done, your complete ViewController.h should look like this:

```
#import <UIKit/UIKit.h>

@interface ViewController : UIViewController<UITextFieldDelegate>
@property (strong, nonatomic) IBOutlet UITextField *txtAddress;
@property (strong, nonatomic) IBOutlet UIWebView *webView;
- (IBAction)AddressChanged:(id)sender;
- (IBAction)GoPressed:(id)sender;

@end
```

> **Note**   If you're not familiar with some of the text field constructs, such as using the delegate, the delegate methods, or the concept of first responder, check back in Chapter 5, where we go through it in more detail.

Now it's time to edit the "ViewController.m" file

# Editing the Code

In this section you're going to edit the code in ViewController.m. You'll set up the delegate functionality and handle UITextField events. You'll also write a custom method that will be shared between multiple actions.

## Managing the UITextFieldDelegate

First off, because you set it up to be a UITextFieldDelegate, you should do a little setup and housecleaning.

Within your viewDidLoad method, as you called the textfield txtAddress, set the delegate for txtAddress to be self.

```
- (void)viewDidLoad
{
    [super viewDidLoad];
        // Do any additional setup after loading the view, typically from a nib.
    _txtAddress.delegate = self;
}
```

In order for the "Return" key to work on the keyboard, you also need to create a textFieldShouldReturn method. As this class is a UITextFieldDelegate, there's a specific syntax that you need to call. Go to the bottom of the file, just above @end, and start typing the letters -te; a hint window will pop up. See Figure 11-6.

```
-textFieldShouldReturn:
M  (BOOL)textField:(UITextField *)textField shouldChangeCharactersInRange:(NSRange)range replacementString:(NS...
M  (void)textFieldDidBeginEditing:(UITextField *)textField
M  (void)textFieldDidEndEditing:(UITextField *)textField
M  (BOOL)textFieldShouldBeginEditing:(UITextField *)textField
M  (BOOL)textFieldShouldClear:(UITextField *)textField
M  (BOOL)textFieldShouldEndEditing:(UITextField *)textField
M  (BOOL)textFieldShouldReturn:(UITextField *)textField
M  (NSString *)textInputContextIdentifier
Asks the delegate if the text field should process the pressing of the return button. More...
```

*Figure 11-6. Adding the textFieldShouldReturn method*

Choose the textFieldShouldReturn method from the list and press "Enter" to insert the declaration.

Within this code you should read the address of the textField. Then use this to generate a call to the Internet for that address and load the results into the web view. However, because you will also be doing the same thing in the "Go" button, you're not going to write all that code in the textFieldShouldReturn method. Instead, in a few moments you'll write a method called "CallWeb" and use that to manage the web view. Within textFieldShouldReturn, you'll just call this method.

Enter this code:

```
-(BOOL)textFieldShouldReturn:(UITextField *)textField
{
    NSString *addr = _txtAddress.text;
    [_txtAddress resignFirstResponder];
    [self CallWeb:addr];

    return true;
}
```

Let's look at this line by line:

```
NSString *addr = _txtAddress.text;
```

This will simply take the text that the user entered and use the `NSString` variable `addr` to reference it.

```
[_txtAddress resignFirstResponder];
```

You learned about first responders in Chapter 5. This line simply resigns first responder status from `_txtAddress`, having the effect of dismissing the keyboard.

```
[self CallWeb:addr];
```

This will give you an error at the moment because you haven't written the `CallWeb` method yet. Don't worry about that for now; just make sure you enter the code as shown. This will call the `CallWeb` method and pass it the address that was typed in.

```
return true;
```

The method has finished executing, so just return true to let the operating system know you're done, and everything is fine!

## Creating the Custom CallWeb Method

The custom text field method that you just wrote calls a method named `CallWeb`, which hasn't been created yet. It used the syntax `[self CallWeb:addr]`, which gives a hint as to where and how you should write the code for this method.

First, as it is in "self," it should be written in `ViewController.m`. Second, as you pass `addr` to it, which is an `NSString*`, you should create it to be able to accept an `NSString*`.

Here's what that should look like:

```
-(void)CallWeb:(NSString *)addr
{
}
```

When using the web view control, you can tell it to go to a page using an `NSURLRequest` object. This object can be initialized using an `NSURL` object, which contains the URL of the resource that you want to load.

---

**Tip**    If you're not familiar with the term "URL," it means *Uniform Resource Locator*, and it's a way of defining addresses on the Internet. URLs are commonly confused with addresses, and they're not exactly the same. When using a URL, the protocol used to determine the content also needs to be specified. Typically when thinking of web sites, where the protocol is http://, we refer to URL and address interchangeably, but this not exactly correct. Http stands for *Hypertext Transfer Protocol*, and, along with its secure cousin https://, where the "s" stands for *Secure*, it is the standard method for browsing pages on the Internet.

---

So, for example, the web site ios7developer.com has ios7developer.com as its address, but http://ios7developer.com or http://www.ios7developer.com as its URL.

Consider the case of an FTP site—for the preceding site, the address of the ftp site is still ios7developer.com, but the URL is ftp://ios7developer.com.

So, our addr variable has the address of the site, but we need to turn this into a URL by using an NSURL object before we can create a web request using an NSURLRequest object.

In Objective-C we can do that like this:

```
NSURL *url = [NSURL URLWithString:addr];
NSURLRequest *theRequest = [NSURLRequest requestWithURL:url];
```

The first line simply creates an NSURL object called url and initializes it using the string addr. Similarly, the second line uses an NSURL object to generate a request.

Now, to use this request so as to have the web view load the page, we simply use the loadRequest message on the web view, like this:

```
[_webView loadRequest:theRequest];
```

This would work very well, but it requires the user to type the http:// before every address, because if you remember the preceding example, a name like ios7developer.com is an address, and not a URL, and if you ask the web view to load ios7developer.com it'll get confused and do nothing.

So let's do a little coding and take a look at the address that comes in. If it has the text "http://" in it, we'll use it. If not, we'll add "http://" to the front of it.

Here's the code:

```
NSString *urlString;
addr = [addr lowercaseString];
if([addr rangeOfString:@"http://"].location == NSNotFound)
{
    urlString = @"http://";
    urlString = [urlString stringByAppendingString:addr];
}
else
{
    urlString = addr;
}
NSURL *url = [NSURL URLWithString:urlString];
```

First, we create a new NSString called urlString and leave it uninitialized and empty. Then we convert the address that was passed to the method (addr) to lower case. This makes it easier to compare, and because typical URLs are not case sensitive, we can do this.

Then, using the rangeOfString message on addr, we can determine if the text "http://" is present. If it isn't, the result of its location will be NSNotFound. In that case, urlString will be set to the text "http://," and then addr will be appended to that. If it is present, then urlString will just be set to whatever was in addr.

Then we go ahead and create the NSURL as before.

Here's the complete method:

```
-(void)CallWeb:(NSString *)addr
{
    NSString *urlString;
    addr = [addr lowercaseString];
    if([addr rangeOfString:@"http://"].location == NSNotFound)
    {
        urlString = @"http://";
        urlString = [urlString stringByAppendingString:addr];
    }
    else
    {
        urlString = addr;
    }
    NSURL *url = [NSURL URLWithString:urlString];
    NSURLRequest *theRequest = [NSURLRequest requestWithURL:url];
    [_webView loadRequest:theRequest];
}
```

You're almost done. Before running the app, you'll just need to add code to the actions you already created.

## Coding the Action Methods

Earlier, you created action methods called GoPressed for when the user pressed the Go button and AddressChanged for whenever the contents of the text field changed. In this case, if the user changes the contents of the text field and then taps elsewhere on the screen, the event will fire.

For both of these methods you do pretty much what you did in textFieldShouldReturn—get the address, resign the first responder, and call the CallWeb method.

Here's the code:

```
- (IBAction)AddressChanged:(id)sender {
    NSString *addr = _txtAddress.text;
    [_txtAddress resignFirstResponder];
    [self CallWeb:addr];

}

- (IBAction)GoPressed:(id)sender {
    NSString *addr = _txtAddress.text;
    [_txtAddress resignFirstResponder];
    [self CallWeb:addr];
}
```

And that's everything you need. Run the app and give it a try.

> **Note** You have the same lines of code in AddressChanged, GoPressed, and textFieldShouldReturn. This is violating a general principle called DRY (don't repeat yourself). As an exercise, how would you avoid this? Hint: Some of this code could be added to CallWeb. We'll give you the answer in the next section.

# Running the App

Now if you run the app you just created, you'll see that you have a basic web browser of your own! Try it by typing an address and then either pressing the "Return" key on the keyboard or clicking the "Go" button. See Figure 11-7 to see it in action!

*Figure 11-7. Using your embedded browser*

This isn't just a dumb rendering of HTML—it's a fully functional browser. For example, in Figure 11-7, we visited Amazon.com and searched for a book using Amazon's search engine. The results are shown in the mobile browser view.

> **Note**   Yes, that's a real book, and it's one of my novels, so I guess this is a shameless self-plug. Sorry about that. ☺ *Laurence Moroney*

For your convenience, here's the full code, with changes made to prevent DRY.

```objc
#import "ViewController.h"

@interface ViewController ()

@end

@implementation ViewController

- (void)viewDidLoad
{
    [super viewDidLoad];
        // Do any additional setup after loading the view, typically from a nib.
    _txtAddress.delegate = self;
}

- (void)didReceiveMemoryWarning
{
    [super didReceiveMemoryWarning];
    // Dispose of any resources that can be recreated.
}

- (IBAction)AddressChanged:(id)sender {
    [self CallWeb];
}

- (IBAction)GoPressed:(id)sender {
    [self CallWeb];
}

-(BOOL)textFieldShouldReturn:(UITextField *)textField
{
    [self CallWeb];
    return true;
}

-(void)CallWeb
{
    NSString *addr = _txtAddress.text;
    [_txtAddress resignFirstResponder];
```

```
    NSString *urlString;
    addr = [addr lowercaseString];
    if([addr rangeOfString:@"http://"].location == NSNotFound)
    {
        urlString = @"http://";
        urlString = [urlString stringByAppendingString:addr];
    }
    else
    {
        urlString = addr;
    }
    NSURL *url = [NSURL URLWithString:urlString];
    NSURLRequest *theRequest = [NSURLRequest requestWithURL:url];
    [_webView loadRequest:theRequest];
}
@end
```

# Creating an Internet-Connected App

In the previous section, you saw how to create an app that used a web view to connect to the Internet and render the contents of a web site. But how about if you don't want your app to show a web page, and instead want it to render data that it gets off the web? In this section, you'll learn how to do that by building an app that serves random inspirational quotes from Martin Luther King, Jr., sourced off the web.

You can see the quotes by visiting `http://ios7developer.com/book/quotes.php` or `http://mlk-quotes.appspot.com/quotes`.

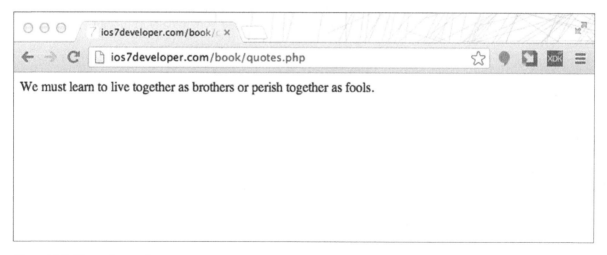

*Figure 11-8.  The quotes service*

To create an app that consumes this service and gives you a random Martin Luther King, Jr. quote, create a new single view application. Open its "Main.storyboard" file and add a label and a button.

Make the label large enough to fill the top half of the screen and add the button beneath it. Change the title for the button to "Get Quotes." Your screen should look like Figure 11-9.

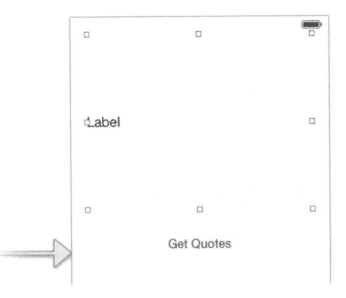

*Figure 11-9. Adding the label and the button*

With the label selected, open the attributes inspector and change the number of lines to 0 (it was 1 when you placed the label), and then set the "Line Breaks" setting to "Word Wrap." See Figure 11-10. Setting the number of lines to 0 like this makes the label size itself dynamically to fit your text.

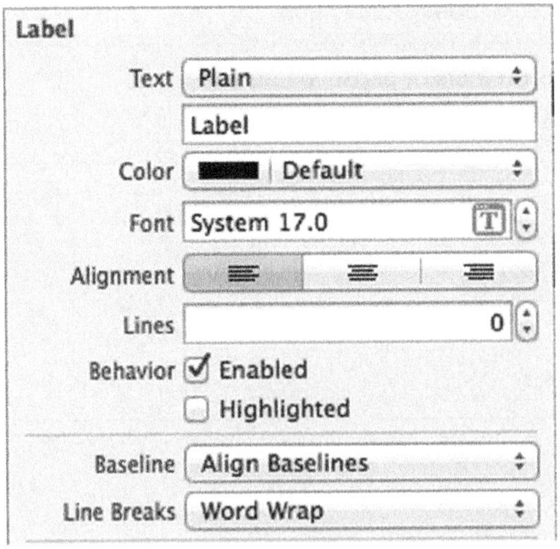

*Figure 11-10. Setting the label attributes*

Next, create an outlet for the label and call it "lblQuote."

Create an action for the button and call it "btnGetQuote."

When you're done, your ViewController.h should look like this:

```
#import <UIKit/UIKit.h>

@interface ViewController : UIViewController
@property (strong, nonatomic) IBOutlet UILabel *lblQuote;
- (IBAction)btnGetQuote:(id)sender;

@end
```

Once you've finished editing that, it's time to edit your "ViewController.m" file to implement the code that will execute when the user clicks the button.

You'll be using the stringWithContentsOfURL message on the NSString object to get the data. This requires you to have an NSError object, which will catch any communications errors, so declare that first. All this code will be in the btnQuote method.

```
NSError *error=nil;
```

Next, you'll create an NSURL object and initialize it with the string containing the address of the service.

```
NSURL *theURL = [NSURL URLWithString:@
        "http://mlk-quotes.appspot.com/quotes"];
```

Once you have the NSURL, you can use it to populate a string. You'll have to specify an encoding and the place to put any errors. *Encoding* is how text is represented on your computer and how it is transmitted across the Internet. The most common format for straight, English text is called ASCII (American Standard Code for Information Interchange), which is represented by the NSASCIIStringEncoding constant.

Here's the code:

```
NSString *theQuote = [NSString stringWithContentsOfURL:theURL encoding:NSASCIIStringEncoding
error:&error];
```

If you have a connection to the Internet, and if the service is running correctly, you'll get a string returned to theQuote—otherwise the string will be empty.

You can check this by inserting if(theQuote), which will return true if there's something in the string and false otherwise. If there's something in the string, you can load it into the label. If there isn't, you can load the details of the error into the string.

Here's the code:

```
if(theQuote)
{
    _lblQuote.text = theQuote;

}
else
{
    _lblQuote.text = [NSString stringWithFormat:@"Error, can't get quote. Details:%@",error];
}
```

Here's the full btnGetQuote function:

```
- (IBAction)btnGetQuote:(id)sender {
    NSError *error=nil;
    NSURL *theURL = [NSURL URLWithString:@"http://mlk-quotes.appspot.com/quotes"];
    NSString *theQuote = [NSString stringWithContentsOfURL:theURL encoding:NSASCIIStringEncoding
error:&error];
    if(theQuote)
    {
        _lblQuote.text = theQuote;

    }
    else
    {
        _lblQuote.text = [NSString stringWithFormat:@"Error, can't get quote. Details:%@",error];
    }
}
```

Now if you run the app and click the "Get Quotes" button, you'll see a random, inspirational quote.
See Figure 11-11.

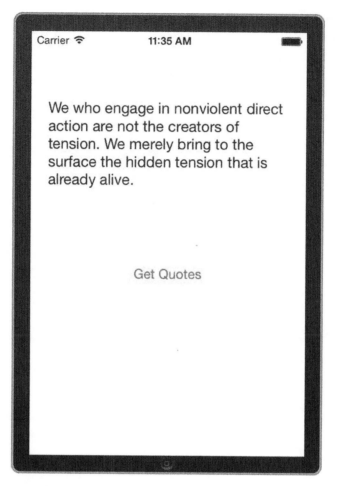

*Figure 11-11. The Internet-connected quote app*

This service has 33 quotes and serves one at random each time it's called. See which one is your favorite!

I personally like "The time is always right to do what is right." See if you can get the app to render it!

String data is relatively trivial, so let's look at one more example—one in which you download an image from the web and render it in your app.

# Download an Image from the Web

In this section you'll create an app that's similar to the one from the previous section, in which you press a button to download content from the web. In this case, the content will be a bit more sophisticated than a string—you'll download an image.

Create a new single view application and call it "downloadImageTest." Open Main.storyboard and add an "image view" control and a button to it.

Make the image view about 2/3 of the height of the screen. Center the button and give it the title "Get Image." See Figure 11-12.

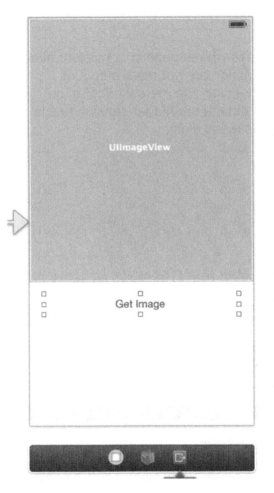

*Figure 11-12.  Laying out the image view app*

Create an outlet for the image view and call it "imgPic."

Create an action for the button and call it "btnGetImage."

When you're done, your ViewController.h should look like this:

```
#import <UIKit/UIKit.h>

@interface ViewController : UIViewController
@property (strong, nonatomic) IBOutlet UIImageView *imgPic;
- (IBAction)btnGetImage:(id)sender;

@end
```

Now it's time to edit your ViewController.m to implement the code for btnGetImage.

First, create an NSString to hold the address of the image:

```
NSString *urlString = @"http://mlk-quotes.appspot.com/mlk.jpg";
```

This string can be used to create an NSURL object, as follows:

```
NSURL *url = [NSURL URLWithString:urlString];
```

Data can be downloaded into an NSData object, and this, similar to the string earlier, can be initialized using a URL. So, to load the binary data that represents the picture, you can create an NSData object like this:

```
NSData * imageData = [[NSData alloc] initWithContentsOfURL: url];
```

At this point, it's not a picture—it's just the data representing the picture. To turn the NSData object into a picture, you can use it to create a UIImage object. This object can be assigned to the image property of the image view in order to render the image.

Here's the code:

```
_imgPic.image = [UIImage imageWithData: imageData];
```

At this point the image view has the image and will draw it.

Here's the entire code for btnGetImage:

```
- (IBAction)btnGetImage:(id)sender {
    NSString *urlString = @"http://mlk-quotes.appspot.com/mlk.jpg";
    NSURL *url = [NSURL URLWithString:urlString];
    NSData * imageData = [[NSData alloc] initWithContentsOfURL: url];
    _imgPic.image = [UIImage imageWithData: imageData];

}
```

Now if you run the app and click the button, you'll see the image get downloaded and rendered into the image view.

See Figure 11-13.

*Figure 11-13. The image download app in action*

Hopefully this has whetted your appetite for the types of apps you can build with Internet connectivity!

# Summary

In this chapter you learned about connecting your app to the web. You saw how to use the "Web View" control to create a simple web browser app, which allowed you to render web sites. You then went under the hood to learn how to write code that downloaded data from the web, first by calling a cloud service that gave you a random inspirational quote, and then by downloading a web image and rendering it in your app. While these scenarios are relatively simple, they give you the building blocks for typical web applications. Hopefully these examples have been as inspirational as the quotes from the cloud service!

# iPad Considerations

You're almost at the end of this book; congratulations for making it this far! While the book is described as being for iPhone *and* iPad development, you've mostly focused on iPhone thus far. The good news is that this is because the skills for an iPhone developer are almost 100% the same as those for an iPad developer. There are a few minor differences that you need to take into account when dealing with the iPad, and they revolve around the different screen size, also known as the *form factor*.

In this chapter you'll take a look at a typical iPad application, and you'll explore the differences for some common scenarios by building them yourself.

## App Navigation on the iPad

In Chapter 9, you looked at the "Table View" control and saw how it is used for in-app navigation to content. Perhaps the biggest difference between building for the iPad and building for the iPhone lies in how you do this. To see an example, consider the email app that ships with your iOS device. Figure 12-1 shows how this looks on an iPhone.

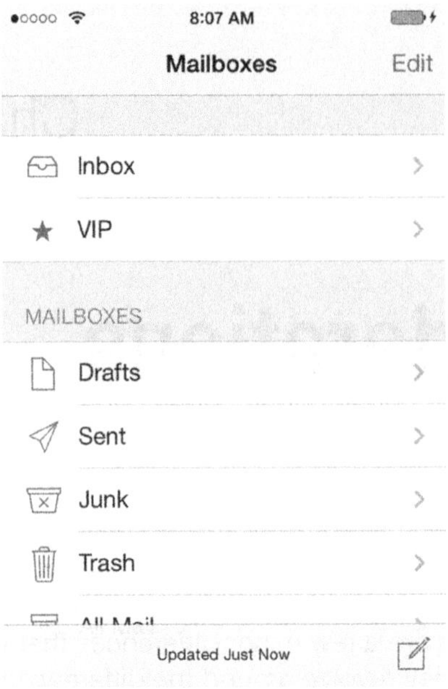

*Figure 12-1.  The email app on an iPhone*

As you can see, it's basically a table view with a number of sections. When you select a section—for example, "Inbox"—the same table-based navigation as you saw in Chapter 9 occurs—the table slides away revealing the next set of content. So, for example, if we choose the inbox, we'll see something like Figure 12-2, which is also a table view!

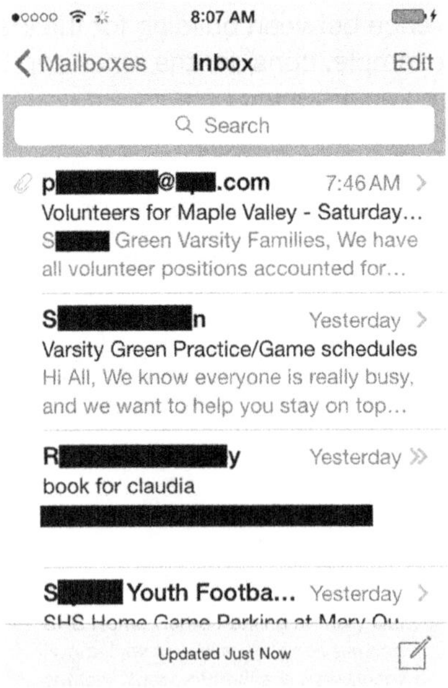

*Figure 12-2.  The email inbox is a table view*

And, as you can see, each mail item is a cell in the table view. Selecting it navigates to the email item, as shown in Figure 12-3.

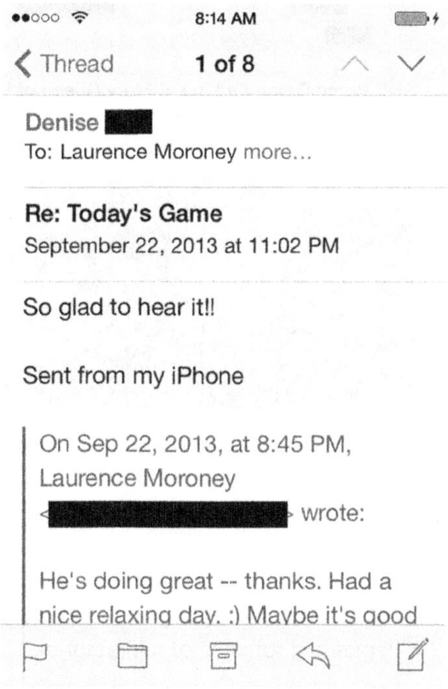

*Figure 12-3. An email item on the iPhone*

Consider how different things are on the iPad with the same application. Figure 12-4 shows the email application on the iPad. Notice that because the list of mailboxes doesn't need to take up the entire screen, a preview of a mail item can be shown on the right-hand side. On the iPad, the last email item that you read is shown on the screen.

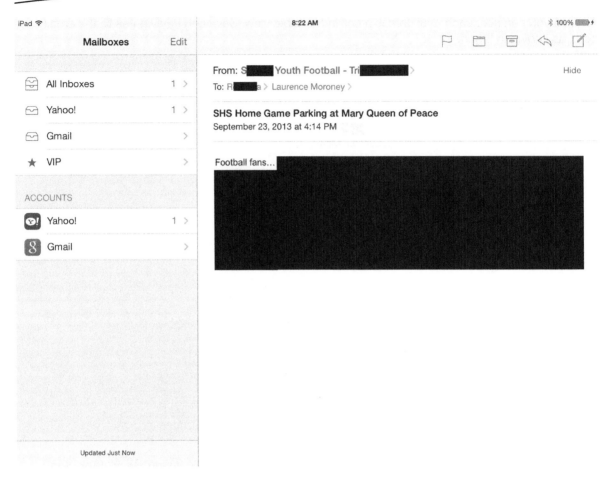

*Figure 12-4. The email App on the iPad*

The list of mailboxes is still a table view, so you can navigate within it. Selecting a mailbox yields the view in Figure 12-5.

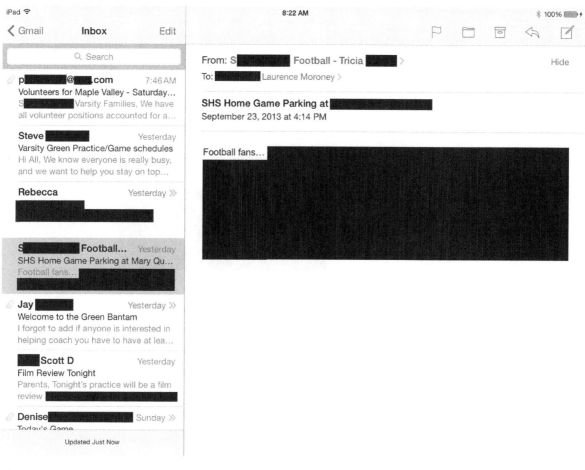

*Figure 12-5. Inbox view*

The table view on the left navigates to the view of your inbox, just as it did on the iPhone version of the app. The right-hand side is used to view the email, so you don't need an additional click to move "in" to the mail and back "out" to the inbox like you do with the iPhone.

The iPad version also needs to consider portrait orientation, where you hold the iPad so that the horizontal axis is shorter than the vertical one. You can see this in Figure 12-6.

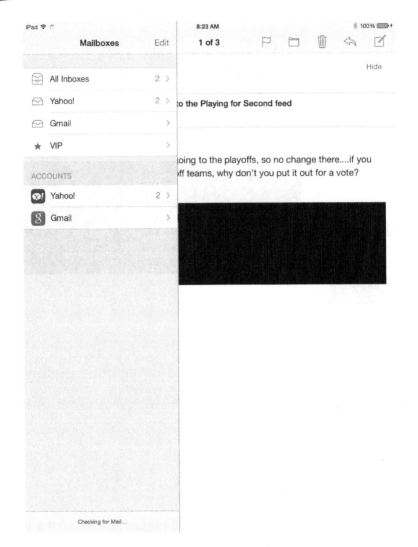

*Figure 12-6.* *iPad in portrait mode*

In this case, the menu to the left, while still a table view, becomes a pop over: it lies on top of the underlying content, instead of being to the left of it. This is more apparent when you navigate to a mail item. You can see this in Figure 12-7.

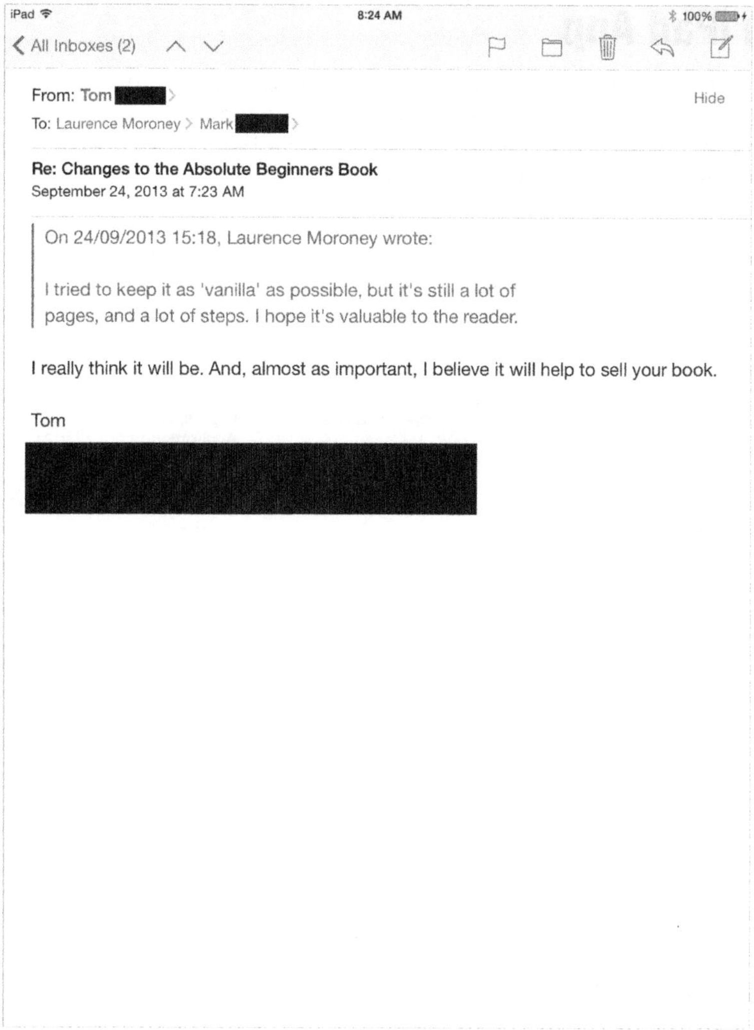

*Figure 12-7. Looking at a mail item in portrait mode*

On the top right-hand side of the screen, you can see a link "back" to all inboxes. On an iPhone, this would move you away from the mail message to show the inbox or list of inboxes, as that is all the screen real estate allows. On the iPad, the list will pop over the mail item as you saw back in Figure 12-6.

To be able to build for the iPad, you'll need to understand how to do this common scenario for yourself, so in the next section you'll do exactly that.

# Building an iPad App

Start up Xcode and create a new project. Instead of the Single View Application you've been building throughout this book, let's go a little deeper. While any of the templates can be used on an iPad, we'll use one that is very similar to the email app that you've been looking at. Select the Master-Detail Application type, as shown in Figure 12-8.

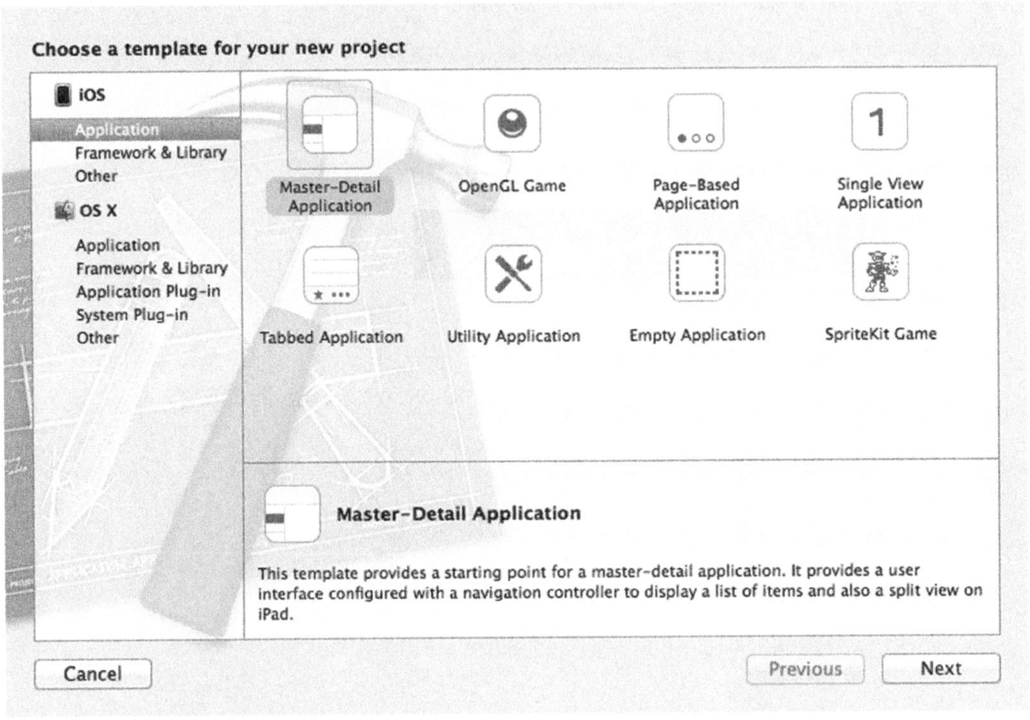

*Figure 12-8.* Building a new app

When asked to choose options for your new project, use the Product Name "characters" as shown in Figure 12-9. Ensure that the Devices selection is set to "iPad." The "Universal" setting creates an app that builds for both iPad and iPhone, with different storyboards for each. For the sake of simplicity, we're just doing iPad here. If "Use Core Data" is selected, uncheck the box.

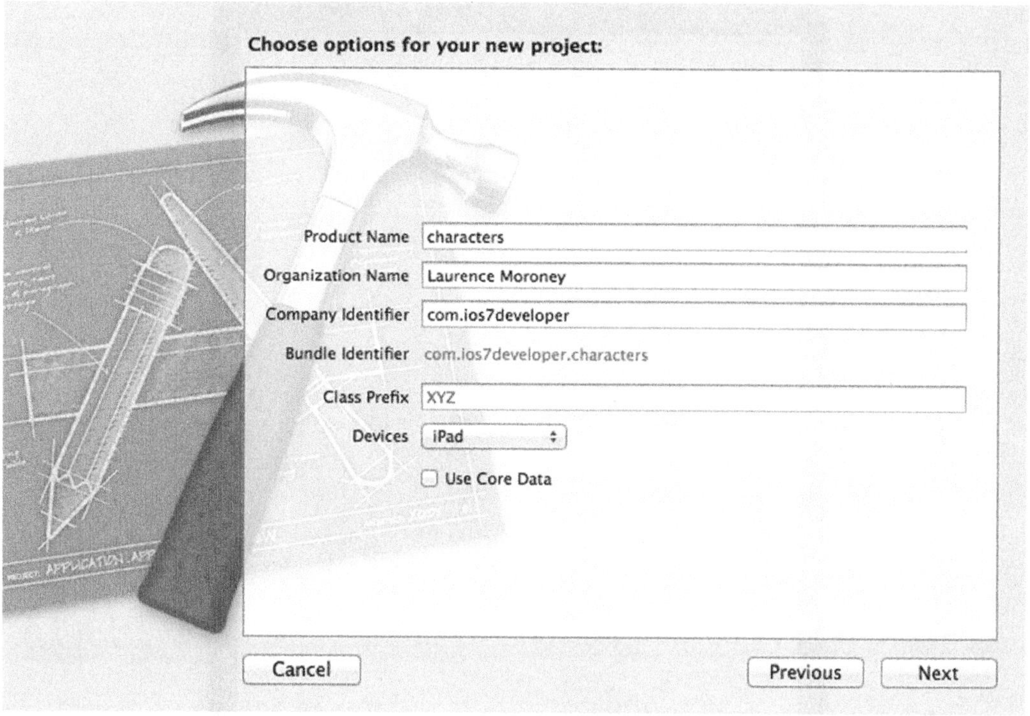

*Figure 12-9. Options for your new project*

Finish the steps and Xcode will create the app for you. Run it on the iPad simulator, where you should see something like Figure 12-10.

*Figure 12-10. Running the master-detail app*

As you can see, it is running in portrait mode, which the simulator defaults to. The detail view is analogous to the email message within the mail app, and the master content is analogous to your inbox. You can see "Master" in the top left-hand side of the screen, and, if you click on it, the master list will pop up. See Figure 12-11.

*Figure 12-11.* *Viewing the master list*

Clicking on the "+" will add new details to the master list, with the current time stamp. Select any of these, and the detail view will show that content.

To see the iPad in landscape mode, you can select "Rotate Left" under the hardware menu. In this orientation, the master list is "docked" to the left of the screen, and selecting any item will show its content in the detail area. See Figure 12-12.

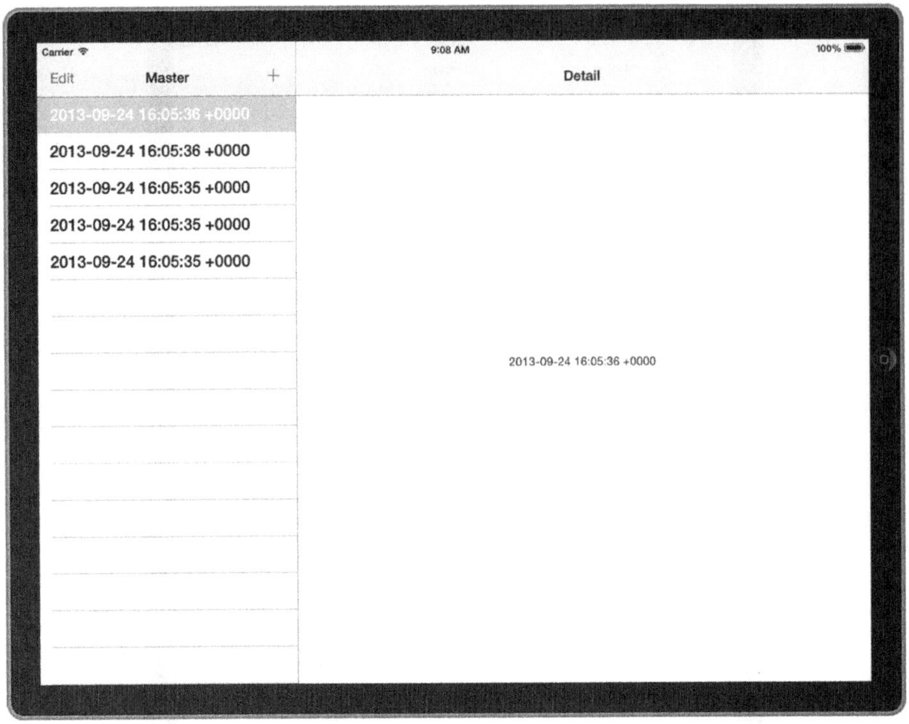

*Figure 12-12. Viewing the master-detail app in landscape mode*

Now that we see how the master-detail sample app works, let's edit it to create a simple app of our own.

## Investigating the Storyboard

Open Main.storyboard, and you'll see something like Figure 12-13. The storyboard in this app is very complex, but don't worry, you'll get the hang of it by working through apps like this one.

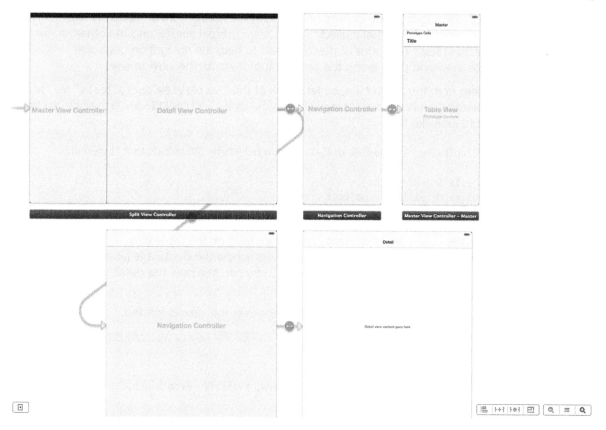

*Figure 12-13. The master-detail storyboard*

The box on the top left might look familiar—it's the overall app, with the master view controller docked to the left of the detail view controller. Navigation in the app is controlled through a table view, as shown on the top left, and the navigation controller regulates the contents of the detail view, as shown at the bottom.

The detail view has a label that says "Detail View Content Goes Here." Before going further and editing the storyboard, consider how that gets updated.

Take a look at DetailViewController.h, and you'll see this code:

```
#import <UIKit/UIKit.h>

@interface DetailViewController : UIViewController<UISplitViewControllerDelegate>

@property (strong, nonatomic) id detailItem;

@property (weak, nonatomic) IBOutletUILabel *detailDescriptionLabel;
@end
```

Note that even though there is only one control on the view, the label, there are actually two properties. One is the outlet for the label (called "detailDescriptionLabel"), and the other is something called "detailItem." The latter of these is used to help the navigation controller communicate with the view and pass along the content that it wants the view to see.

The user picks the item from the master list, so let's look at the "MasterViewController.m" file, where the code resides. Selecting an item on a table view fires the didSelectRowAtIndexPath code, so take a look at that. It should look like this:

```
- (void)tableView:(UITableView *)tableView didSelectRowAtIndexPath:(NSIndexPath *)indexPath
{
NSDate *object = _objects[indexPath.row];
self.detailViewController.detailItem = object;
}
```

As you can see, when the user selects an item, the current item on the table view is selected and is set to the detailItem of the detailViewController. This is how the content is passed to the view. When you look at the "detailViewController.m" file, you can see how the detail view controller handles it.

Take a look at its viewDidLoad method. This is called whenever the view is loaded.

```
- (void)viewDidLoad
{
    [superviewDidLoad];
        // Do any additional setup after loading the view, typically from a nib.
    [selfconfigureView];
}
```

Every time you've seen that function so far in this book, you've probably seen the [super viewDidLoad] call, but the [self configureView] is new. So let's take a look at it:

```
- (void)configureView
{
// Update the user interface for the detail item.

if (self.detailItem) {
self.detailDescriptionLabel.text = [self.detailItemdescription];
    }
}
```

As you can see, this function checks to see if something has been passed into it, and if something has been, the function sets the text of the label to the description of the item that was passed in.

Let's now change the app so that instead of allowing the user to add random times and dates to the master list, you'll add a static list of people that are characters from a book.

---

**Tip** If you haven't already looked at Chapter 9, it's a good idea to do so before continuing. Many of the concepts of building table view content that you'll use in this section are already covered there.

There are a few changes you'll need to make to MasterViewController.m. First, go to the viewDidLoad method. It should look like this:

```
- (void)viewDidLoad
{
    [superviewDidLoad];
        // Do any additional setup after loading the view, typically from a nib.
self.navigationItem.leftBarButtonItem = self.editButtonItem;

UIBarButtonItem *addButton = [[UIBarButtonItemalloc]
initWithBarButtonSystemItem:UIBarButtonSystemItemAddtarget:selfaction:@selector(insertNewObject:)];
self.navigationItem.rightBarButtonItem = addButton;
self.detailViewController = (DetailViewController *)[[self.splitViewController.
viewControllerslastObject] topViewController];
}
```

Delete all but the first and last lines. The code you are removing provides the user with the ability to add or remove content from the master list. You're going to provide a static list of names instead. You can initialize that static list in viewDidLoad. When you're done, your code should look like this:

```
- (void)viewDidLoad
{
    [superviewDidLoad];
_objects = [[NSMutableArrayalloc] initWithObjects:
@"Fintan",
@"Zack",
@"Ayako",
@"Nizhoni",
@"Sinclair",
@"Iara",
nil];

        self.detailViewController = (DetailViewController *)[[self.splitViewController.
viewControllerslastObject] topViewController];
}
```

If you run your app on the iPad simulator, you'll see something like Figure 12-14.

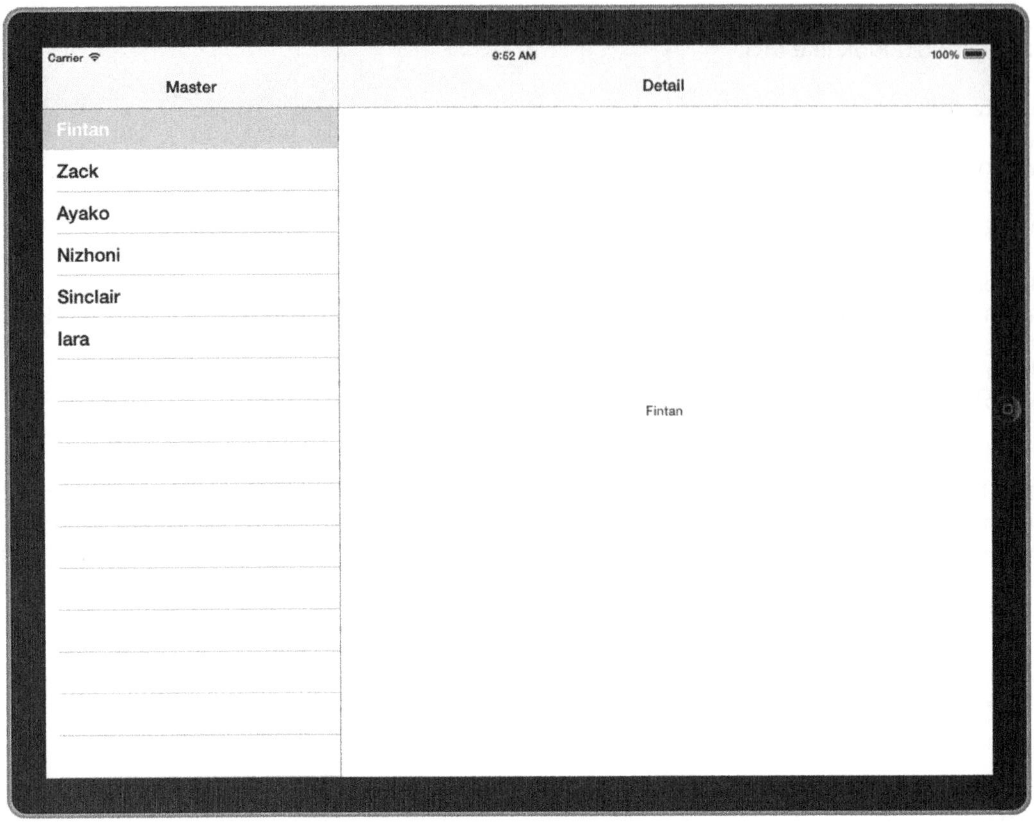

*Figure 12-14. The characters app with a static master list*

You'll notice that when you select a character name, the name appears in the detail view. But let's make that a little more interesting and have it render a picture of that character instead.

As you might recall from earlier in this section, the configureView method in DetailViewController.m executes when someone makes a selection from the list. Select DetailViewController.m from the project navigator and take a look. It sets the text of detailDescriptionLabel based on the description of the navigation item. That's why it now renders the name of the character instead of the time and date as it did earlier. As a recap, here's the code:

```
- (void)configureView
{
// Update the user interface for the detail item.

if (self.detailItem) {
self.detailDescriptionLabel.text = [self.detailItemdescription];
    }
}
```

Let's update it so that it renders the address of an image instead. The address of the image will be `http://ios7developer.com/book/<character name>.jpg`, so the code to do that is here:

```
- (void)configureView
{
if (self.detailItem) {
NSString *imageAddress = [NSStringstringWithFormat:@"http://ios7developer.com/book/%@.jpg",
[self.detailItemdescription]];
        imageAddress = [imageAddress lowercaseString];
self.detailDescriptionLabel.text = imageAddress;
    }
}
```

This builds an NSString called "imageAddress" with the preceding format and then converts it to lower case.

> **Tip** The `stringWithFormat` message on `NSString` is used to construct strings. Locations in this string with the characters %@ will be replaced by strings, so in this case you can see that the filename `%@.jpg` will become <character name>.jpg

The code then renders the address into the detailDescriptionLabel. See Figure 12-15 for how that will appear at run time.

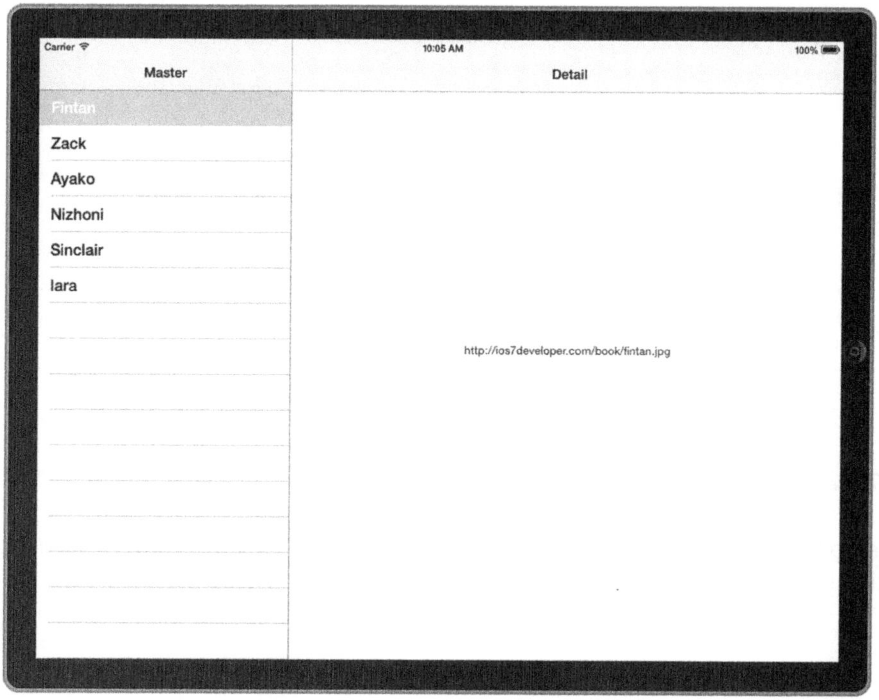

*Figure 12-15.* *Rendering the address of the image*

Of course, it would be much better if the code rendered the image instead of the address, so you'll do that next.

---

**Tip**    Many web servers are case sensitive for paths, so the file `http://ios7developer.com/book/Fintan.jpg` might be different from `http://ios7developer.com/fintan.jpg`. As such, it's somewhat of a standard that you use all lowercase in defining URLs in order to keep things simple. The master list capitalized the names, as it should, so we convert that to lowercase in order to create the URL.

---

Go back to your Main.storyboard file and zoom in on the detail view design. See Figure 12-16.

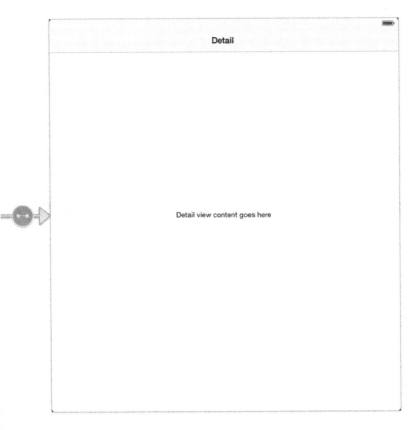

*Figure 12-16. The detail view controller design*

Drag the label toward the bottom of the view and make the font larger. Also add a UIImageView and change the title to read "Picture." See Figure 12-17.

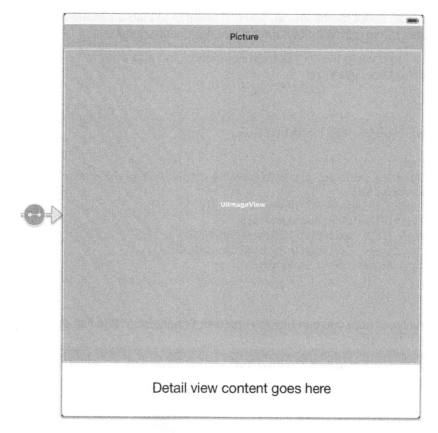

*Figure 12-17. Designing the detail view*

Using the assistant, CTRL-drag the UIImageView to DetailViewController.h and create an outlet
called "imgCharacterPicture."

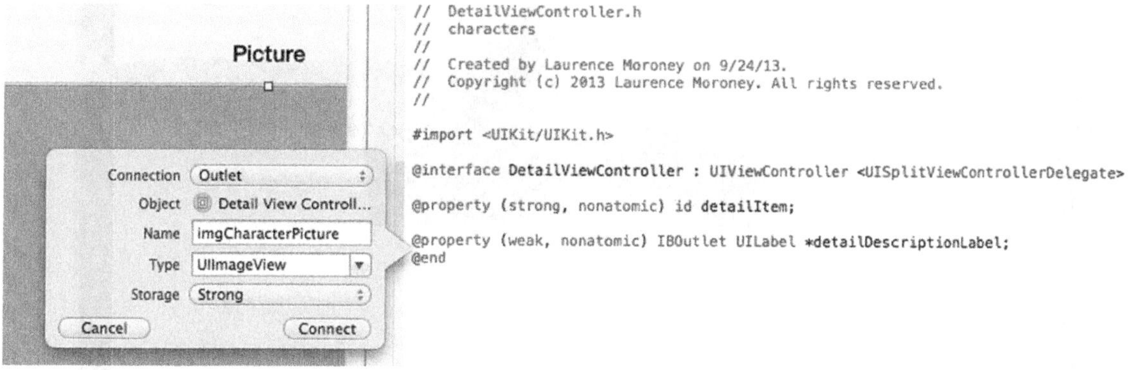

*Figure 12-18. Creating the outlet for the image*

Now that you have an outlet for the image, you can use this to load an image from a URL. This was covered in Chapter 11, so review that chapter if you need more detail.

To load the image, go back to the configureView function and add code to have it load the image into imgCharacterPicture, like this:

```
- (void)configureView
{
// Update the user interface for the detail item.

if (self.detailItem) {
NSString *imageAddress = [NSStringstringWithFormat:@"http://ios7developer.com/book/%@.jpg",
[self.detailItemdescription]];
        imageAddress = [imageAddress lowercaseString];
NSURL *url = [NSURLURLWithString:imageAddress];
NSData * imageData = [[NSDataalloc] initWithContentsOfURL: url];
_imgCharacterPicture.image = [UIImageimageWithData: imageData];
self.detailDescriptionLabel.text = imageAddress;
    }
}
```

Now when you run your app, you can browse images of characters. See Figure 12-19.

*Figure 12-19. Running the "Character Browser" app on an iPad*

The app works naturally in portrait mode too, as you can see in Figure 12-20.

*Figure 12-20. Running the app in portrait mode*

And that's it! You've just built your first iPad app, which has some of the same basic functionality as the email app that comes with iOS. Congratulations on taking this step in your journey.

> **Note**    These characters are from the novels *The Fourth World*, *The Million-Year Journey,* and *The Legend of the Locust*, of which I'm the author. They are renders that were done to support a potential animated movie. *–Laurence Moroney*

# Summary

In this chapter you took a look at some of the differences in building iPad applications, a skill set that is an enhancement to the iPhone development skill sets that you've been working on throughout this book. You saw how to build a master-detail application that works in landscape and portrait modes and that uses the common design pattern of an iPad navigation app. In the next chapter, you'll wrap up your beginner's learning by stepping through the process of app store deployment.

# 13

# Deploying Your App to the App Store

Once you've built your app, you will probably want other people to use it. There are two ways of distributing your app. The first was outlined in Chapter 3, where you saw how you could deploy to a device. The process required you to have the device on hand so that you could add provisioning profiles to it. You were also limited to 100 devices for your entire developer account, so that option was somewhat limited. The second, and more typical, approach is to deploy your app to Apple's app store. It doesn't cost anything to do this, other than the developer account subscription of $99 per year.

If you haven't worked through Chapter 3 yet, you really need to do so before continuing with this chapter. The processes of signing up for a developer account and deploying to a physical device need to be completed before you can submit to the app store. You can't compile an app for the simulator and then deploy it to the store. It must have been built for a physical device first.

In this chapter, you'll see how to prepare your app for app store submission, including the attributes that you'll need to add to it. You'll also see how to use the iTunes Connect portal to define the app, before finally using Xcode to deploy the app to the app store.

## Preparing Your App for Store Deployment

There are a number of steps that you have to go through to prepare your app for store deployment. In this section, you'll go through what needs to be done for the typical iPhone app. This involves setting the application graphics for icons and for the launch screen, as well as signing the application with your deployment certificates.

# Setting the General Settings

The first step in preparing your app for store deployment is in the "General Settings" tab. To access this, ensure that your project is selected in the project navigator. See Figure 13-1, where we're working with the "Magic 8 Ball" app from Chapter 6.

*Figure 13-1.* *Selecting your project*

Once it's selected, you need to select the target compilation for your app. This is sometimes hard to find, because it's very discreet. Immediately to the right of the project navigator, you'll see the settings and a number of tabs, such as "General," "Capabilities," "Info," etc., as in Figure 13-2.

*Figure 13-2.* *Settings for your project*

You'll notice, to the left of where it says "magic8," there is a little right-pointing triangle. If you have this, click it, and a sidebar will appear with the target settings. See Figure 13-3. If you already have this sidebar, you're in good shape!

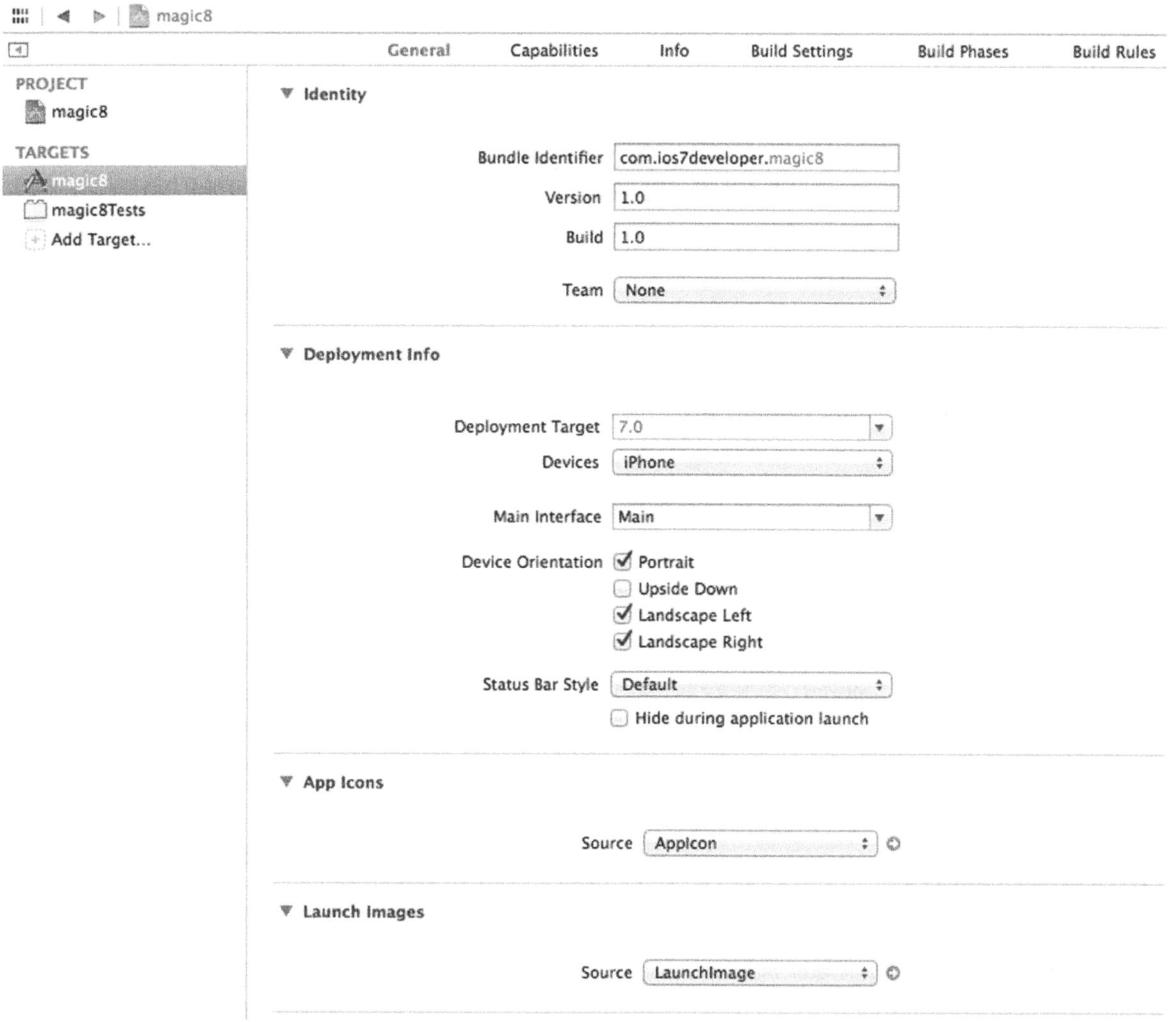

*Figure 13-3.  Project settings with sidebar*

You'll likely see two targets, as in Figure 13-3. One will be the name of your project, and one will be the name of your project postfixed with "Tests." If you don't see the latter, don't worry. You just need the main one, as shown in Figure 13-3.

## Editing App Identity

The "Identity" section has four main settings.

The "Bundle Identifier" is the name that you gave the app when you created it. If you want to change it, you can do so here, but it isn't necessary to do so at this point. You can see the "Version" and "Build" items are defaulting to 1.0. As you create updates to your application, you can change them here. For your first deployment, it's good to keep them at 1.0.

It's important to set the "Team" setting in order to be able to deploy to the app store. Here is where you specify who you are—and your certificate is used to sign the application. If you are a solo developer (like this example), Apple treats you as a team of one.

Select this setting and you should see your identifier with your account details for the iOS developer portal, as set up in Figure 13-4.

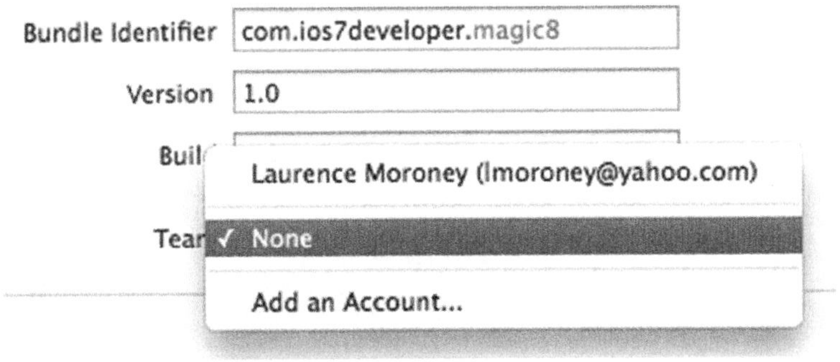

*Figure 13.4. Setting the "Team" settings*

If you don't see anything here, you should work through Chapter 3. If you see an entry, such as the "lmoroney@yahoo.com" one above, use it.

## Editing App Icons

Your app needs a number of icons for use by the app store, and for your end-users' iPhone home screens from which they will launch your app. You can set these up through the "app icons" section of the "General Settings" tab. See Figure 13-5.

*Figure 13-5. The app icons settings*

You'll see the setting reads "AppIcon" and has a right-pointing arrow beside it. Click this arrow, and you'll be taken to the icon editor.

*Figure 13-6. The app icon settings*

Here you'll see that there are three types of icon you need to set. The dialog isn't very clear on what size it wants them to be, so the best approach is to create three icons: one at 58x58, one at 80x80, and one at 120x120. They should all be in the PNG format.

> **Tip**  If you need a graphics application to create the required graphics, you don't need to buy an expensive one. There's a terrific, simple, lightweight app called Paintbrush that is open sourced and available for download from `http://paintbrush.sourceforge.net/`. This is what we have used throughout this book.

Once you have these images, you can drag and drop them onto the dotted boxes on the right-hand side of the screen. You can see what this would look like in Figure 13-7.

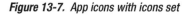

| 58 | 80 | 120 |
|---|---|---|
| 2x | 2x | 2x |
| iPhone Spotlight – iOS 5,6 Settings – iOS 5–7 29pt | iPhone Spotlight iOS 7 40pt | iPhone App iOS 7 60pt |

*Figure 13-7. App icons with icons set*

Once you've dropped your icons into the boxes, you'll see a preview of them in place of the dotted boxes. So, for example, in Figure 13-7, my 58x58 image has the number 58 in it, and so forth.

You also need to set the LaunchImage, so on the left side of the screen (see Figure 13-6 for an example), immediately below AppIcon, you'll see LaunchImage. Select it and you'll see the LaunchImage settings. See Figure 13-8.

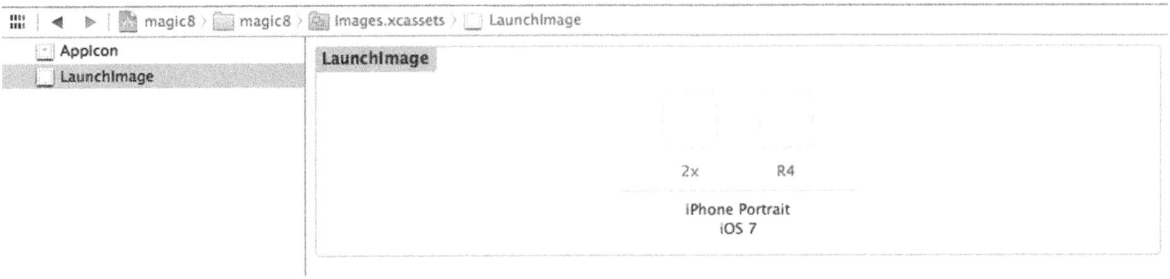

*Figure 13-8.* *The LaunchImage settings*

You'll see that there are two settings—one for 2x and one for R4. Again, it's not very clear, but what Xcode is expecting here is a 640x960 image for 2x and a 640x1136 image for R4. Create these images and drop them onto the dotted boxes. When you're done, your screen should look something like Figure 13-9, with previews of your images replacing the dotted boxes.

*Figure 13-9.* *LaunchImage with images set*

You should now compile your app and run it on either the simulator or your device. You should see one of your configured icons for the app on the iPhone's home screen. See Figure 13-10. You'll also see your launch screen graphics when the app launches.

*Figure 13-10.* *Your app on the home screen*

You've now finished the first set of steps that you need to follow to get your app ready for the app store. In the next section, you'll take a look at what you need to do to get the app store ready for your app!

# Creating Settings for Your App on iTunes Connect

iTunes Connect is the portal that you use to configure your apps in the app store marketplace, as well as to manage their availability, banking details (so that you can get paid), and all legal documents that you need to agree to in order to sell in different countries.

> **Note** To use iTunes Connect and the iOS developer center, you need to be a registered iOS developer. The process for signing up for this is documented in Chapter 3. You won't be able to access most of the functionality in this section until you do so.

iTunes Connect is integrated with the developer portal that you sign into as a registered user. You can find this portal at: `https://developer.apple.com/devcenter/ios/index.action`. When you sign in to this site, you'll see a sidebar for the iOS Developer Program on the right-hand side. See Figure 13-11.

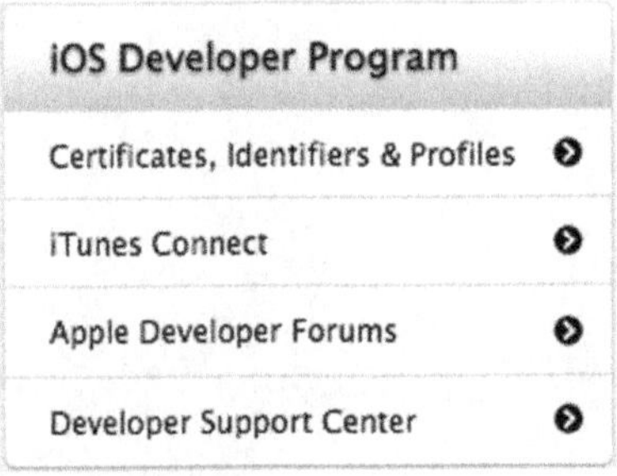

*Figure 13-11.  Finding iTunes Connect on the developer portal*

Select the iTunes Connect link and you'll be taken to the iTunes Connect portal. You can also link directly there by visiting `https://itunesconnect.apple.com/WebObjects/iTunesConnect.woa`. Sign in with the same Apple ID and password that you use to sign into the iOS developer center.

When you're signed in, you'll see the iTunes Connect portal. It should look like Figure 13-12.

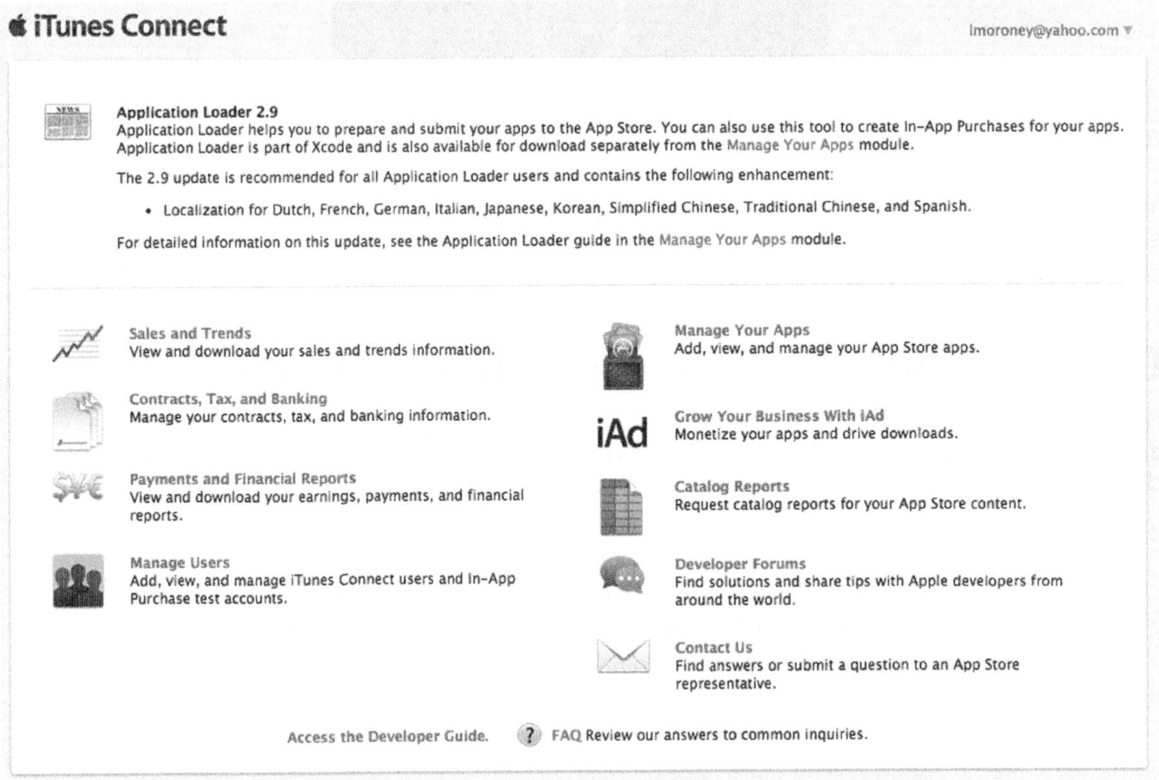

*Figure 13-12.  The iTunes Connect portal*

There's lots to do in here, including monitoring your sales and trends, handling taxes and banking, and so forth. There's a lot that goes beyond the scope of this book, so to focus on app deployment, you're going to select the "Manage Your Apps" option.

This will take you to a site that lists your recent iOS app activity, which shows, for example, which of your apps have recently gone on sale or have been removed from sale. At the top of the screen, you'll see a blue "Add New App" button. See Figure 13-13.

*Figure 13-13. Managing your apps in the iTunes Connect portal*

To add a new app, click the button, and if, like me, you subscribe to both iOS and Mac OS development, you'll be asked to select the app type. If you don't see this step, don't worry—it just means that you subscribe to one or the other, and the portal has taken you directly to the right place.

You can see this choice in Figure 13-14.

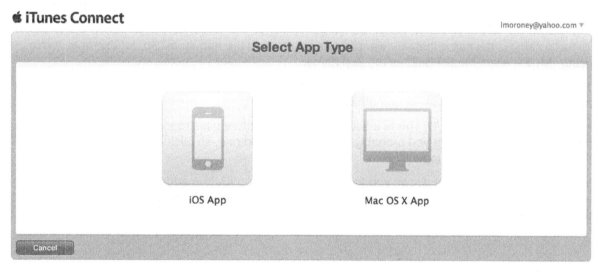

*Figure 13-14. Selecting the app type*

Select "iOS App" and you'll be taken to the App Information screen. See Figure 13-15.

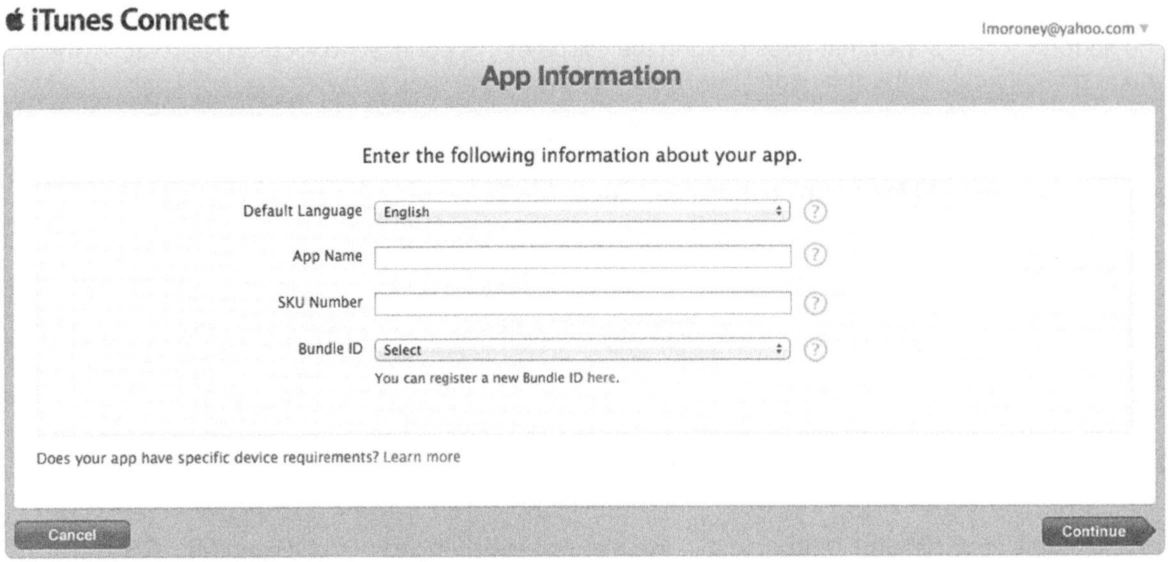

**⚹ iTunes Connect**                                                    lmoroney@yahoo.com ▾

## App Information

Enter the following information about your app.

Default Language    [ English                                    ↕ ]  (?)

App Name    [                                                      ]  (?)

SKU Number    [                                                    ]  (?)

Bundle ID    [ Select                                         ↕ ]  (?)
             You can register a new Bundle ID here.

Does your app have specific device requirements? Learn more

[ Cancel ]                                                    [ Continue ▸ ]

*Figure 13-15.* *App Information screen*

You need to specify the default language, app name, SKU number, and bundle ID in this section.

The *default language* should be, as expected, the language that your app is built for. In this case, we're leaving it as English.

The *app name* is the name that you want to give your app in the app store. So, for example, we're using "My Excellent Magic8Ball" as the app name.

The *SKU* is a code that you enter that helps you track your app amongst others if you deploy a lot of apps. You can just use "1234" or something similar here.

Finally, you need a *bundle ID*. This is a setting that the app store uses to identify your app and any future updates. At this point you probably haven't developed one, so click on the link where it says "You can register a new Bundle ID here."

You'll be taken to a site that allows you to register an iOS App ID. The address of this site is: https://developer.apple.com/account/ios/identifiers/bundle/bundleCreate.action. You can see this in Figure 13-16.

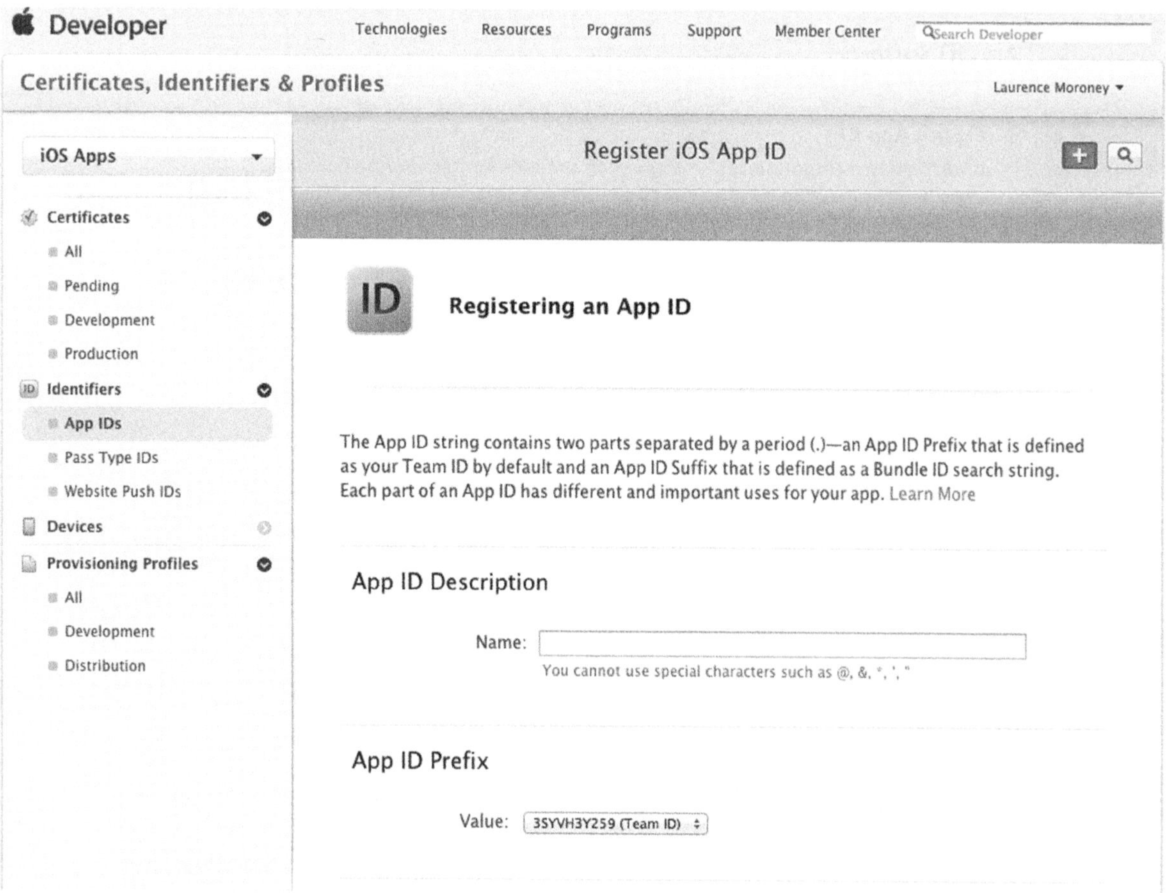

**Figure 13-16.**  *Registering an App ID*

You'll need to give the app a name. We'd recommend using the same name as you're using in the app name section. Apple also gave you a team ID when you set up your developer account. This will be the default setting in the "App ID Prefix" field. You can keep this setting.

As you scroll down, you see settings to use an explicit App ID or a wildcard App ID. As the site explains (see Figure 13-17), explicit App IDs are good if you want to specifically identify a particular app with an App ID. If you don't mind bundling a bunch of apps with an App ID, you can use a wildcard.

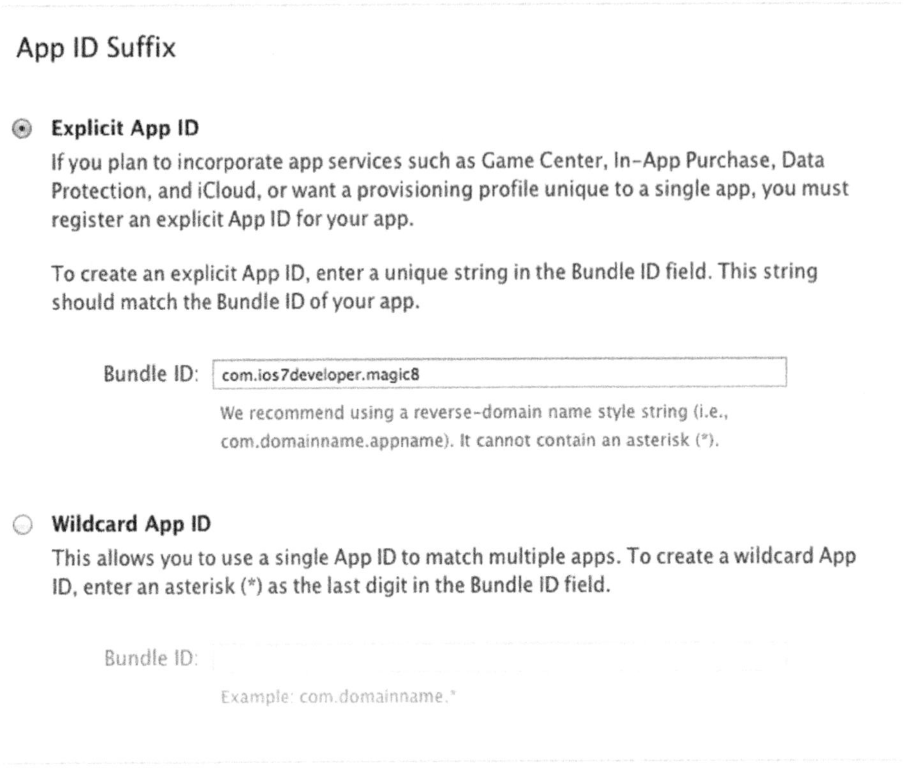

## App ID Suffix

⦿ **Explicit App ID**

If you plan to incorporate app services such as Game Center, In-App Purchase, Data Protection, and iCloud, or want a provisioning profile unique to a single app, you must register an explicit App ID for your app.

To create an explicit App ID, enter a unique string in the Bundle ID field. This string should match the Bundle ID of your app.

Bundle ID: | com.ios7developer.magic8 |

We recommend using a reverse-domain name style string (i.e., com.domainname.appname). It cannot contain an asterisk (*).

○ **Wildcard App ID**

This allows you to use a single App ID to match multiple apps. To create a wildcard App ID, enter an asterisk (*) as the last digit in the Bundle ID field.

Bundle ID:

Example: com.domainname.*

*Figure 13-17. Setting the App ID suffix*

As you've already used a reverse-domain-name approach to name your app, we'd recommend using an explicit App ID and using that name. In my case, the "Magic 8 Ball" app was called com. ios7developer.magic8, so we'd set that as the explicit App ID.

See Figure 13-17.

Next you'll see App Services. By default you app is set to allow game center and in-app purchases. Depending on your app, you'll use different settings. Pick what is appropriate for your app and click "Continue." You can see these settings in Figure 13-18.

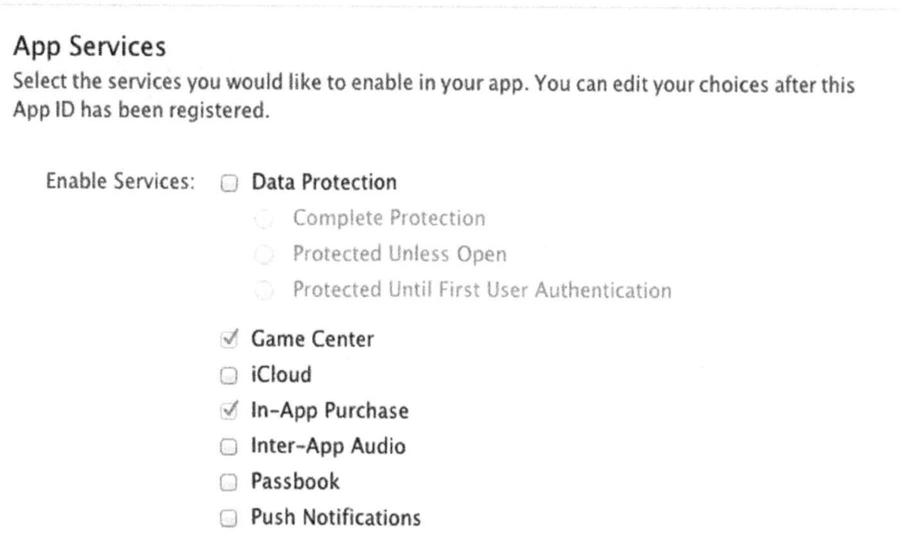

## App Services

Select the services you would like to enable in your app. You can edit your choices after this App ID has been registered.

Enable Services:  ☐ **Data Protection**
         ○ Complete Protection
         ○ Protected Unless Open
         ○ Protected Until First User Authentication

      ☑ **Game Center**
      ☐ **iCloud**
      ☑ **In-App Purchase**
      ☐ **Inter-App Audio**
      ☐ **Passbook**
      ☐ **Push Notifications**

*Figure 13-18. App Services*

When you're done, click the "Continue" button, and you'll see a screen with your App ID details where you can confirm your App ID. You can see this in Figure 13-19.

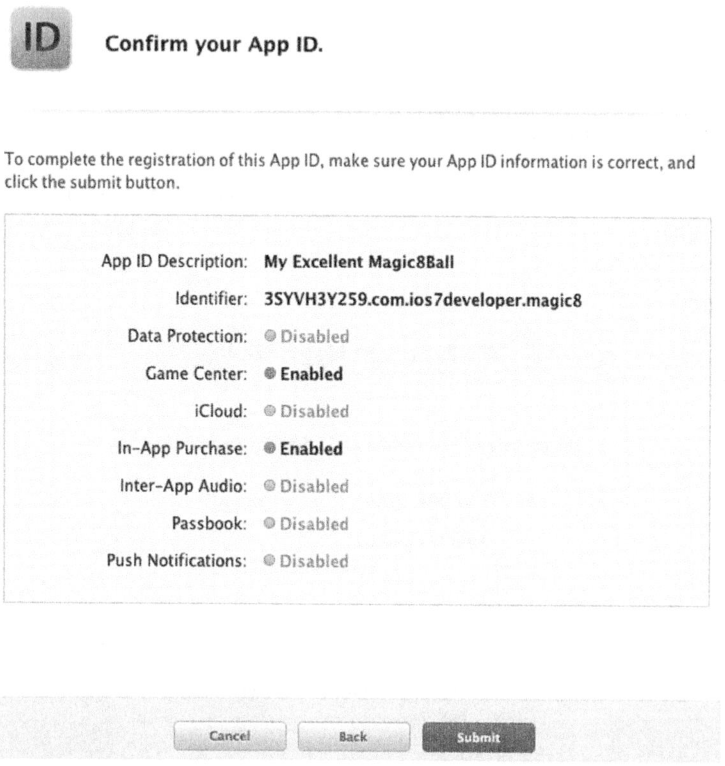

 **Confirm your App ID.**

To complete the registration of this App ID, make sure your App ID information is correct, and click the submit button.

| | |
|---|---|
| App ID Description: | **My Excellent Magic8Ball** |
| Identifier: | **3SYVH3Y259.com.ios7developer.magic8** |
| Data Protection: | ○ Disabled |
| Game Center: | ● **Enabled** |
| iCloud: | ○ Disabled |
| In-App Purchase: | ● **Enabled** |
| Inter-App Audio: | ○ Disabled |
| Passbook: | ○ Disabled |
| Push Notifications: | ○ Disabled |

Cancel     Back     Submit

*Figure 13-19. Confirming your App ID*

If you're happy with the settings, click "Submit" to continue. Your App ID will be created for you.

Now, if you return to the App Information screen, as in Figure 13-15, you'll be able to specify this App ID as your bundle ID. If you don't see it, just go back to the iTunes Connect portal and attempt to add a new app again.

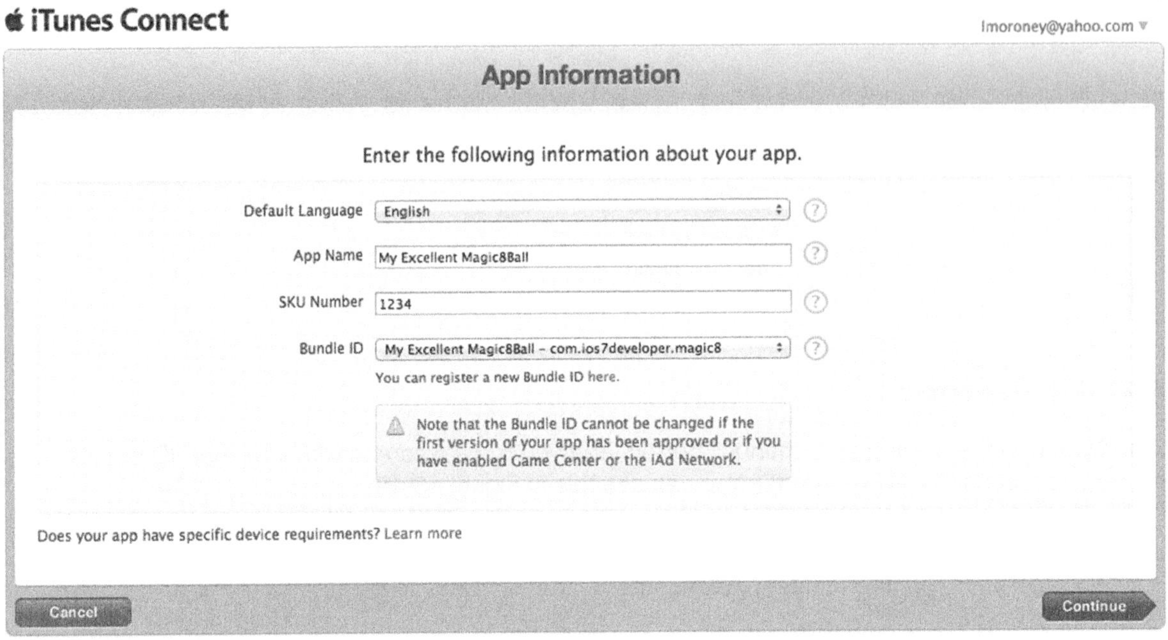

Figure 13-20. *Setting the app information*

When you're done, click "Continue." At this point, you'll be taken to the availability date and pricing information for your app.

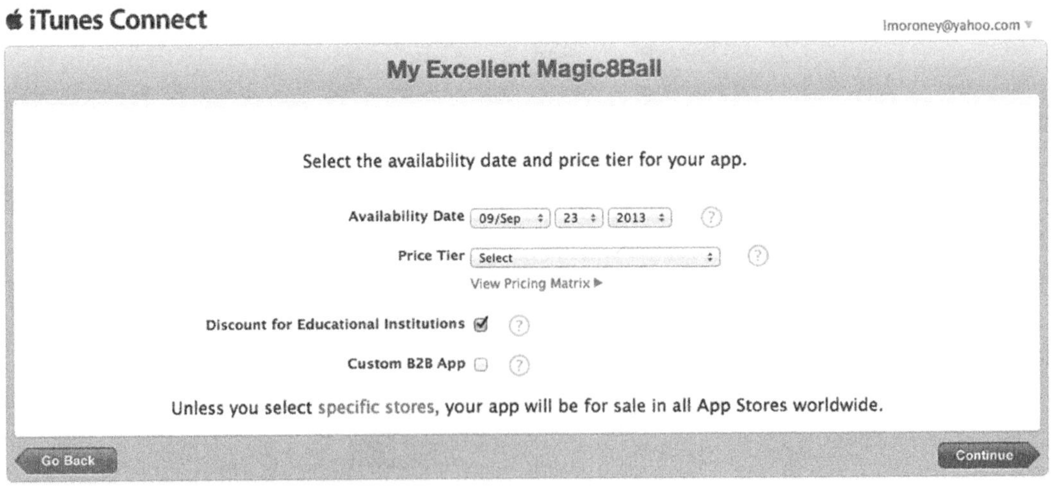

Figure 13-21. *Availability and pricing for your app*

Set it the way that you want, including pricing and discounts, and click "Continue."

You'll then have to set various metadata for your app, including copyright and descriptions that will be used to set an app rating. See Figure 13-22.

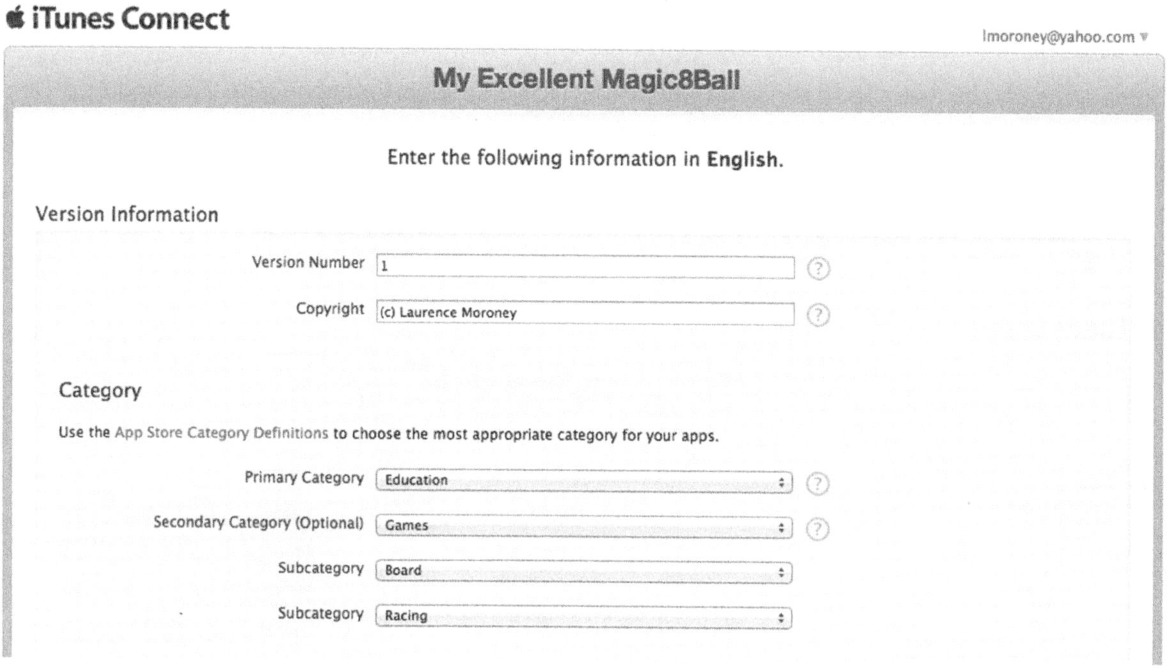

Figure 13-22. *Setting your app metadata*

> **Important**   For the "Version Number" setting, make sure you put exactly the same value as you put within the app settings in Xcode. So, if you used "1.0" in Xcode (see Figure 13-3), you should use "1.0" here. Or, if you have "1" here, then you should edit your Xcode settings to have a "1."

For the "Category" section, you should pick what's most appropriate for your app. Follow the guidelines given.

You'll need to fill out the rest of the form with sensible data for your app, including metadata to describe it and contact information for you. The engineer who reviews the app may need to contact you. In one circumstance, we were asked to shoot a video of our app in action and send it to them. It's good to put as many review notes in as possible, so that the reviewer has what they need to "pass" your app into the store.

Before finishing, you need a number of graphics.

First is the *large app icon*. This is a 1024x1024 image of at least 72 DPI (dots-per-inch). If you use Paintbrush, the default image created for you has this DPI, so you can easily create one.

Next are the *3.5-inch retina display screenshots*. You can create these using the simulator. With your app running in the simulator, go to the File menu and select "Save Screen Shot." The simulator will save a screen shot on your desktop called "IOS simulator screenshot" with the date of capture postfixed. You can save a few of these and upload them here.

Do the same for the *4-inch retina display screenshots* and *iPad screenshots*. Just rerun your app in the simulator for those devices and take some screenshots.

Some apps can be restricted to only run within specific geographic locations. The "Routing App Coverage" file governs this. You can safely ignore that for now.

Click "Save" when you're done. You'll be returned to the iTunes Connect portal, and you'll see that your app's status is set to "Prepare for Upload."

See Figure 13-23.

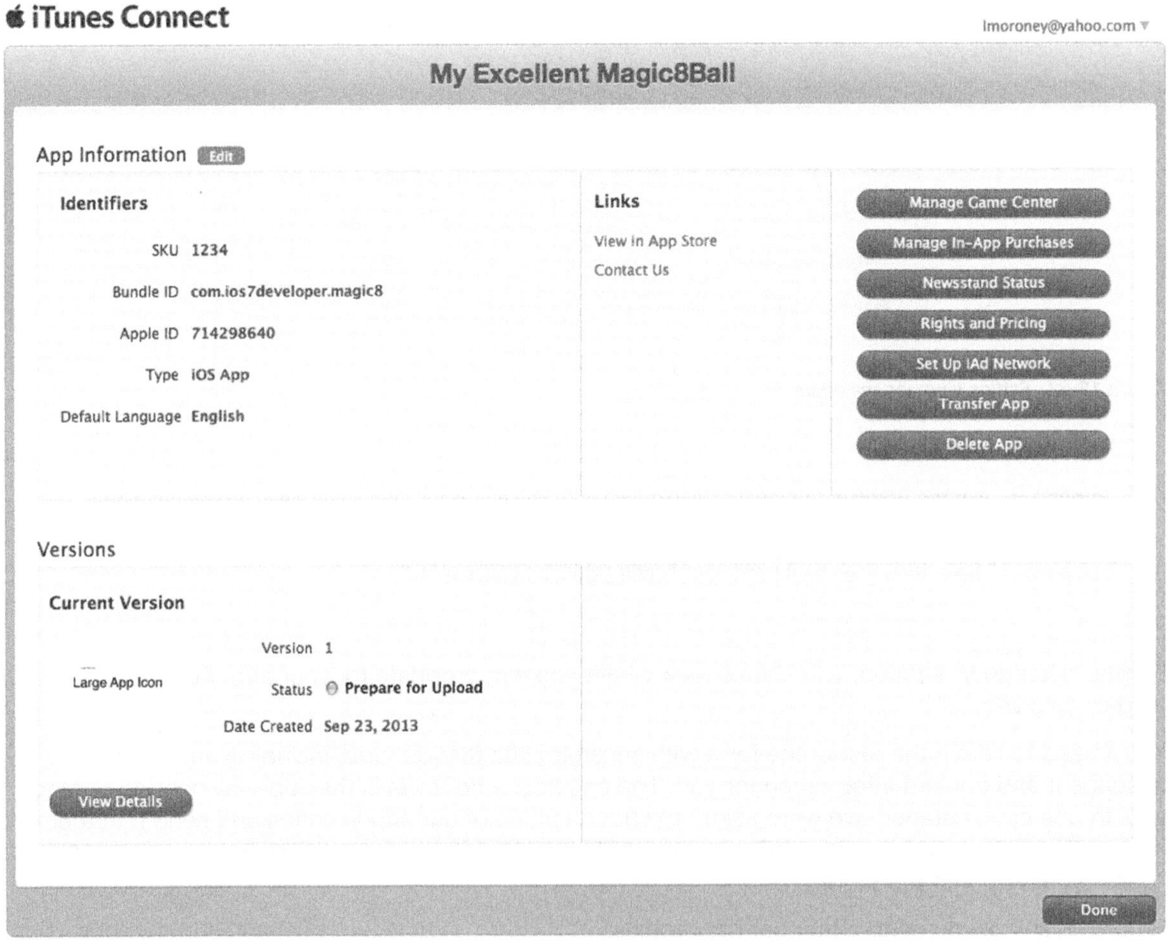

*Figure 13-23. Your app has a "Prepare for Upload" status*

Below your large app icon, you'll see a button that reads "View Details." Select this and you'll be taken to the details screen for your app. See Figure 13-24.

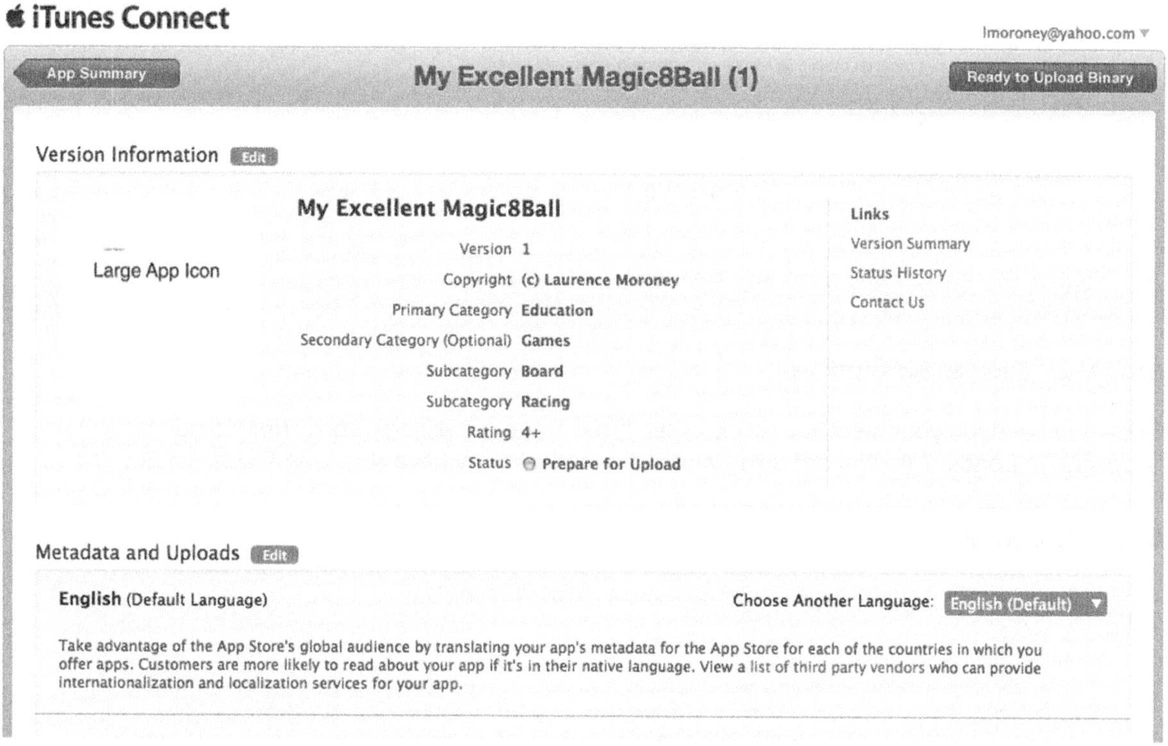

Figure 13-24. *Getting your app ready for upload*

On the top right-hand side, you can see a button that reads "Ready to Upload Binary." Click this, and you'll be asked some questions. First, you'll be asked if your app is designed to use cryptography. If it is, say "yes." In most cases it isn't, in which case you'll say "no." For the magic 8-ball, no cryptography is used.

See Figure 13-25.

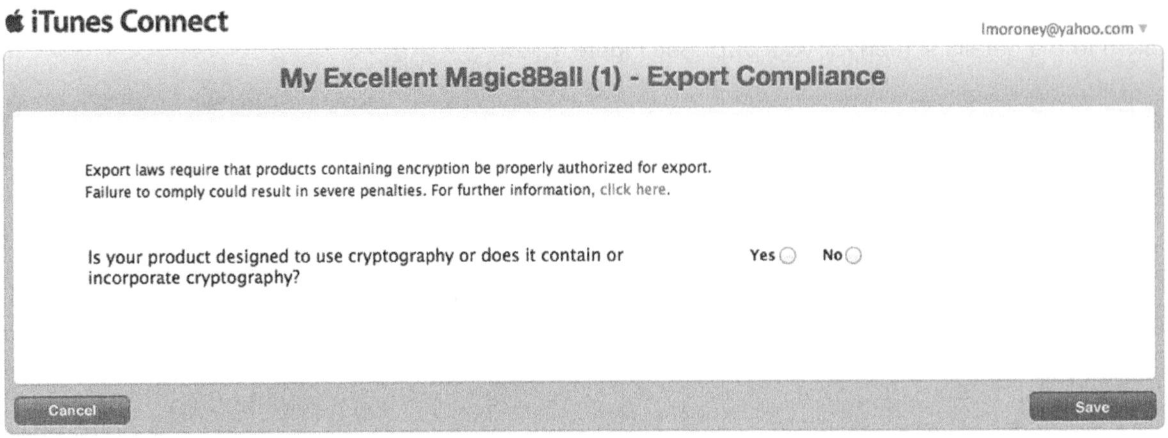

**🍎 iTunes Connect**                                                            lmoroney@yahoo.com ▾

## My Excellent Magic8Ball (1) - Export Compliance

Export laws require that products containing encryption be properly authorized for export.
Failure to comply could result in severe penalties. For further information, click here.

Is your product designed to use cryptography or does it contain or                Yes ○    No ○
incorporate cryptography?

Cancel                                                                                    Save

*Figure 13-25.  Export settings for your app*

Once you've made your selection, click "Save." You'll see a message about uploading using
"Application Loader." As you are using Xcode 5, you'll already have this. See Figure 13-26.

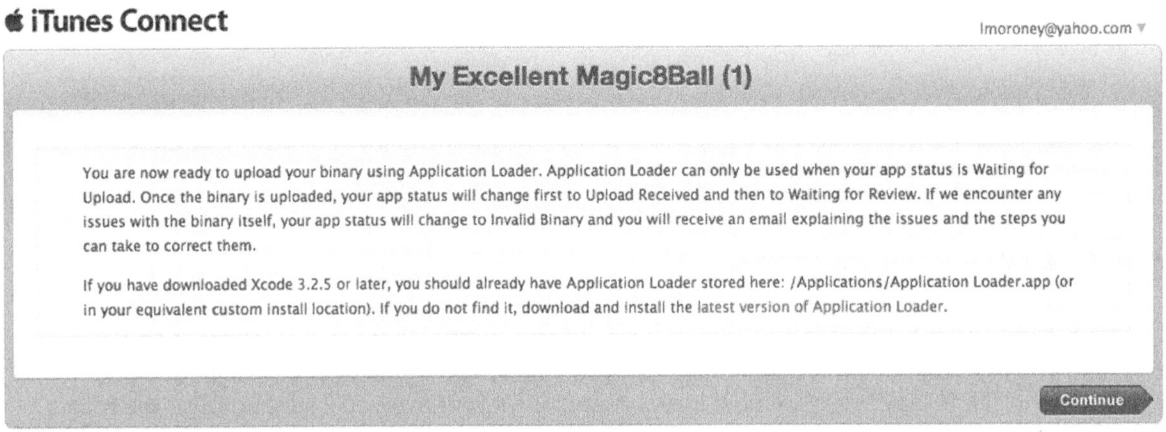

**🍎 iTunes Connect**                                                            lmoroney@yahoo.com ▾

## My Excellent Magic8Ball (1)

You are now ready to upload your binary using Application Loader. Application Loader can only be used when your app status is Waiting for
Upload. Once the binary is uploaded, your app status will change first to Upload Received and then to Waiting for Review. If we encounter any
issues with the binary itself, your app status will change to Invalid Binary and you will receive an email explaining the issues and the steps you
can take to correct them.

If you have downloaded Xcode 3.2.5 or later, you should already have Application Loader stored here: /Applications/Application Loader.app (or
in your equivalent custom install location). If you do not find it, download and install the latest version of Application Loader.

Continue

*Figure 13-26.  Getting ready to upload*

Click "Continue," and you'll return to the details screen. You'll see that the application is now in the
"Waiting for Upload" state. See Figure 13-27.

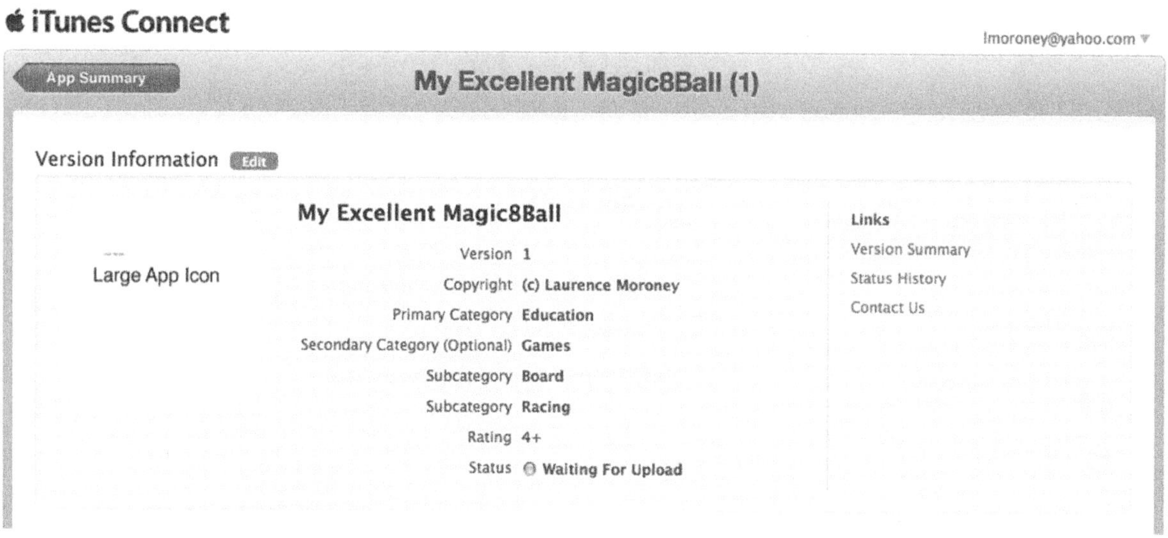

**⊛ iTunes Connect**

App Summary                    **My Excellent Magic8Ball (1)**

Version Information  (Edit)

**My Excellent Magic8Ball**                              Links

                                                        Version Summary
Large App Icon          Version  1                      Status History
                        Copyright  (c) Laurence Moroney
                 Primary Category  Education             Contact Us
      Secondary Category (Optional)  Games
                     Subcategory  Board
                     Subcategory  Racing
                          Rating  4+
                          Status  ⊝ Waiting For Upload

*Figure 13-27.  Your app is now waiting for upload*

Now that the app store is waiting for you to upload, the next step will be to go back to Xcode and have it build, sign, and upload your app for store verification.

# Building Your App for Store Distribution

Now that the app store is waiting for you to upload your app, the next and final step is to build your app, sign it for store delivery, and deploy it to the store.

To start, you'll need a *distribution certificate*. With Xcode open, select "Preferences" on the File menu. From this, select the "Accounts" tab. See Figure 13-28.

*Figure 13-28. The accounts settings*

Select your name and a list of signing identities will pop up. Your development certificate that you created in Chapter 3 will be listed. Click the "+" button and you'll see a list of potential certificates that you can add. Yours may be different, but you will see "iOS Distribution" as an option. See Figure 13-29.

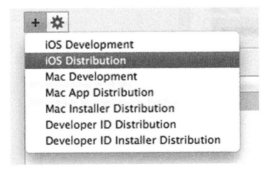

*Figure 13-29. Picking an iOS distribution certificate*

A distribution certificate will be created for you and added to the list. You can see what it will look like in Figure 13-30.

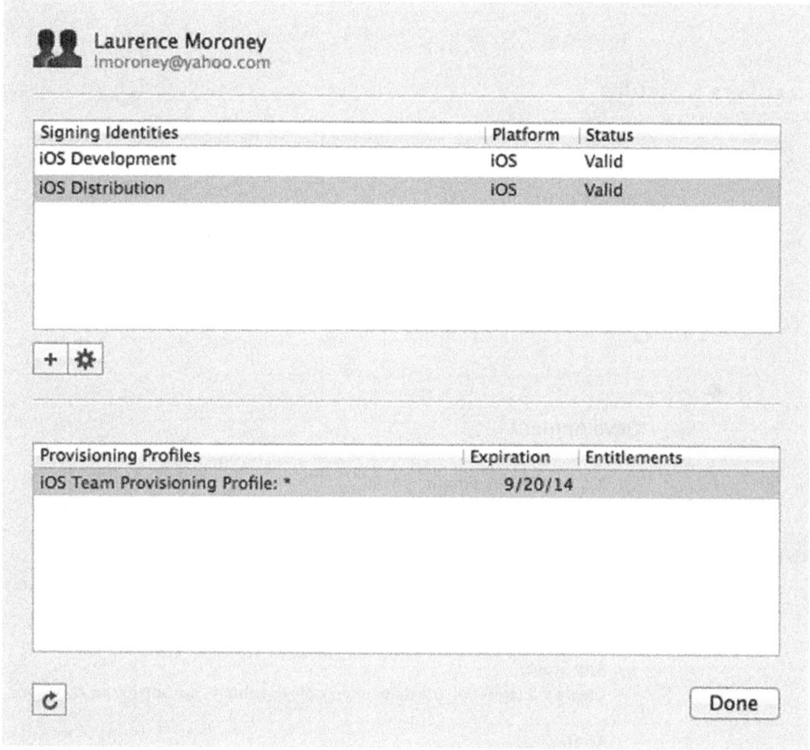

**Laurence Moroney**
lmoroney@yahoo.com

| Signing Identities | Platform | Status |
|---|---|---|
| iOS Development | iOS | Valid |
| iOS Distribution | iOS | Valid |

| Provisioning Profiles | Expiration | Entitlements |
|---|---|---|
| iOS Team Provisioning Profile: * | 9/20/14 | |

*Figure 13-30. Creating a distribution certificate*

Next you'll need to create a *store distribution profile*. To do this, go back to the iOS dev center (`https://developer.apple.com/devcenter/ios/index.action`) online. On the right-hand side of the screen there's a link to "Certificates, Identifiers & Profiles." Select this and you'll be taken to `https://developer.apple.com/account/overview.action`, from where you can select "Provisioning Profiles."

You'll be taken to the iOS Provisioning Profiles screen. See Figure 13-31.

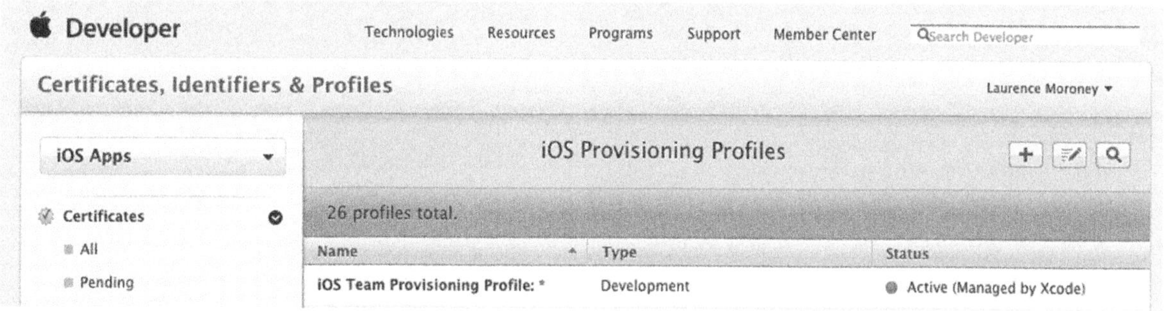

 Developer          Technologies    Resources    Programs    Support    Member Center    Search Developer

**Certificates, Identifiers & Profiles**                                      Laurence Moroney ▼

| iOS Apps ▼ | iOS Provisioning Profiles | + 📝 🔍 |
|---|---|---|

Certificates    ◉       26 profiles total.

  All
  Pending

| Name | Type | Status |
|---|---|---|
| iOS Team Provisioning Profile: * | Development | ● Active (Managed by Xcode) |

*Figure 13-31. iOS Provisioning Profiles screen*

At the top right-hand side of the screen, there's a "+" button to allow you to add a new profile. You'll be asked what type of provisioning profile you need. See Figure 13-32.

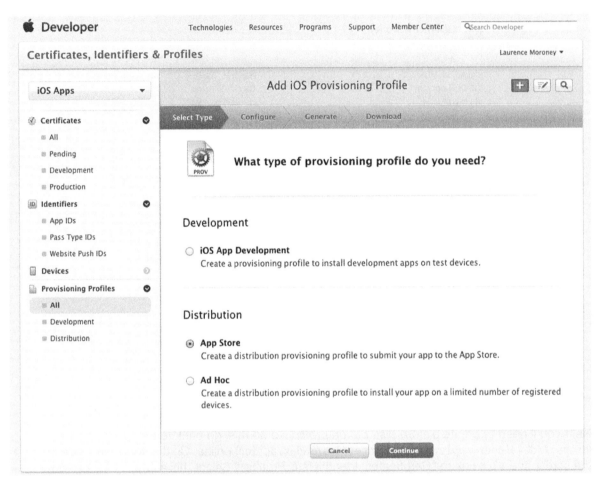

*Figure 13-32. Setting the provisioning profile type*

Select "App Store" as the distribution type and click "Continue." You'll be asked to select an App ID. Use the one that you created earlier. See Figure 13-33.

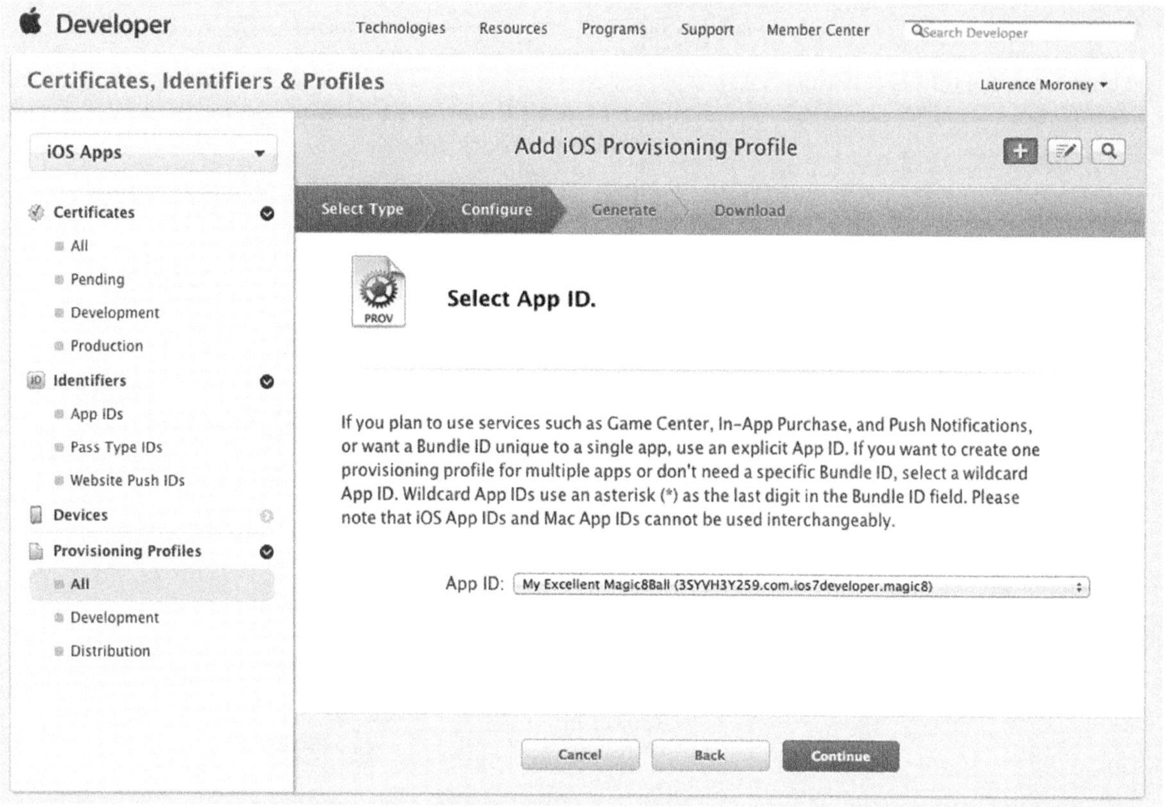

*Figure 13-33.* *Selecting your App ID*

You'll be asked which certificate you want to include in the profile. The one you created earlier should be listed. See Figure 13-34.

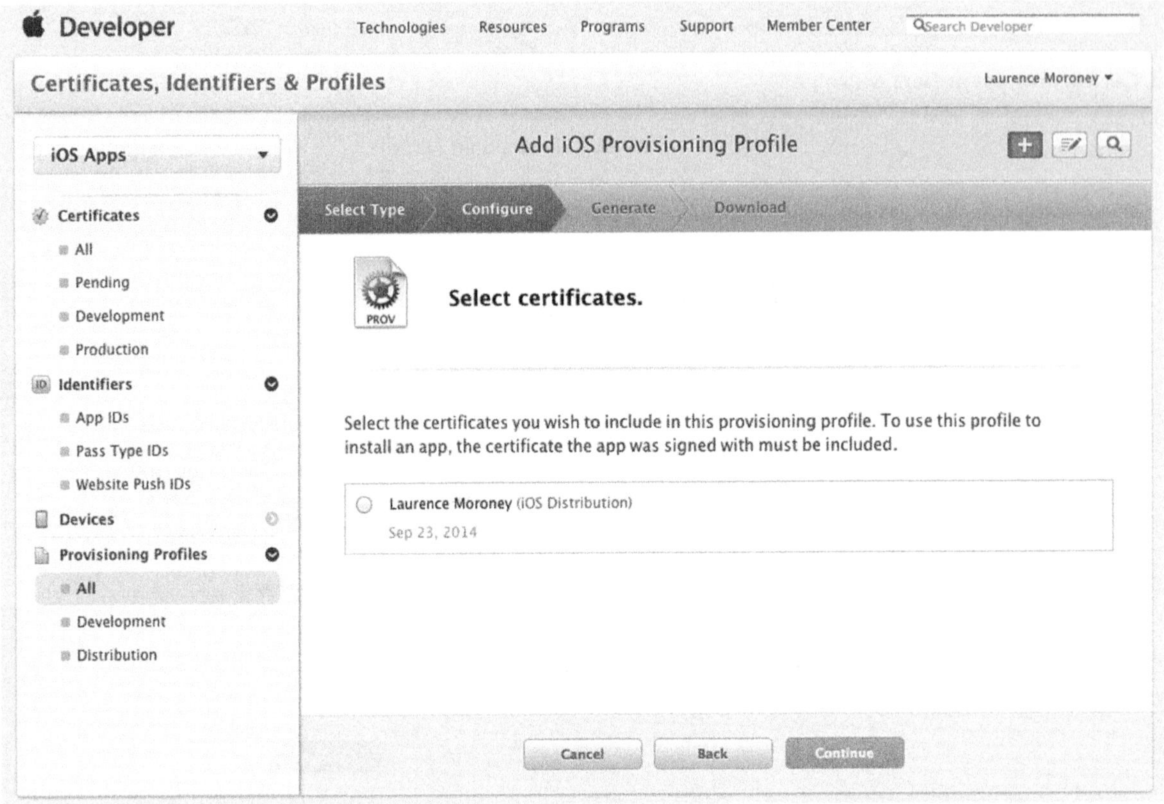

*Figure 13-34. Selecting your certificate*

Select your certificate and click "Continue." You'll then be asked to name the profile and to generate it. See Figure 13-35.

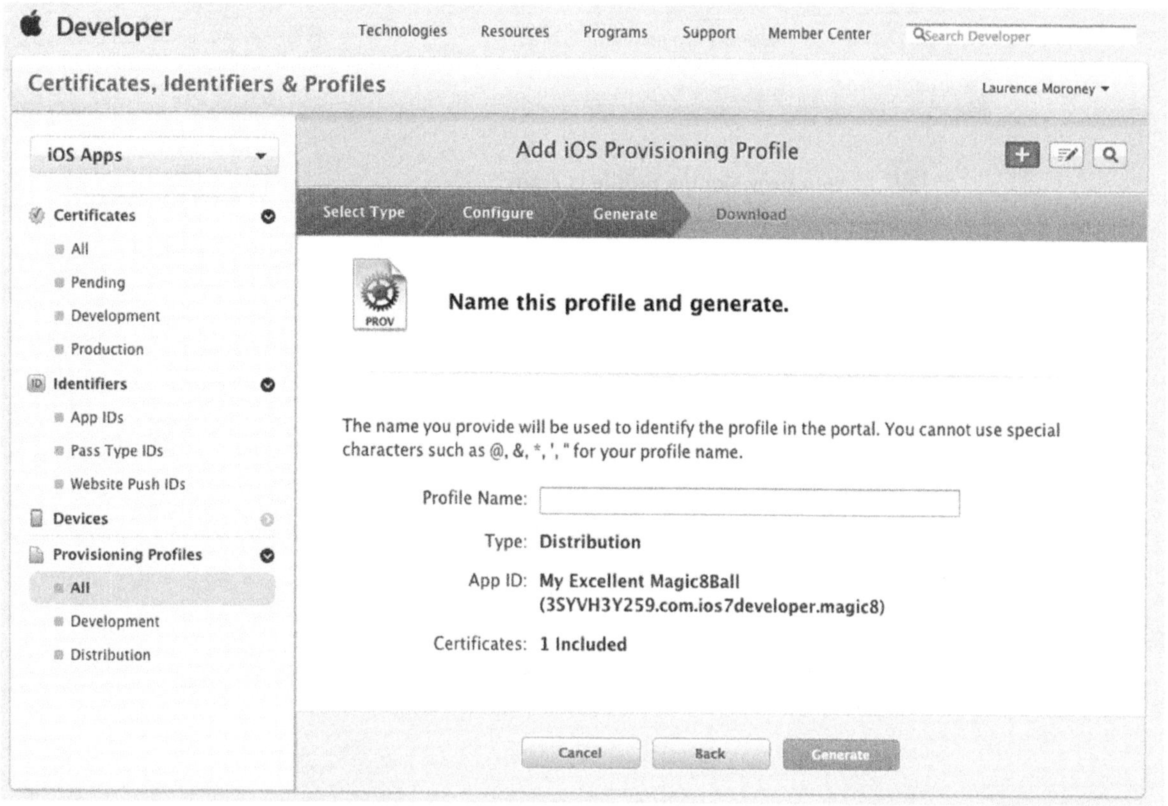

*Figure 13-35. Naming and generating a profile*

Give it a name and click the "Generate" button. In this case, we used the name "8Ball." The portal will work for a little while and then return with a screen telling you that your profile is ready, including a link to download and install it. See Figure 13-36.

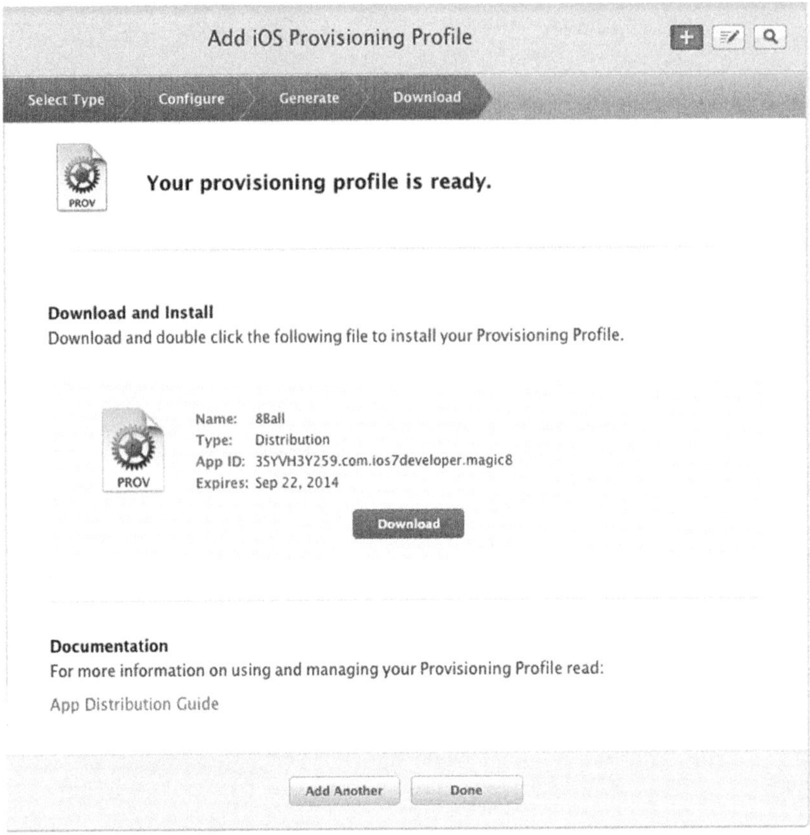

*Figure 13-36.  The provisioning profile is ready*

Press the "Download" button, and your browser will download a file with the `.mobileprovision` extension; for example, if your name is "8Ball," the file will be called "8Ball.mobileprovision."

After it downloads double-click on it, and the provisioning profile will be opened by Xcode. You may not see anything happen, but it's okay—the provisioning profile details are there.

Go back to Xcode, open your app, and ensure that it is selected to run on your device, as shown in Chapter 3. On the product menu, select "Archive," and your app will be archived. You'll be asked to sign the app with your certificate. Go ahead and do so. The archive will complete, and organizer will open with the "Archives" tab selected.

See Figure 13-37.

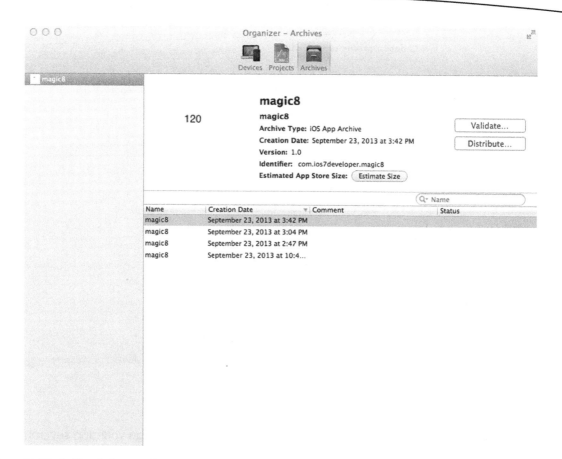

*Figure 13-37. Archives in the organizer*

Every time you archive, you'll see an entry added to the list. In Figure 13-37, we have four of them listed. You'll likely only have one at this point, and that's fine. Select it and click the "Validate" button.

The app store requires your app to be fully validated before it can be submitted, so you do need to go through this process.

When you press the "Validate" button you'll get a dialog asking you to log in to iTunes Connect. Use your developer credentials and click "Next."

You should see the dialog from Figure 13-38, which shows you the provisioning profile. If you don't see this, you'll see a screen that gives you an option to import the profile. In that case, import the .mobileprovision that you created earlier.

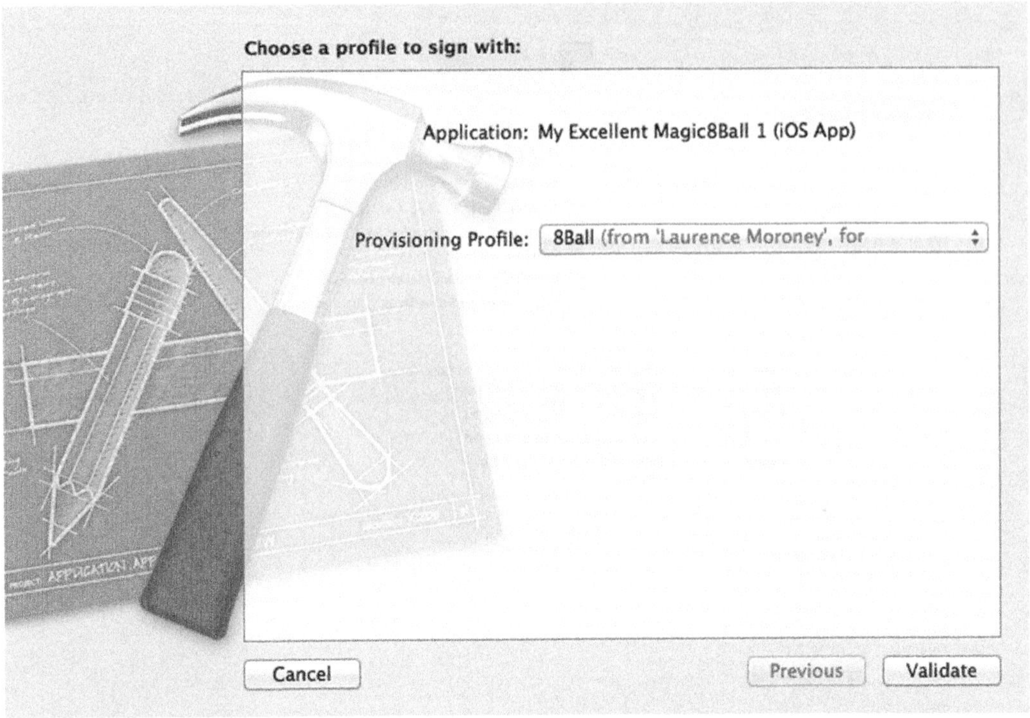

*Figure 13-38. Choosing your profile*

Click the "Validate" button and the process will begin. You'll be asked to sign your app several times. If it validates successfully, you'll see something like Figure 13-39.

*Figure 13-39. Validation has succeeded*

There are some common errors you might encounter here, including a warning about version numbers not matching. If that is the case, you should ensure that your version setting in Xcode (see Figure 13-3) exactly matches your version setting on iTunes Connect. If this happens, change the setting, clean the project (select "Clean" on the "Product" menu), and try again.

Another error could be one saying that "The entitlements specified in your application's code signing entitlements file do not match those specified in your provisioning profile," or similar. If you see this, select your project in Xcode and select the project name as the target. Then, on the "Build Settings" tab, make sure that you have selected "iOS Distribution" in the "Code Signing Identity" section. See Figure 13-40.

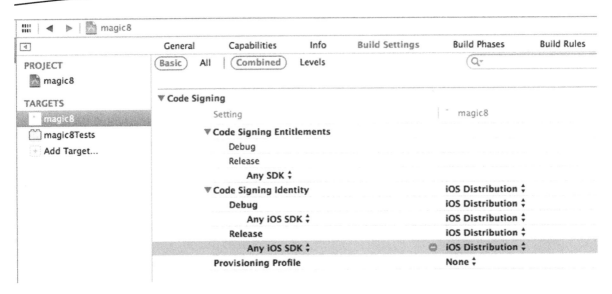

*Figure 13-40. Ensuring your code signing identity is correct*

Once you've passed validation, you can select "Distribute..." on the organizer. You'll be given the choice between submitting to the app store, saving for enterprise or ad hoc deployment, or exporting as an Xcode archive. See Figure 13-41.

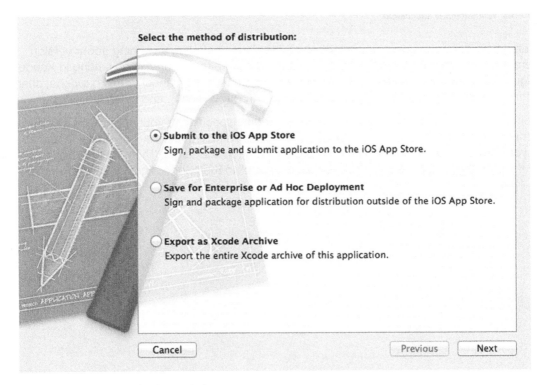

*Figure 13-41. Selecting your distribution method*

Select "Submit to the iOS App Store" and click "Next." You'll be asked to sign in to iTunes Connect. Use your developer ID and password. You'll then be asked, as with validation, which profile to sign with. Use the provisioning profile that you created earlier and click the "Submit" button.

As you've already passed validation, the package will be created and then uploaded to the app store. When it's done, and the submission succeeds, you'll see something like Figure 13-42.

**Submission Succeeded**

No issues were found in "magic8".
"magic8" has passed validation and has been submitted to the App Store for further review.

| Cancel | Previous | Finish |

*Figure 13-42. Submission to app store succeeds*

Now it's time to sit back and wait for the app store reviewer to give you feedback. Most apps get feedback within ten business days. Depending on issues found, you may go straight into the store; otherwise, they'll give you feedback via the email address on your Apple ID. In that case, you'll have to fix your app, rebuild it, and resubmit it.

# Summary

Perhaps the hardest part of being an iOS developer is understanding all the concepts that you need to know in order to submit an app to the app store. This long chapter is a guided tour through the typical scenario. Don't worry if you didn't get it all the first time. As you deploy more apps, repetition will become the key in learning it all.

Congratulations on getting this far. You're well on your way to being a professional iOS 7 developer!

# Index

# ■ T

# Get the eBook for only $10!

Now you can take the weightless companion with you anywhere, anytime. Your purchase of this book entitles you to 3 electronic versions for only $10.

This Apress title will prove so indispensible that you'll want to carry it with you everywhere, which is why we are offering the eBook in 3 **formats** for only $10 if you have already purchased the print book.

Convenient and fully searchable, the PDF version enables you to easily find and copy code—or perform examples by quickly toggling between instructions and applications. The MOBI format is ideal for your Kindle, while the ePUB can be utilized on a variety of mobile devices.

Go to www.apress.com/promo/tendollars to purchase your companion eBook.

Apress®
THE EXPERT'S VOICE™